BLOODY PAYBACK

The young woman lay mostly in the bedroom with her feet extending into the hall and her shorts pulled down around one ankle. Her white T-shirt was drawn up tightly under her arms, as if she had been dragged, exposing her bloody, naked torso. Melody Wuertz's slight body had been mutilated by savage thrusts of a knife blade. One large wound, roughly in the shape of an inverted cross, extended across both breasts. A symbol, roughly in the shape of an R had been cut into her abdomen. Her genitals had been deeply sliced. She had been hit in the face and shot twice: once in the back of the neck and once in her left ear.

In a small pool of blood nearby lay her eleven month old daughter Jessica, shot twice in the head.

The autopsy report would show that Melody Wuertz had only been incapacitated by the first bullet to her neck. She was alive and conscious when the butcher killed her daughter . . . alive and conscious when the monster then took his sharp knife to her own body.

REAL HORROR STORIES!
PINNACLE TRUE CRIME

OVER THE EDGE

Bill G. Cox

Pinnacle Books
Kensington Publishing Corp.

http://www.pinnaclebooks.com

Some names have been changed to protect the privacy of individuals connected to this story.

PINNACLE BOOKS are published by

Kensington Publishing Corp.
850 Third Avenue
New York, NY 10022

First Printing: September, 1997
10 9 8 7 6 5 4 3

Printed in the United States of America

As always, to my wife, Nina I. Cox, who is a masterful copy reader and a very patient lady with the mood changes that occur within a working (and at times, non-productive) writer.

ACKNOWLEDGMENTS

I acknowledge with sincere thanks the many people who contributed information and other assistance during my research of this book in Oklahoma City and Edmond, Oklahoma.

Foremost, I want to thank Oklahoma County District Attorney Robert Macy, a hard-hitting prosecutor and distinguished gentleman in the legal profession, and the courteous and helpful secretarial staff of the District Attorney's Office; also, Larry W. Andrews of the District Attorney's Office, who was an investigator and who also headed the competent Task Force of investigators from the Edmond Police Department, the Oklahoma State Bureau of Investigation and the District Attorney's Office in its latter time of operation.

Also, Detective Captain Ron Cavin; and Detectives Theresa Pfeiffer and Richard Ferling, the lead investigators in the case, all members of the Edmond Police Department, who spent uncountable hours from the beginning of the murder investigation through the trial three years later. And the operators and dispatchers of the Edmond Police Department, who were courteous and patient during my many follow-up long distance phone calls to the department's investigators.

My special thanks goes to Rockie J. Yardley of the Edmond Police Department, one of the finest crime scene investigators in the country, who guided the collection and identification of crime scene evidence with the cooperation of State Bureau of Investigation and FBI forensic experts and crime scene analysts and profilers. Yardley in the past received special recognition from the U.S. Postal Department and the FBI for his crime scene work on the Edmond Post Office massacre in August 1986, and he also assisted at the Murrah Federal Building bombing site in Oklahoma City in 1995.

My hat goes off to John W. Coyle, the Oklahoma City criminal attorney who headed the defense team representing the defendant and who, along with his efficient secretarial staff, helped so much in my documentary research. Also, the competent county employees who work in the Old Records department of the District Clerk's Office in Oklahoma City.

My thanks also go to Leo and Colleen Smith of Bethany, Oklahoma, and Mr. and Mrs. W. U. McCoy of Oklahoma City for special courtesies and help during the two weeks my wife Nina and I spent in the Oklahoma City area.

And to the helpful staffs of the University of Central Oklahoma Library at Edmond, and the Oklahoma City Downtown Public Library, and the reference department of the Amarillo, Texas Public Library, whose members always are a tremendous research help.

Also to Mr. James Coburn of the photographic department of the *Edmond Evening Sun*.

And I am grateful for the coordinating work of Consulting Editor Karen V. Haas and Editor-in-Chief Paul Dinas on this book.

And, as always, a special thanks to my wife, Nina, a former newspaperwoman and also freelance writer, for her help in research and copy reading and bearing with me during the occasionally bleak days of the project.

Chapter 1

As usual she felt the fear, almost like a presence lurking out there in midnight's darkness. Melody Wuertz, twenty-nine years old, a petite and pretty brunette, walked rapidly to her car in the parking lot and drove away from the sprawling U.S. Veterans Administration Hospital in Oklahoma City, Oklahoma. It was a few minutes past 12 A.M. on Tuesday, July 2, 1991.

Her shift as a ward clerk at the large, red-brick hospital just concluded, she was exhausted, more from the recent weeks of high tension, she thought, than the work.

Driving along the darkened streets and turning onto the expressway, she fought against the hopeless feelings, tried to push the engulfing fright from her mind. She lived in Edmond, a small town to the north of the Oklahoma City limits, only a short driving distance. She made this familiar drive twice a day, five times a week. But the night was always a bad trip.

Fifteen minutes later Wuertz pulled up at a house in

Edmond, the residence of her tiny daughter's baby-sitter, Phyllis Davis. She tapped lightly at the front door.

It wasn't Davis who came to the door. "Mother's already in bed," the young woman who met Melody said. "Dad and I were sitting up looking at family wedding pictures. Your little angel is asleep."

The blond-haired baby girl fussed sleepily when her mother picked her up. "Now, now, honey, Momma's here."

Jessica Rae, you are so beautiful, Wuertz thought. Beautiful and so pure and unaware of life's troubles. The infant barely gurgled as her eyes closed again in sleep.

"See you tomorrow afternoon, Melody. Don't forget the party," the woman reminded. "It's the last chance we will get to see you'all for two weeks."

Driving the few blocks to her own home, Wuertz thought about the pending trip back to her hometown in Indiana to visit her parents, and tried to crowd out the foreboding feeling that made her shudder for a second. She and Jessica would be in a much happier environment soon, thank goodness, in that secure place where life had been so simple and sweet and full of God's love.

What is that old saying, she thought: You can't go home again? But Wuertz certainly was looking forward to doing just that; and the quicker she reached that safe haven from her past, the better. Earlier last night she had phoned her mom from the hospital during a break, telling her the departure and arrival times of Thursday's flight.

Mom and Dad were planning a big birthday party there for Jessica on July 7, her actual birthday. One year old. Wuertz could hardly believe it.

Such a perfect and loving baby, cheerful and always bubbling over with friendliness, now learning to walk on her chubby little legs, a tot full of big smiles and hugs for everyone. Recently, several of Wuertz's "ooh-ing and ah-ing" women coworkers—after looking at the latest photos of Jessica (one of those studio bargains of one big picture and a dozen little ones)—volunteered to baby-sit any time, gratis. "I would love to have this darling baby for my own," one hefty nurse had said with a big smile.

With such a blessing as Jessica, why did life have to be so complicated and threatening, she wondered.

The young mother turned down West Seventh and eased her car along the quiet, tree-lined residential block. This was the worst time, returning at this lonely hour to a darkened house. She looked forward to when she would begin a new day shift after the vacation trip. It was a promotion, in more ways than one, Wuertz thought.

No lights were on in any of the houses. Her own house was almost concealed by tall hedges on both sides of the front walk. She pulled into the carport connected to the modest, gray, wood-frame home.

Her heart was pounding. The danger was out there waiting in the black shadows, or—even a more terrifying possibility—in the house.

Only the sounds of insects broke the night's silence. Wuertz opened the car door and stepped out. She jumped as a sudden night wind stirred the tree branches overhead. The night was hot and sultry. With one more quick look around, she scooped up her daughter from the buckled baby seat, walked briskly to the front entrance, unlocked the outer glass door and then the dead-bolt lock on the inner wooden door, and rushed inside.

She flipped on the light and saw nothing to cause her to turn and flee. But she didn't even put down the sleeping baby until she latched the outer door and secured the dead-bolt on the inside door, with a sigh of relief.

"Sleep tight, precious darling," she whispered, bending to lay Jessica in her crib and gently kissing her forehead. As Wuertz lay in her bed, her mind roamed once more to the pastoral bliss of Indiana. Even as anxious and beat as she was, she smiled. The next two weeks would be joyful ones for her and Jessica. Later, Wuertz stirred in her sleep. Something had caused her to rouse. Fully awake, she listened with her heart in her throat.

Then she realized it was only the low rumble of thunder, the prelude to an approaching summer thunderstorm.

She arose and looked at her sleeping baby. Jessica was breathing evenly, her tiny face one of peaceful composure in the dim light from the window.

The concerned mother finally slipped into sleep, in spite of the rolling thunder coming closer, though her sleep was fitful.

Not during the blackness of night, but in the full light of midday, on this same Tuesday at high noon, the terror Melody Wuertz had feared so long invaded her house. It arrived through the always-locked front door and struck with blitzlike fury and unimaginable horror, unleashing a savagery that would shock all those who viewed the pitiful, bloody results.

Chapter 2

Phyllis Davis was frustrated. Too many things to do, too few hours in the day. Now, here it was already 1:15 P.M. Davis's 10:30 A.M. dental appointment had run much longer than she thought it would.

She still had to get everything ready for Jessica's party. She phoned the residence of Melody Wuertz, just to make sure the mom and her special little party-honoree would arrive early enough before Wuertz had to leave for her hospital shift. One . . . two . . . three rings . . .

Davis knew that Wuertz had a set routine for getting ready: feeding Jessica, getting down and playing with her on the floor, dressing Jessica and herself, dropping the baby off on the way to work. Wuertz had it down perfectly, like a minute-by-minute drill, and still found time to keep her house sparkling clean. You could always count on Wuertz's punctuality.

When Wuertz's phone had rung several times with no answer, Davis was puzzled. Maybe Wuertz had taken her baby on an errand. That hardworking gal had said she still had so many things to accomplish for tomorrow's trip to see her folks in Indiana.

As the day moved on, Davis called Wuertz's number several times without receiving an answer.

To Davis it seemed highly improbable that Wuertz would not come by for the party, at least not without calling; perhaps something unavoidable had delayed her, or even made it impossible to get here early.

The baby-sitter got busy and didn't notice the time. She was really startled when Wuertz's boss at the hospital phoned and asked if she knew why Wuertz wasn't at work yet. My lands, it was 4:30 P.M.! Wuertz should have been on the job an hour ago.

"I have no idea at all," she said.

After hanging up, Davis had an ominous thought: What if Wuertz had suffered one of her epileptic seizures? Passed out or fallen, and couldn't get to the phone for help? She knew the young mother took medication to prevent these attacks, and seemingly had the lifelong malady well under control.

But Davis recalled one such episode several months ago, when she had to bring Wuertz home from the hospital after she was stricken with a seizure while on duty.

Worried, Davis couldn't go over and see about her friend. She was caring for other small children whom she couldn't leave. Fortunately, the baby-sitter's teenage daughter, Jill, came home, and Davis asked her to go to Wuertz's house, to make sure she hadn't become ill.

Several minutes after her daughter left to walk the several blocks to Wuertz's address, the phone rang. When Davis answered, she was met by an hysterical outpouring of almost incoherent words:

"Someone has killed Melody!" blurted Jill Davis, sobbing uncontrollably. The girl's high-pitched words tumbled forth as she screamed, "And they killed Jessica, too!"

Phyllis Davis shouted to her oldest son, who happened

to be at home, "Something terrible-bad has happened over at Melody's house! Hurry! Go over there! Jill is there by herself! She's hysterical! She's screaming and crying! Oh, something awful has happened!"

The son dashed from the house, followed by a younger brother. They intended to run all the way to the West Seventh location, but a neighbor said he would drive them.

Lisa West, who lived across the street from Melody Wuertz, was in her backyard hanging out clothes. She was glad that this morning's rainstorm was over, and the sun was breaking through.

The Wests had moved into the rental house two weeks ago. One thing that irked Lisa West considerably was that there was only an electrical plug-in for her gas-operated clothes dryer, no gas connection at all. Therefore, she had to turn to the old-fashioned way: hanging out the wash to dry.

Her three small children and a visiting young girl from down the street were playing in the house. As she pinned the wet laundry to the clothesline, West was interrupted by the visiting girl who came out and said: "There's a lady at your door and she said she needs help."

West left her clothes basket, wondering what in the world was going on as she hurried inside. She was startled by the sight of the sobbing and obviously scared-out-of-her-wits Jill Davis. West saw that the teenage girl was visibly shaking all over as she managed to get out the words, "You've got to help them! You've got to help them!" The girl cried the desperate message over and over.

West and her husband, who had barely arrived home from work, ran with Jill Davis to the gray house across the street. The inner wooden door was open, and the Wests opened the outside glass door and went in.

They immediately saw the small baby on the floor in the hallway near the bathroom door.

At first, West thought the infant was taking a nap: one small arm was extended above its head as the baby lay facedown, eyes closed. But as she stooped over the unmoving baby, she saw a small round hole in the baby's temple, and blood!

"Oh, Lord, she's been shot!" she exclaimed.

As she extended her hand to check for breath, or signs of life, she realized she still had some clothespins in her hand. She laid the clothespins on the floor near the baby.

As she raised up and glanced down the hall, West saw the body of a woman.

The woman was lying mostly in the bedroom with her feet extending into the hall, her shorts pulled down around one ankle, a white T-shirt drawn up tightly under her arms; there was blood covering the entire front of her body from below the neck to her exposed crotch, the blood obliterating from sight the breasts and abdomen and pubic region.

"Oh, good Lord above . . . Lord, Lord," West moaned.

She rushed to the telephone located between the living room and kitchen and dialed the 911 emergency number. Her husband went to where the woman was sprawled to see if he could do anything. But he saw that she obviously was beyond help. He stepped back, almost gagging at the sight of the horrible mutilation.

After telling the 911 operator that there was a dead baby and a dead, bloody lady whose clothes were torn off—"We think she has been raped"—West listened for a few seconds. The operator told her to give CPR and try to resuscitate the baby.

West interrupted him: "I can't. You need to tell me how to do this. I don't know how. I don't want to do it wrong." And she added, "I'm going to have to get the baby closer to the phone . . . just a minute. . . ." She put the receiver down and walked over to carefully slide her hands under the tiny body, which was stiff and cool.

She winced as she felt something wet and sticky on her fingers. She lifted up the baby and carried it to the phone, gently lowering the body to the carpet. Now she saw that the stickiness on her hands was blood.

Some other voices joined the operator, assisting in the CPR on-line instructions. But West finally said she didn't think it was going to do any good, the baby was gone.

Chapter 3

Rockie J. Yardley, crime-scene technician for the Edmond Police Department, was on his way home. It was a few minutes after 5 P.M. when his regular shift had ended.

Yardley is a pleasant-faced, stoutish man with a mustache and hair graying at the temples; he likes to wear vests and open-at-the-neck shirts.

On this hot July afternoon, he was thankful for the air-conditioning in his own car and for air in the police unit he used while on duty. He wondered how cops in the old days ever made it, before air-conditioning was installed in police cars. Come to think of it, they didn't have two-way radios, either.

Suddenly his pager went off. They didn't have pagers, either, Yardley thought. Maybe their life wasn't so bad, after all.

The police dispatcher informed him of a double homicide—and possibly a rape—on West Seventh. The call came at 5:14 P.M.

Yardley was only a few blocks away and he arrived at the

address in minutes. At the same time Lt. Terry Gregg, a detective supervisor, pulled up in his unit. As they alighted from their cars, they were met by two patrolmen and a patrol sergeant, the first officers on the scene. There were people, civilians—probably neighbors—standing in the front yard.

One of the uniform officers said, "It's a bad one. A woman and her little baby girl. The baby was shot. It looks like the lady was raped and someone tried to butcher her. She's all cut up, and may have been shot."

The contingent of police officers grew by the minute as department supervisors and detectives in the Criminal Investigation Division (CID) were called back. Detective Capt. Ron Cavin had not left the police station yet. He had a late meeting in his second-floor office and was notified there of the double-homicide call.

Edmond police chief Bill Vetter also came to the scene.

Within a short time, Oklahoma County district attorney Robert Macy, a white-haired, distinguished-looking official with a long record as a tough prosecutor, also arrived.

Macy had heard the call on his own police band in his automobile, on the way home from his office in the County Office Building, which adjoins the Oklahoma County Court House in downtown Oklahoma City.

Yardley had been a policeman for twelve years; before that, he had been with the Edmond ambulance service for seven years. He had seen his share of violent death and brutality. But, in all of Yardley's professional experience of viewing human carnage, nothing had equaled the impact of this death scene that greeted him.

It was overkill, to the worst degree.

Though stilled in death's finality, the bodies in the house

screamed overkill. The baby looked as though she was taking a nap on the floor—that is, until you counted the two bullet holes in the head. Not much blood here—a small stain on the front and back of the one-piece outfit the baby was wearing.

But who would shoot to death an innocent baby, what kind of person could do it, Yardley and the other homicide investigators wondered.

Why execute a nearly one-year-old baby that could never be a witness against anyone? No motive was plausible. The killer obviously had wanted that baby dead—two shots in the head left no doubt of the intent.

But the woman's murder was wholly different. The heartless killer had wanted more than only death for the young woman sprawled on the floor, her body hideously mutilated by slashes and savage thrusts of a knife blade, or some other sharp instrument. Unmerciful fury spurred by white-hot hatred was apparent in the killer's Ripper-like bloody slaughter.

As they looked at her, the officers saw that a large wound, roughly in the shape of an inverted cross, extended across both breasts, slicing through the right nipple.

Less definable was an odd-shaped symbol, roughly in the shape of an R, that had been etched on the abdomen, almost as if the killer was doodling for his entertainment. A single loose, long dark hair was visible on the abdomen, which could have been left by the attacker during a sexual assault.

Then there was the perverted act of torture. The pubic area and genitalia had been mutilated, and a powerful and deep thrust of a scalpel-sharp instrument, probably a hunting knife, had penetrated the vagina.

There was a minor contusion over her lower lip, probably the result of a blow to the face.

She also had been shot twice—once in the back of the neck and again in her left ear. Her right leg was bent upward at an angle, exposing the bloody crotch and inside of her legs; a pair of light-blue shorts was pulled down around the ankle on the left leg. The white T-shirt she wore had rolled up tightly beneath her armpits and up on her back when she was apparently dragged into the southeast bedroom. It looked as if she had been pulled down the hall by one arm, which was extended over her head. The detectives also observed another sign that the body had been dragged—the woman's watch was askew and pushed up and beyond the tan line on her wrist.

With the body sprawled faceup, and the one leg spread outward, with the shorts down around her ankle, and her breasts and pubic area exposed, it was easy to see why Lisa West had told the 911 operator that the woman might have been raped. It certainly was suggestive of a sexual attack, but could not be determined until the autopsy was performed later.

The bullet wounds in both victims appeared to have been made by a small-caliber gun, the investigators noted.

The short hallway obviously was the site of the initial attack. Both the baby and mother apparently had been shot just outside the bathroom door leading into the hall.

Probably the woman had been curling her hair when she was rushed by the killer, because a curling iron, plugged in and still on, was lying on the counter beside the lavatory.

On the floor of the bathroom was a purple pillow with what looked like gunpowder residue on it, leading the investigators to think the pillow had been used to muffle the sound of a gunshot.

Two small bloodstains on the hall carpet in front of the bathroom door marked the spot where the infant had been shot and from where Lisa West had moved the body to the phone in the living room, as she had related. Visible in one blood pool, where Jessica had been shot, was the imprint of her tiny left hand.

West had not known the victims' names; she recalled having seen the woman and the baby outside working in a flower bed one Sunday, but she had not become acquainted with them.

However, positive identification was made by Jill Davis and other witnesses, who arrived at the scene. The dead woman and child were Melody Wuertz, a twenty-nine-year-old ward clerk at the U.S. Department of Veterans Affairs Medical Center in Oklahoma City, and her eleven-month-old daughter, Jessica Rae Wuertz.

Jill Davis recalled that the front doors—the glass screen that opened outward and the wooden door that opened inward—were unlocked when she arrived to check on Wuertz.

The first patrol officers to respond had seen that the back door was still locked and the security chain in place, and all windows were closed and locked. There were no signs that the unknown killer had forced his way into the small home. Entry obviously had been by the front door.

A video and still photographs of the crime scene were made by Yardley and a member of the Oklahoma State Bureau of Investigation (OSBI). The Edmond police had requested the assistance of the highly efficient and scientifically-equipped state agency, which dispatched its lab experts to help gather the forensic evidence.

During the next several hours when Yardley was in the murder house, he made crime-scene drawings, carefully triangulating all evidence locations. This is a procedure in which a series of directional measurements are made to mark all pertinent items accurately on the crime-scene sketch for future reference and reconstruction of the murder locale as originally seen. Later, a computer-generated crime-scene drawing or "map" would be produced from the criminalist's sketch.

The bedroom where Melody Wuertz lay was sparsely furnished with a bed, a small chest of drawers, a shoe rack behind the door containing women's shoes, a sewing machine, an end table beside the bed, a chair and a small bookshelf. A hair dryer was still plugged in.

The room at first glance was a grab bag of possible clues. Yardley and the detectives saw a man's black hair comb with a wad of black hair enmeshed in the teeth. It was on the floor near Melody Wuertz's body. They also observed several packages of condoms, of varying brands, eight packs in all, scattered on the bedroom floor.

On the bed was a light-colored pillow with a blackish smear. The pillow, like the one found in the bathroom, had been used possibly as a silencer to reduce the sound of a gunshot.

In sharp contrast to the murder's ugliness, which filled the room, was a handwritten inspirational poem taped on the wall above Melody's bed. It was titled, "Don't Quit."

In later talks with a detective, Susie Wuertz, Melody's heart-broken mother, would identify the poem as one written by Melody's grandfather Buddy, and given to her when she was a child, fighting hard to make a normal life for herself after developing epilepsy at the age of thirteen. "She never let the threat of having a seizure keep her from doing anything," her tearful mother later recalled.

Discovered on the floor underneath the bed was a pair of dirty, white, size-thirty man's Jockey underwear. The criminalists working the room also bagged for later examination and testing a pair of white cotton gloves such as photographers use to handle negatives to prevent smudging, and another pair of latex gloves—the kind used in hospitals or doctors' offices.

Yardley observed that a rectangular-shaped electric

alarm clock sitting upright on the bedroom floor and still plugged into a wall socket was flashing on and off, with the digital numbers showing two o'clock. Seemingly, the floor was the regular place for the clock; it had not been knocked over or cracked, nothing to suggest it might have been disturbed during the murder of Wuertz.

The detectives remembered the morning's round of thunderstorms. They guessed a power surge or a temporary outage during the stormy weather might have started the clock flashing at the unchanging time of two o'clock. Later in the probe, the two o'clock flashing time would take on an important significance to the case.

On the remote possibility that the clock someway figured in the crime, it was dusted for fingerprints. But just as other items and surfaces tested, no prints were found.

Yardley estimated the small home consisted of less than 700 square feet, including a small front room and kitchen; a short hall leading to two bedrooms opposite each other (the smaller bedroom obviously was Jessica's, with a baby bed, a diaper pail that held two dirty diapers, and baby toys strewn about); a utility room with a washer, a dryer and an ironing board that was set up; and the bathroom.

As the investigators examined all of the rooms, one thing stood out like a black spider on an angel food cake: The killer had not left behind any weapon, no knife, no gun.

The absence of any weapons indicated that the crime was more planned and organized than they believed when making the initial "walk-through" of the murder scene. The detectives' conclusion was that the killer brought the gun and a knife—or some other sharp instrument—with him, and carried them away. These were not the actions at all of what the FBI violent-crime analysts call a "disorganized," hit-at-random killer.

Based on their first look at the crime scene, the first and

most logical theory was that mother and baby had been slain by a random intruder bent on rape. That idea rapidly was becoming questionable. Nor did burglary or theft appear to be involved in the double murder.

The TV, a stereo, a VCR and other valuable household items, which normally would be taken by a thief or burglar, had not been disturbed. No drawers had been opened and ransacked.

And the officers found Melody Wuertz's purse containing $157 in cash, some of the currency lying on top of the purse, and a black tote bag containing various documents on a high-back wicker chair in the kitchen. Inside the purse was a prescription in Melody Wuertz's name for Tegratol, an anticonvulsant drug used to control epileptic seizures.

A set of keys, later identified as Wuertz's house and car keys on a key ring, was in plain sight.

The purse, the visible currency, and the keys—plus Wuertz was wearing fresh makeup—strengthened their deduction that the mother had been attacked as she was preparing to leave the house to go to work.

Probably, the officers thought, she was curling her hair, and Jessica was playing on the floor near the bathroom door, when the unknown intruder unexpectedly burst in. The bruise over the young mother's lip suggested she had received a hard blow that staggered or knocked her down before being shot. Her glasses lying on the hall floor backed up this theory.

Adding to the horror of the murderous rampage was the possibility that Jessica was probably shot to death on the floor only inches from her still conscious but incapacitated mother. Melody Wuertz witnessed the execution of her baby.

* * *

Yardley and the OSBI lab techs dusted for fingerprints on all surfaces that the killer might have touched, especially around the front door. But Yardley had a feeling that none of the monster's prints would be found. If there had been careful preplanning by the murderer, he probably was wearing gloves—maybe even one of the pairs in the bedroom.

Under the direction of Lieutenant Gregg, outside searches for the missing weapons and other evidence were conducted by patrolmen as the work inside the home went on. A thorough examination of the home's exterior, as well as scrutiny of the front porch, the yard and driveway, the street and the backyard, were made. The premises and neighboring yards were combed by the picket line of officers working shoulder to shoulder.

Melody Wuertz's car was searched and examined, inside and outside.

Another team began a neighborhood canvass, going door-to-door in the neighborhood to see if any of the residents had heard or seen anything that might be a lead—be it an unknown vehicle or a stranger in the neighborhood.

When a detective knocked at another home on West Seventh, a lanky teenage boy came to the door.

Asked if he had noticed anything out of the ordinary earlier in the day, Joe Randall, said, "Yes, sir, I did."

The answer caught the detective by surprise. Maybe they were getting lucky. "You noticed something?"

"I heard what I thought was a gunshot. I think it was around eleven-thirty or twelve-thirty just before or right after noon or so."

The thirteen-year-old youth said he was in the living room with his sister and a pal, watching TV. The morning had been rainy, so the kids had turned to the TV.

"How are you sure about the time?" the officer asked.

"Because I remember what I was watching. I looked in a TV guide to see what time it was playing, so I knew around what time it was."

"What made you think it was a gunshot?"

"I've heard gunshots before. It was just loud."

The boy said the volume of the TV was tuned "just normal, not too low or too loud, and I could hear the shot over the TV. I opened up my door and looked out the screen door to see if I could tell where it was coming from. It sounded like it came from the front somewhere. I didn't see anything unusual, so I just closed the door, and that's it."

He said he heard only one shot.

The house-to-house check turned up other neighbors who thought they might have heard gunshots around noon or shortly after, but they weren't sure, it being so near to the Fourth of July and firecrackers popping frequently.

But Randall was adamant that what he heard was a gunshot, not a firecracker.

"I know when I hear a firecracker," he said.

With the boy's recollection, the investigators believed they now had some idea of the time period in which the murders might have happened.

The critical time element seemed to be further pinpointed by a young resident who lived next door to the Wuertz house. She told detectives about her pet dog, who was barking excitedly in a manner she recognized as how the animal acted when barking at a person.

Suddenly the dog, its tail tucked between its legs and yipping frantically as if in fright, came dashing into the house through a hinged pet-entrance and ran under a bed, the owner said. She added that was the way her dog responded when it had been scared by a person.

"I was concerned at the time because my dog started barking at the back fence next to where Melody and Jessica live," the girl said. "I knew that Melody had been afraid of something lately and I was worried."

She looked out but had not seen anything suspicious.

Chapter 4

District Attorney Macy did not immediately enter the Wuertz home.

Having been a cop for several years before he became a lawyer, the district attorney (D.A.) knew the importance of keeping human traffic at a crime scene to the bare minimum in the first stages of an investigation. It is vital to give the lab people early access and enough time to stake out and secure evidence so they can do their job properly.

Cops know it, prosecutors know it, defense attorneys have nightmares about it. Forensic evidence can be more reliable than eyewitnesses.

Trace evidence (hair, fibers, blood types and patterns, wounds on a body, all kinds of stains and human secretions, carpet sweepings and scrapings, fingerprints, discharged bullets, shell hulls, gunpowder residue) can tell a story to the police scientists who have the experience for processing and interpreting it. In this manner, the dead do speak.

The scientific brain trust available to homicide detectives—the forensic wizards such as pathologists, serologists, entomologists, fingerprint and firearm experts, trace-evidence analysts, psychological analysts, and criminal profilers—is a powerful crime-fighting task force never to be underestimated.

Microscopes and test tubes probably solve more baffling murder cases than do the deductive talents of detectives; and no one realizes this more than the detectives themselves.

That's why the crime-scene techs are the fair-haired men and women everywhere that human bodies turn up—dead under suspicious or violent circumstances.

When District Attorney Macy did go inside, he was struck by the inhumanity of the killings. The apparent cold-blooded execution of a tiny, helpless baby and the monstrous mutilation of the small-statured young woman sickened and angered him.

In his street days, then policeman Macy had known the devastation that envelops victims and families of victims. He would always remember the time when a brutally assaulted woman could not speak but gripped his hand and would not let go. He would never forget when a heavy truck had collapsed and crushed the young man working beneath it, and the emotional agony of the victim's father who was present and moaned over and over, "Johnny, don't leave me! Johnny, don't leave me!"

From the moment he took in the full horror of the murders in the Wuertz home, Macy knew that he would seek the death penalty for the killer when that time came.

He told reporters at the scene, "It's the most horrible crime scene I have ever seen. It is certainly one that will live on in my memory."

*   *   *

Dozens of photographs had been taken inside and outside the house. Tammie Wright, an investigator for the Oklahoma County Medical Examiner's Office, examined the bodies and then authorized their removal. Before this was done, the victims were wrapped in clean sheets to preserve any trace evidence such as hairs and fibers from falling off.

To the spectators outside, especially to the friends who had known the mother and baby, it was a heartrending tableau when gurneys bearing the wrapped and strapped-on bodies—one so tiny—were wheeled from the house to waiting ambulances.

Melody and Jessica Wuertz were leaving their cozy home for the last time, only one day before they should have been on their way to the planned happy vacation in Indiana.

The timing of the double tragedy would become a factor in the murder probe ahead.

One of the technical experts who helped Yardley with the collection of evidence was Douglas J. Perkins of the OSBI, an expert on Luminol testing. He had been called by Yardley to conduct Luminol tests to look for bloodstains that might be overlooked by the naked eye.

Luminol is a mixture of chemicals that when sprayed on surfaces causes any previously undetected blood spatters or blood trails or blood masses to glow in the dark, much like the eerie glow of a Halloween mask. The discovery of any blood traces is essential to investigators in reconstructing events at a violent-crime scene.

In one Oklahoma City murder case several years ago that Yardley was aware of, homicide detectives believed that a woman had been killed by her husband, who reported her missing after she left to go to a supermarket close by and never returned.

The detectives suspected the woman had been killed

inside her home by her spouse, and her body disposed of in some unknown location. There were some minor bloodstains, but it was learned the house had been scoured recently by a professional clean-up crew hired by the husband.

However, when a bedroom was sprayed with Luminol, the walls began to glow with such intensity that a person could read a book by the glowing light. Samples of blood found in the bedroom were matched to the missing woman by a reversed DNA process in which blood types can be cross-matched with parents or siblings of the victim. With the tremendous blood loss, the sleuths knew she had been killed in the house.

However, the Luminol testing by Perkins in the Wuertz home, done long after dark when other technicians and detectives had finished their work, literally did not throw much light on what already was surmised from the visible bloodstains.

The investigators were puzzled by the lack of a blood trail in the hallway, which they thought would have been left when Melody Wuertz was dragged into the bedroom, that is, if the killing had happened as they believed.

But the absence of any blood trail was cleared up by a blood-pattern expert, Capt. Tom Bevel of the Oklahoma City Police Department.

Bevel, after looking at crime-scene photographs and the autopsy report on Melody Wuertz, explained that external bleeding, if any, from the gunshot wound in her neck would have been soaked up by the victim's hair before reaching the carpet.

The more excessive bleeding had been in the bedroom, where the elder Wuertz was slashed and stabbed by the killer before a second shot was fired into her left ear, the blood expert said.

When Det. Theresa Pfeiffer got out of her car at the West Seventh address on that hot and muggy July 2 evening, a knot of officers and civilians was outside, among them her CID supervisors and the police chief.

Whatever it was, it was big. One of those top-priority cases that can grab full and unrelenting attention in a small town, she sensed.

She had planned a quiet evening at home with her twelve-week-old baby girl and her husband, a city fireman who worked shifts of twenty-four hours on and twenty-four hours off. With his shifts and her never knowing when emergencies would tear her away from hopes of domesticity, it seemed like sometimes they just waved and said, "hello, goodbye," and went their individual ways.

The attractive blonde investigator also had another daughter, six years old, at home, but it seemed to her that motherhood experienced again was every bit as fulfilling as her firstborn had been, as full of surprises and unexpected experiences, promising so many wonderful moments with her newborn child.

Pfeiffer had been back to work barely more than a month.

As she started toward the gray house, Rockie Yardley came out the front door and intercepted her. She noticed his face was pale. She had never seen him like that. She didn't know any details of the double-homicide call, but if the shaken appearance of her fellow officer was any indication, it must be pretty bad inside.

In the ten years they had been colleagues in the Edmond Police Department, Yardley and Pfeiffer had worked numerous violent death scenes together.

Having worked as a patrol officer before becoming a detective, gory accident scenes were not all that rare. Neither were brawling drunks, calls where she sometimes came out on top of the pile in a Donnybrook bar fight, sometimes on the bottom.

But she had never backed away, and the guys knew that and respected her for it. She had earned the patrol badge she wore. She didn't try to throw her weight around, either. She couldn't, in fact. She wasn't all that big. She took pride in being a woman, in looking and feeling like a woman.

But now Yardley said to her, "Theresa, we've got a dead baby in there. I don't think you need to go in there."

Police Chief Vetter and supervisors of the Criminal Investigation Division were standing nearby. Chief Vetter supported Yardley's suggestion, saying, "You've just had a baby yourself, Theresa. You don't have to go in there and see that. Another detective can do that. There are plenty of other things to do right now, and there is plenty of help inside. Let the scene go for the time being, okay?"

They were emphatic: Now wasn't the time for her to view that crime scene, with her own new baby in its crib at home.

Considering the prospects for a few seconds, she took their advice.

She could stand up to it—she knew that, and so did her colleagues who had worked with this spirited young lady, when as a uniform officer she never shied away from any fight or danger that the car-beat cops face regularly.

"Okay," she said. She trusted their perceptions, these tough cops who never allowed themselves the luxury of emotion in their professional duties. Though there was hardly a police officer anywhere who didn't take the tragedies of the shift home with him.

She realized if her fellow cops were that concerned about the scene's effect on her, they must have good reason to be. She noticed that anyone who emerged from the house had the same look and pallor.

Later, when she finally did see photographs of Jessica Wuertz, she was glad of the warning she received, and more glad she had taken it seriously.

For months on end, as she worked this case, those pictures of that pitiful little form in a pool of blood would be the first thing that flashed into her mind when she awakened, and the last thing she thought of before finally going to sleep.

Chapter 5

Edmond, Oklahoma, site of the University of Central Oklahoma, is an affluent small city of about 40,000. Most of the time it is a peaceful and quiet place to live, where life is not too fast paced, and melodic church chimes ring out the hour.

In recent times the biggest local controversy was when a group of citizens of a non-Christian religious faith filed suit against the Edmond City Commission to force the officials to remove the Christian cross that was part of the official city seal. The litigation went all the way to the Supreme Court, and finally the cross was removed.

Then, one church wanted to construct a 157-foot-high concrete-and-steel cross near Interstate 35, but the city officials ruled it would have to be smaller in size.

Edmond's City Hall, at First and Littner, is a neat-looking white-brick building with wide and shallow steps across the front, facing south on First. The Edmond Police Department also is on First and directly west across Littner Street from City Hall. Both municipal buildings have on-street parking for the public.

Inside the police building, friendly clerks are on duty behind a glass window opposite the entrance. There is a soft-drink vending machine and a public phone in the lobby.

An elevator to the right of the entrance accesses the Criminal Investigation Division on the second floor, where detectives work out of individual, partitioned cubicles. The detective captain and administrators have separate offices across a corridor.

It is a fairly modern and typical small-city police department that frequently finds itself dealing with big-city crime because of Edmond's proximity to Oklahoma City, the state capital fifteen miles to the south. Crime in Edmond is mostly run-of-the-mill stuff—burglaries, thefts, family fights, kids speeding.

But as one police officer said, "Those times that crime gets hairy, it's *real* hairy."

Like that morning of Wednesday, August 20, 1986, around seven o'clock, when a disgruntled postal worker, an ex-Marine, walked into the Edmond Post Office with two guns and a box of ammunition. Within minutes he shot to death fourteen fellow postal employees, wounded six others, and then killed himself.

Rockie Yardley was the evidence officer working that bloody massacre; later he was given special recognition by the U.S. Postal Department and the FBI for a job well done.

Now, five years later, Yardley and Edmond detectives were in the middle of a murder investigation that would land the town once again in the national news focus.

The execution-style murders of a young mother and her

baby were bad enough, but other shocking developments in the case lay ahead.

On this particular Tuesday, July 2, 1991, with the long summer day of daylight saving time finally waning and slipping into late dusk, just about all members of the Edmond Police Department were up to their necks in trying to unravel one of Edmond's most heinous homicide mysteries in recent years.

Already the Oklahoma City and Edmond news media were clamoring for more details. Detective Capt. Ron Cavin, who doubled as the department's public-information officer, had his hands full.

With the technical hunt for incriminating clues continuing in the Wuertz home, the few detectives assigned to CID were trying to come up with something that would bring down the killer who could callously execute an infant and torture and butcher the mother.

Theresa Pfeiffer's regular partner was Det. Richard Ferling, a thirty-nine-year-old quiet, almost stoic investigator who primarily worked white-collar crime when more demanding cases such as a brutal murder didn't call out everyone in CID. Their supervisors felt that the styles of the two detectives complemented each other.

The Edmond department was not large enough to justify full-time homicide detectives. There weren't that many murders in Edmond. In the past, Ferling had worked maybe ten homicide cases over his years of service; Pfeiffer nine.

On this day, before the bottom fell out of all routine duties, Ferling had conducted several interviews in general-assignment cases. Pfeiffer had finished up a rape case affidavit before ending her regular stint. She often was involved in sex-crime investigations because she had a knack for relating to children and female victims.

Ferling had heard the double-homicide call on the police scanner, but he wasn't immediately called to the scene. It was about 7 P.M. when Lieutenant Gregg dispatched him to the VA Medical Center in Oklahoma City to interview coworkers of Melody Wuertz, who, investigators learned, had been employed at the big hospital as a ward clerk.

When he arrived on the fifth-floor unit where Wuertz had worked, he was unprepared for the emotional scene unfolding around the nurses' station. One nurse was on her knees on the floor, crying and praying.

Other people were crying and trying to console each other. The usually professionally efficient nurses and various assistants were in a state of near shock from the stunning news of the brutal slayings of Melody Wuertz and her baby, Jessica.

Only a few days earlier, the hospital workers remembered, the proud mother had displayed the latest photographs of her charming baby girl. One of Melody Wuertz's nurse friends was enamored with little Jessica and had paid for the photographs, since the baby's mom was always short on cash and barely making ends meet.

Only meager facts had been available on the 6 P.M. TV newscasts, but the impact on the hospital ward was one of disbelief and emotional devastation. The shocking news had temporarily halted normal hospital routine. It would take a while for Ferling to get people to talk to him about their on-job relationships with Melody Wuertz, the friendly, little ward clerk.

Pfeiffer, meanwhile, encountered a similar emotional wave when she knocked on the door of Phyllis Davis, the woman who had been Jessica's baby-sitter since the autumn of 1990, and had watched Jessica grow to the point that she was beginning to walk and say words such as "Mama."

The baby-sitter was hysterical with grief, and it took a few minutes before she could control her sorrow. But when she was able to talk to the detective, the words tumbled forth about a male nurse who had worked with Melody Wuertz at the hospital and was the father of her baby.

The sobbing baby-sitter repeated the words over and over, through her tears:

"He had the key. Melody didn't get the locks changed. She couldn't afford it."

Davis said that Melody Wuertz and the male nurse, Jimmie Ray Slaughter, the one who "had the key," had been embroiled in a paternity dispute of escalating hard feelings that recently had caused Melody to fear for her safety. That fear had increased markedly after Wuertz took legal action in an attempt to force Slaughter to pay child support for the infant he had fathered.

Pfeiffer could not help but notice the irony of the male nurse's name relative to the exceedingly brutal murders under investigation. But at this point it seemed almost ludicrous to think that a domestic-type fuss about paying child support could be the motive for the fiendish murders of the mother and baby.

The distressed baby-sitter was unable to go into all the details, but Pfeiffer did learn that Nurse Slaughter was an older married man with whom the somewhat naive Wuertz had become romantically involved a short time after she went to work at the Veterans Hospital.

Before ending the interview, the detective obtained the name of a close friend of Melody's who lived in Edmond. The sympathetic detective cut short her interview with the grieving baby-sitter with a pat on the shoulder and some comforting words.

* * *

Dianna Angell also was fighting back tears when questioned at her house by Pfeiffer. Angell said that she and Wuertz had been friends when they both were living in St. Louis, Missouri, before coming to Oklahoma City.

Angell and her husband had moved to Oklahoma City first, followed later by Melody Wuertz when a job opportunity opened at the Veterans Medical Center where Angell's husband held an administrative job.

As she talked about Melody Wuertz and their friendship, Angell suddenly exclaimed:

"I know who did this." She looked up and said, her voice quavering, "Do you understand that? I know who killed Melody and Jessica! I know who killed them!"

Pfeiffer said in the same quiet tone in which she had been questioning Angell, "Who do you think did it, Dianna?"

"Well, Jimmie Slaughter. He's the father of Jessica."

"Why do you think Jimmie Slaughter killed them?"

The distraught friend recalled that Wuertz had told her many times during conversations over the past few weeks that she thought Slaughter was capable of harming someone, and she was "somewhat afraid of him."

"Melody seemed to be more apprehensive after she filed that paternity suit naming Jimmie Slaughter as the daddy of her baby and asking for child support," Angell said. "She seemed real scared after that, much more apprehensive."

Angell remembered that Wuertz especially was frightened at night, when she came home after midnight from her hospital shift, because Slaughter still had a key to her front door.

"She was scared to death that he would be inside her house, waiting for her. She talked about it all the time.

We all told her to get the locks changed, but Melody hardly had enough money to keep food in the house, much less change the locks.''

After thanking Angell and telling the witness she would talk to her again when she was calmer and feeling better, Pfeiffer returned to the police station to report on the remarks of Phyllis Davis and Dianna Angell pointing to the hospital nurse named Jimmie Slaughter as the one they thought had killed Melody and Jessica.

Detective Ferling, who had checked back from his questioning of nurses and others at the Veterans Hospital, said that Slaughter's name had come up offhand, but no direct accusations had been made.

But Ferling had been aware of what seemed like growing fear among the hospital personnel, prompted by the horrible murders of one of their fellow workers and her lovable baby.

One thing was for certain, said Lieutenant Gregg, who was in charge of the investigation: "We need to know everything we can find out about this nurse, Jimmie Slaughter.''

This early in the murder probe, he thought, it almost was too much to hope for that the suspect would pan out.

People at the Veterans Affairs Medical Center had said Slaughter at present was assigned as a nurse in Irwin Army Hospital at Fort Riley, Kansas, 300 miles to the north of Edmond. His former coworkers said the ex-Army major had asked to be reactivated at the time of the Desert Shield crisis in the Middle East.

He had been gone from the VA Medical Center for several months. No one could say for sure whether his urge to go back into the service was based on patriotism or merely an opportunity to get far away from the growing heat of Melody Wuertz's paternity suit.

* * *

Pfeiffer finished her reports and didn't get home until
3 A.M. on Wednesday, July 3.

Her baby girl was sound asleep in her crib, alive and
beautiful. The detective felt a tug in her heart for that
young mother and her baby daughter, whose lives had
been snuffed out so terribly.

Chapter 6

Edmond police Sergeant Matthew Griffin was at home when he heard a news report about the murders and knew that his coming night shift was going to be a busy one, with most everybody tied up on the homicides.

When he went on duty at 9 P.M. he was summoned by Police Chief Vetter.

After a conference at the police station with Lieutenant Gregg and his detectives, it was decided to send Det. Sgt. Mike Meador to Fort Riley, Kansas, to see what could be learned about Jimmie Ray Slaughter, assigned as a nurse to Irwin Army Hospital there, the chief informed the patrolman.

"I want you to drive him and be available to help with whatever's needed," the chief said. He told the officer to use the department's newest police car.

Griffin and Meador stopped by the detective sergeant's home briefly, then started for Fort Riley at 2 A.M. on July 3.

* * *

It was daylight when they were met at a Junction City convenience store by members of the Army Military Police. Junction City adjoins the sprawling complex that is Fort Riley. The MPs escorted the Edmond officers onto the military installation.

After arrangements were made for the civilian officers to talk to Slaughter, he was brought into an office.

Meador and Griffin saw that the male nurse was an imposing figure, a large man who stood about six feet two inches tall and weighed 240 pounds. He was bald on top of his head and had dark brown hair on the sides. He wore black-rimmed glasses.

Slaughter worked as a psychiatric nurse in the Irwin Army Hospital, the same job he held during his years of employment at the VA Medical Center in Oklahoma City in the alcohol- and drug-abuse unit. The officers could see that the muscular male nurse was physically well qualified to handle any patient who might have to be restrained.

From the beginning the soft-spoken and obviously well-educated Slaughter was amiable to the policemen, seeming willing to tell them anything they wanted to know.

"Very cooperative" is how the investigators would describe him later to their supervisors. But he acted puzzled as to why the lawmen would want to talk to him.

Slaughter displayed no emotion when he heard the reason for their visit: the murders yesterday of Melody Wuertz and her baby in their Edmond home.

But he had a question himself: "Can you tell me how this woman and her child was killed?"

The Edmond officers noticed his using the words "this woman" instead of the given name he certainly knew.

He admitted he had dated Melody, and he said that after she had a baby, "I did something really dumb. I signed that paternity affidavit," implying that he did so just to give the child a name. No, his wife knew nothing about his relationship with the hospital-ward clerk or her claim that he was the father of her baby.

"Do you know the baby's name?"

Slaughter paused a second or two before replying. "I think she calls her Jessica."

Slaughter said he had not been in Edmond or any place near it on Tuesday, July 2. He had been with his wife, Nicki, and their two young daughters, Betsy and Caroline, all day. His family had arrived at Fort Riley on June 30 to visit over the holidays, he explained.

The wife and children still lived in the Slaughter home at Guthrie, Oklahoma, which they had kept when Slaughter was reactivated at the time of Desert Shield, the prelude to Desert Storm.

The Army nurse said that he and his wife had slept late Tuesday. In fact, he had placed a "Do Not Disturb" sign on the door of his apartment quarters in Carr Hall, a base dormitory for officers. Later, taking his wife's Ford Taurus, the family had driven into Junction City to eat lunch, then continued on to Topeka, Kansas, to do some shopping at a mall.

Later on Tuesday, July 2, Slaughter had reported for his regular shift at Irwin Army Hospital from 7 P.M. to 7 A.M.

Answering the officers' questions, Slaughter said he owned some knives. He was a collector of knives, and guns, as well. It was a hobby. He thought there was a .22 revolver in the trunk of his car.

Questioned separately, Nicki Slaughter corroborated her husband's statement that he had been with his family all day on July 2.

But there was one difference in her version of the day's activities. She said that they had been in Slaughter's Dodge Shadow automobile when they went shopping at various department stores in Topeka, not her Taurus.

Asked if she knew Melody Wuertz and Jessica, the wife said she had never heard of them.

Interviewed again, Slaughter was asked if he had any idea as to who might have done the murders.

He shook his head slowly back and forth and said, "Look at the black acquaintances she had." He implied she had a sexual preference for African-Americans.

He said that Wuertz had expressed an interest in "being involved with black men," despite the fact that he had made it clear he would have nothing to do with a woman who admitted involvement with a black man.

He recalled Wuertz once asked him if she could borrow a gun, the only thing he had ever denied her while they were seeing each other, he said.

"Why did she want a gun?"

Slaughter answered that Wuertz had mentioned "some agile sucker (Slaughter's reference to a black man) jumping fences in her neighborhood and making the dogs bark."

Permission was obtained to search Slaughter's quarters which consisted of a living room, a bedroom and a bathroom off of the bedroom.

During the search, Griffin served as the searcher and Det. Sgt. Meador took notes about where different items were found. The Edmond officers found twenty-two knives and numerous sheaths for knives in the nurse's quarters, and also in the vehicles of Slaughter and his wife.

One knife was removed from a briefcase that was on a desk in the living room.

The .22 mentioned by Slaughter was not found—there were no guns in his car.

But two knives and an assortment of knife sheaths were taken from his car; one knife was underneath the driver's seat, and another knife was behind the sun visor. The knife sheaths were on the floorboard.

The officers observed odd-looking symbols carved on several of the knife sheaths, weird designs with half circles and straight lines and reversed or inverted letters.

In the ashtray of Jimmie Slaughter's car were several keys on a ring. The investigators intended to check later to see if any of the keys might fit the door of Melody Wuertz's house.

The searchers also took a book titled *Complete Book of Magic and Witchcraft*.

Glancing through the book, they noticed drawings of some symbols similar to those etched on the knife sheaths owned by Slaughter, and not all that different from the one carved on Wuertz's abdomen.

In a living-room wastebasket Griffin discovered four receipts for various purchases from stores in Topeka, all dated July 2 and bearing the time that the sales slips were issued.

Numerous photographs were taken of Slaughter's living quarters and the couple's two automobiles. Detailed diagrams were made of the apartment and the vehicles, showing where each recovered item was found.

Although Slaughter's wife had backed her husband's story of their being together in Kansas on July 2, during the hours when the murders were believed to have occurred in Oklahoma 300 miles away, one important fact was undisputed: The duty records kept by the Army base showed that Slaughter definitely was not on duty on July 2 until the beginning of his night shift at 7 P.M. that date.

Officially, at least, his whereabouts on July 2 were unaccounted for up to the start of his night shift.

It remained to be seen how Slaughter's own account of his activities on that day checked out. Detectives would visit the stores named on the recovered merchandise receipts and talk to clerks to see if they remembered the Slaughter family.

But there was something about Slaughter and his smoothness, and his denials, that set off alarm bells in the investigative natures of Meador and Griffin.

Chapter 7

Robert H. "Bob" Macy, the district attorney, already had made an important decision in the double-homicide case at Edmond, a town in which he had spent eight years of private law practice before becoming a public official.

Although the investigation was nowhere near the stage of filing murder charges, Macy knew from the time he first viewed the murder scene on the previous afternoon that he would seek the death penalty for the killer. Growing forensic evidence indicated that the murders of the baby and mother had been premeditated, cold-blooded executions with the overtones of a professional "hit" job prompted by a motive unclear at this point. The earlier theory of a random sex attack that ended in murder was losing ground among the investigators.

In this distinguished career, Bob Macy had been a private practice lawyer, an employee of the U.S. Department of Justice in Washington, and an assistant county attorney in Pontotoc County, Oklahoma.

He also had been an assistant state attorney in the Oklahoma Attorney General's Office, the deputy Public Safety Administrator for the city of St. Petersburg, Florida, and an assistant to the superintendent of the Indiana State Police.

Governor George Nigh of Oklahoma appointed Macy as Oklahoma County District Attorney in 1980, to replace the incumbent, who had resigned to seek the office of a U.S. senator. When Macy's name had come up, Governor Nigh, who had been a fellow law-school student with Macy at the University of Oklahoma, appointed him with the reported verbal observation, "Bob Macy is the most honest man I know."

The sixty-six-year-old Macy is a past president and former chairman of the board of the National District Attorney's Association and was appointed by Pres. George Bush as a member of a Presidential Commission on Model Drug Laws. Former U.S. attorney general William Barr once described Macy as "a great American and one of the most outstanding law-enforcement leaders of our time."

Macy rose to the top of the legal profession the hard way. His years as a cop with the Oklahoma City Police Department influenced his views on criminal prosecution. Seeing what violent crime can do to ordinary people had been Macy's boot-camp training for his future courtroom wars with crime.

He had gone to work as a night-shift patrolman to pay his way through daytime studies at the University of Oklahoma law school.

The police encounter he dreaded most was any case involving the injury or violent death of a child. Macy never forgot some of the things he had seen.

The hard-core street experiences of the young officer drove home the devastation felt by surviving relatives. He hated those times when he had to carry tragic news to families of victims. Macy felt deeply the vulnerability of people, recognized their need for protection by the law, by the policemen who enforced the law, came to know too well the frustrations cops sometimes feel trying to do their jobs.

Within the six-foot, 225-pound frame of the youthful cop being indoctrinated into society's inhumanity, was a compassionate nature. Outwardly displaying the professional detachment that a law-enforcement officer has to maintain, Macy hurt inside for the victims and the people who had loved them.

When he became a prosecutor, it was a step further for taking action against the predators who wrought havoc against innocent people. His sensitivity to the suffering of crime victims and their families fueled a personal philosophy of hard-nosed law enforcement.

It was a constant factor in achieving a national reputation as the country's leading death-penalty prosecutor. By 1996, Macy personally had sent fifty killers to Oklahoma's Death Row, and other prosecutors in his office added a dozen to that total.

He strongly advocated the death penalty. At the same time, he set for himself a tougher guiding standard for judgment than the one that the law provides for jurors. Before asking for the death penalty, he personally had to be convinced of the defendant's guilt beyond *any* doubt— not just beyond a *reasonable* doubt as specified in the law that jurors must abide by.

Macy believed that society should not have to endure the continuing threat of a convicted murderer, especially the ones so depraved that they could deliberately and without remorse take a human life under circumstances justifying the death penalty.

In Macy's view, there is no hope of rehabilitation for this type of murderer, and he has never felt any regrets for the fifty convicted killers that he personally sent to Oklahoma's Death Row.

The way he and his three brothers were raised by their strict father had a lasting effect on the D.A.'s thinking toward the law and people's personal accountability. He often recalled his dad's well-heeded words:

"You boys will obey me because you respect me, or you will obey me because you're afraid not to."

And that's exactly how Macy the prosecutor felt: If people could not obey the law because of respect for their fellow citizens, then they should obey it out of fear for what will happen if they don't.

Macy in 1996 was serving his fourth consecutive term as District Attorney of Oklahoma County. He won all the elections with high voter pluralities.

The district attorney's office is on the fifth floor of the Oklahoma County Office Building in downtown Oklahoma City, only a few blocks from the site of the nine-story Alfred P. Murrah Federal Building that was ripped apart by a truck bomb on Wednesday, April 19, 1995, killing 167 persons and wounding 675.

The bombing disaster that would rock the nation and the world was still nearly four years in the future on that Wednesday, July 3, 1991, when Larry W. Andrews was summoned to the office of his boss.

Andrews, forty-five years old and a former veteran homicide detective for the Oklahoma City Police Department, was the head of a countywide drug task force based in the D.A.'s office.

As he made his way to Macy's relatively small office at the far end of a large room filled with the desks of assistant district attorneys and secretaries, he wondered what was up.

"Come in, Larry," Macy greeted the slender-faced,

bespectacled investigator. "I need your help on a murder case."

The D.A., wearing his usual Western-style black tie, sat at his desk. On the wall behind him hangs an enlarged color photograph taken at the annual Celebrity Rodeo in Oklahoma, of Macy and actor Ben Johnson, a native Oklahoman who became famous for his character role in the 1960s movie *Hud*. Both men were outfitted in Western regalia.

But Macy was no ordinary dude posing with a cowboy actor. Bob Macy was still an active rodeo competitor— admittedly in the less-strenuous Team Roping event because, as he says, "It's a rodeo event you can compete in as long as you can sit a horse and toss a rope. And once in a while I get lucky and win."

Andrews sat down and the D.A. leaned back and explained the new assignment he had for the drug task force leader. Macy was familiar with Andrews's work in previous years as a homicide sleuth with the Oklahoma City Police. The investigator had come highly recommended.

The D.A. got to the point. It was beginning to look as if the murders of a mother and her baby in Edmond were not done by a strike-at-random, break-and-enter rapist, who freaked out and killed the woman and child.

Andrews had heard about the murders on the TV news the night before, but he knew few details.

Macy said that at first glance there were signs that it was a sex murder—the woman partly unclothed, one leg spread to the side, sexually mutilated. It was understandable why the lady who called the 911 operator had said a woman had been raped and murdered.

"There was evidence at the scene that, right now, we are not sure just what it means," Macy said quietly. "There are conflicts."

He added that the name of a possible suspect had surfaced in the hours following discovery of the bodies. Macy did not mention the name. "This guy may have had a pretty good motive. They say he looks like a good suspect, but I don't know that. The point I'm making is that I don't want us to get overfocused on any one person and ignore someone else. A suspect, as you well know, is just that, a suspect."

Macy said he was concerned with the brutality of the murders: "I went by the crime scene yesterday afternoon. The killings were vicious. Can you believe somebody would execute a little baby with two shots in the head?" The baby's mother had been shot, too, and cut up horribly, butchered was the only word, Macy said.

"But the Edmond police and the OSBI have this idea that things may not be all that they look to be," the district attorney added. "We'll know more about that when the forensic people and the Medical Examiner's Office are finished."

Macy said it seemed likely that the killer had gone to the Edmond residence for the sole purpose of executing the mother and child, and had struck so quickly there had been no chance for resistance or flight.

How the intruder got into the house was a major factor in the probe, Macy said. No evidence of forced entry: Either the killer had been admitted after knocking, or had pushed his way inside when the woman opened the door, or had a key.

No ransacking of the house, nothing missing even though over $100 cash was in plain sight. And the preliminary exam by the medical examiner disclosed the woman, Melody Wuertz, apparently had not been sexually assaulted.

Macy told Andrews, "I want you to go to Edmond and offer the police department our help, any way we can help. The police are running the investigation, and I would like you to be there as liaison for this office. . . ."

The quiet-spoken district attorney paused and looked directly at the investigator.

"And Larry, I want you to stay on the case until it's solved. I want us to give the person that is suspected every benefit of the doubt. I don't want us to push on this one person to the extent that we would overlook somebody else that we haven't heard about yet."

Chapter 8

The autopsies on the bodies of Melody and Jessica Wuertz only confirmed what already was suspected by the detectives.

Melody Wuertz had not been sexually assaulted. Test swabs of her vagina, anus and mouth were negative for male sperm. A lust-driven madman in a sexual frenzy had not raped and murdered the mother and killed the child; instead, the slayings had been a professional job by a cunning and merciless killer, in every respect a "hit"-type homicide.

The autopsy findings indicated the victims had been targeted for death by the killer long before he invaded their small home. Though couched in the medical language used by those who do postmortem work, the pathologist's report nevertheless imparted the conclusion that the slayings had been calculated and cold-blooded executions.

Melody Wuertz had died from two gunshots in her neck and head. The killer had slashed, stabbed, and mutilated her while she was still alive, although probably paralyzed from the gunshot in the neck that struck the second cervical vertebrae in the stem of the spine.

Another gunshot, this one fired into her brain through an ear, had brought death, but only after she suffered unspeakable atrocities to her body. The deep slashes and stab wounds extending from her breasts to her genitals had been inflicted with an instrument that was scalpel sharp.

The weapon had been expertly wielded, as shown by the lack of so-called "hesitation marks" in the incision margins—not the kind of wounds made by a novice or someone out of control or in a sadistic frenzy.

The gaping wounds on her breasts and vagina resulted from decisive, swift and precise use of the weapon, which might have been a single-edge, hunting-type knife with a blade at least eight inches long.

The report related that the gunshot into her ear "left a blackened peripheral abrasion rim to the left earlobe," obviously gunpowder residue that would be deposited if the gun had been held almost against or close to the skin. The other wound on the back of her neck "left a red peripheral abrasion rim but no soot black inner powder stipling."

Slicing across Wuertz's chest was a horizontal stab wound with an overall depth of 5.6 inches, described as a "through and through wound" that penetrated the heart and partially collapsed the right lung.

A gaping cut on the right breast had sliced through the full thickness of the breast and part of the nipple. The vicious swipe of the blade had cut through the ribs and exposed the lungs.

An elongated slash, somewhat cross shaped, gaped to two inches over the left breast.

On the stomach were superficial cuts covering an area about ten by four inches which appeared to be shaped roughly like an R. It looked as if the knifer had been trying to draw a bizarre, cultlike symbol in the skin.

In the pubic region was a slash wound in the shape of a crude X. A gaping, 8.8-inch-long stab wound to the vagina had penetrated all the way through the anus and back of the right buttock. The deep and powerful thrust of the knife blade had completely dissected the vaginal canal.

The only other signs of violence noted on Melody Wuertz's body were bruises over the lower lip and the inner membrane of the lower lip, suggesting that she had been struck a hard blow to the face with a fist.

No injuries were found on her hands and arms, such as would have been present if she had struggled to defend herself. Examination of the throat area (the "hyoid epiglottis and the thyroid cartilage") showed no abnormalities; so there had been no attempt by the assailant to strangle her.

Wuertz's stomach contained some partly digested food including melon litters. Her bladder was empty of urine, and no alcohol was found in her blood.

Baby Jessica had died from two gunshot wounds to her head, one of them passing through both lobes of her brain and being instantly fatal.

There was a rim of gunpowder residue around the wound and in the tissue. The path of the bullet was forward, upward and to the left.

The pooling of blood on the carpet with the baby's left handprint in it meant that Jessica was lying there for several minutes before the killer put a second shot into the back of her head. The killer apparently turned Jessica over and facedown before pressing the gun barrel against the back of her head and shooting. The final shot was described as a "contact wound."

Trajectory of this slug was forward, downward and to the left.

Jessica Wuertz had not been mutilated. It was obvious

that the killer's only intention was to make absolutely sure that she was dead.

Driving to Edmond after his meeting with Macy, Andrews attended a briefing at the Edmond Police Station of all the investigators working on the case. Lieutenant Terry Gregg summarized what was known and had been done so far.

Detective Meador and Sergeant Griffin were on their way back from Fort Riley, where they had questioned Maj. Jimmie Slaughter and his wife, and made a search for evidence.

But at this point, nothing had turned up that would justify taking Slaughter into custody as a suspect, according to the Edmond officers, who had reported by phone from Kansas before starting home.

It was clear that the job ahead would require all the personnel that could be mustered to interview the dozens of potential witnesses: Slaughter's coworkers at the Fort Riley hospital and the Veterans Affairs Medical Center in Oklahoma City, as well as employees of the stores named by Slaughter and his wife as where they had been shopping during the crucial time period when the murders were thought to have been done.

It was vital to find out as soon as possible whether Slaughter was in the clear, as his alibi would indicate.

Already the name of another possible suspect had come to light during the preliminary interviews with friends and coworkers of Melody Wuertz.

Mason Hollinger was a young man who had dated Melody for a while. Only recently they had broken off the relationship with a heated argument, detectives were told. The ex-boyfriend was said to have a quick temper. And so far, the investigators had not been able to locate Hollinger for questioning.

* * *

Andrews went to the house on West Seventh to get the crime scene firmly in mind. As he walked through the residence with Edmond investigators, he had many questions, but he quickly learned that the local detectives and crime-scene techs had done an impressive job of gathering and analyzing evidence at the scene, searching the area, and canvassing the neighborhood for possible leads.

Some residents had not been at home, and those addresses were being revisited by investigators. But from the neighbors who had been questioned, certain things were determined: The boy who thought he had heard a shot, and the woman who recounted the excited barking of her dog, offered the best clues so far as to the time period in which the murders occurred, at noon or not long afterward.

Laboratory technicians of the Oklahoma State Bureau of Investigation had examined some of the possible evidence found on Melody Wuertz's body and in her bedroom.

Three hairs that were not Wuertz's—a long hair and two shorter hairs discovered on the woman's body—had been identified tentatively as Negroid head hairs. The same type of hair was found on the pair of Jockey undershorts and also in the man's black comb that was near her body.

Douglas J. Perkins, the criminalist with the OSBI who had done the Luminol testing in the house and helped Yardley gather and preserve the possible evidence, had pointed out after preliminary analysis that the way the hair was entangled in the comb was unusual.

The hair was in a bunched wad, not evenly dispersed through the teeth as it would be when a person normally combs his hair; rather, it was "a lot of hair that apparently had been pushed onto the teeth of the comb at one end."

This fact alone began to raise the possibility that the crime scene had been staged. And the position of Melody

Wuertz's body and the disarranged clothing made no sense
at all with the autopsy determination that no sexual assault
had occurred. The logical conclusion was that the killer
had done this to lay a false trail for the investigators.

Chapter 9

Captain Ron Cavin, head of the Criminal Investigation Division of the Edmond Police Department, was tired of sitting in the office while all of his detectives were out beating the bushes for leads. There were only a half-dozen detectives available and they were spread thin with all the angles that had to be pursued.

Cavin had wanted to be a policeman from the time he was a boy. One of his uncles had been an Oklahoma City officer, and his stories had stirred Cavin's youthful interest in becoming a policeman. Back then, a cop was one thing that boys wanted to be when they grew up.

Cavin's father was a news cameraman for a TV station, and his adventures in covering crime stories added to the inspirational yarns Cavin heard from his uncle.

Cavin realized as he grew up and spent several successful but comparatively boring years in the grocery business, that it was not what he wanted to do.

He joined the Edmond Police Department as a patrolman on July 1, 1983, when Edmond was a town of only

14,000 with a police department of only fourteen officers. He worked undercover in sting operations and later in narcotics. He became head of the Edmond detective unit in August 1986.

On this July 3, which happened to be his birthday, Cavin decided to walk out the area around West Seventh, looking for weapons and any information that might help unravel the double-murder case.

He chose an area on Fretz Street, which runs into West Seventh. There was a house with a high fence on the corner and an open field across the street. The detective captain concentrated his search around a shed and a patch of trees and brush toward the end of the field, working his way in the direction of houses farther down the street.

He thought it would have been a good place to discard a weapon. As he was checking the spot, he saw three young boys walking toward him along Fretz. Their words were loud and vulgar.

He approached the trio and said, "Hey, you guys watch your language." He threw in a remark that brought concern to the young faces. "I'm a police officer."

Cavin asked the boys if they lived in this neighborhood. One of the boys replied, "Yes, sir. Down the street a few houses on this side."

Cavin asked if they had been out and around yesterday.

"Yes, sir, we was," the youth said.

"Did you see any cars parked along this street, or any people you didn't know?" It was a wild shot at best, and Cavin was startled by the boy's answer.

"Yes, sir, there was a car parked about where we're at now with some geeky-looking, bald-headed old doober in it."

Asked to describe the car, the youngster said it was a gray or blue car, maybe a Dodge. Cavin recognized that the description generally fit the gray-blue Dodge Shadow that Jimmie Slaughter drove, the car that had been searched at Fort Riley by the Edmond officers.

"A skinny-looking guy, maybe?" Cavin asked.

The boy grinned. "No, sir, he was big and kind of fat. He was bald on top of his head and wore glasses."

He said that as they walked by the car, the boys had made remarks among themselves, making fun of the man in the car.

The boy said he had walked close to the driver's side, and as he came abreast of the car, the man suddenly raised up and glared at him.

"He had been bent over, sort of ducked down and doing something like reaching under the seat," the boy recalled.

The man in the car didn't say anything, just glared at him.

Cavin realized the description given by the boy sounded like Jimmie Slaughter, as he had been described by the officers who questioned him at Fort Riley.

The detective captain placed a call for Detective Pfeiffer to come to the location and interview the youngsters in more depth. Pfeiffer was an expert when it came to getting the most out of questioning kids.

Later, after talking to the boys, she asked them to write out in their own words what they had seen.

Suddenly, pure luck had dropped into the sleuths' laps; here was the possibility of a possible eyewitness, who might place Jimmie Slaughter in a car less than one-half block from the Wuertz home on the day of the murders.

And the time that the boys saw the balding man with glasses was about 12:37 P.M. Once again, television had helped a witness relate an event to the time it occurred. The boys remembered a TV program that had gone off as they left one of the boy's house. They knew it went off at 12:30 P.M.

After it became an issue, detectives walked with the youths from the boy's house to the spot where they said the car was parked. Sauntering along as kids do when talking and cutting up, it had taken seven minutes.

If the boys could make a positive identification, the investigators knew they could wipe out Slaughter's alibi story. The boys would be asked to look at a photograph lineup, after a picture of Slaughter was obtained and mixed with other mug shots, to see if they could pick out the man they had seen in the parked car.

There was no question that Slaughter was emerging as the prime suspect in the homicides. But Andrews remembered Bob Macy's cautioning words to "not overfocus" on one suspect to the extent that others might be overlooked.

Jimmie Slaughter might be looking good for the murders to the detectives, but they were a long, long way from being able to prove anything against him. And, when the string was run out to the end, he well might be innocent as claimed. Andrews had seen it happen.

Toward the objective of finding out for sure—however it turned out—Larry Andrews and Det. Theresa Pfeiffer left together for Fort Riley on July 5, three days after the slayings.

They were a unique investigative team, in some ways. Andrews, the veteran and experienced ex-homicide detective from the big-city police department; Pfeiffer, the young woman whose murder investigation experience was far more limited. She had faced a dilemma before agreeing to accept the out-of-town assignment. It was a hard decision for the detective to make, to embark on the biggest case in her police career at the untimely moment when a new baby was competing in her mind and emotions for the motherly love and attention so important in the first months of life.

It had been a tough and painful decision for Pfeiffer to make, and even now, on the way to Kansas, she was wondering if it had been the right decision. Sadly, as it developed, she would wonder about her decision for years to come.

She had been kept from seeing the dead baby at the crime scene by the thoughtfulness of her fellow officers, but necessarily the time came when she had to look at the victim photographs.

The image of that tiny form lying as though sleeping—on her back, eyes closed, one small arm up and the other just to the side of her face, replayed itself in Pfeiffer's mind like a nightmarish video that could not be turned off.

Lieutenant Gregg, the supervisor on the case, had called Pfeiffer into his office when she reported to duty on July 5. Larry Andrews was there, seated in another chair. She had never met him before.

Gregg got right to the point: "You have a new baby, I know, but I really need somebody to go to Kansas with Larry and help to either substantiate this guy Slaughter's alibi or not. You don't have to, but I'm in a bind."

One detective of the small CID unit was on vacation at the time, and others were tied up on assignments.

Gregg knew of the woman detective's capabilities for dealing with delicate situations, for drawing out the facts in an ugly sex-crime case from tearful and humiliated victims, women, and children.

Pfeiffer didn't answer immediately. She was thinking of the demanding responsibilities of baby care. It was hard for her to stay away from her baby even during regular shift hours.

Only a mother could feel it, this overwhelming emotion, feeling so fully every tug and need of her baby, hardly able to wait to get home in the evenings and gather the cuddly bundle in her arms.

But finally she said only, "Well, okay, I'll go."

She had no idea that she would not get home again for a week.

Theresa Pfeiffer had struggled hard to be a good police officer in a profession that historically was mostly a man's world. It would change dramatically in future years, but when she started in her very early twenties, one of the first things that a woman rookie had to fight against wasn't the criminals on the streets but her fellow cops.

Not all of them certainly, but some of them, particularly the older guys who habitually had thought of their jobs as man's work. The same was true in the fire department and the armed forces, and the colleges and universities that were not coeducational.

She recalled the first day she walked to the police car with her field-training officer (FTO), a gruff kind of guy who immediately laid down his own rules when they were seated in the unit: "This is my radio, this is my car, I don't want you touching any of it. And by the way, the last female officer we had here I got fired for cowardliness."

She referred to the training officer after that, not in his presence, of course, but when bemoaning her troubles to other rookie cops, as "the old crudmudgen (sic)."

One day not long after that roughshod introduction to the job, this same field-training officer got into a tough spot trying to restrain an obvious mental case on a call that he and Pfeiffer had answered. It turned out to be a real brawl. Two male officers, who arrived in another car, hung back from what was becoming a fierce struggle, and it was going the wrong way for the training officer.

Pfeiffer jumped in to help. She used to good advantage what she had been taught about defensive combat in the police academy.

Her FTO had a different outlook toward her after that. Before he retired, he and the woman rookie whom he had harshly dressed down at their first meeting became good friends.

Pfeiffer, thereafter had a reputation for carrying her part of any load, and for being a fearless brawler. It was a far cry from the first profession she studied at the University of Oklahoma: pharmacy.

While going to college, she had taken a part-time job as clerk and dispatcher with the Nichols Hills Police Department. Nichols Hills was a small incorporated community of wealthy residents that actually was within the city limits of sprawling Oklahoma City.

One day she had decided she didn't want to spend her life standing and pasting labels on bottles and passing out pills. After a year with the Nichols Hills department, she had come to the Edmond Police Department.

Her first job had been undercover in the narcotics unit then headed by Sgt. Ron Cavin. She was set up in an apartment; only a limited number of people on the Edmond department knew about her assignment. She made a lot of buys.

From the undercover operation she went into the Field Training Program and was a patrol officer for two years. She learned quickly that if she just went out there, not with a chip on her shoulder, not saying she's as tough as any other guy, but just do the job effectively and not lock herself in a patrol car, then the guys would treat her with respect.

After the patrol duty, she was assigned as a detective to CID.

But all the challenges she met while learning to be a competent police officer were nothing like the stress she would encounter as a hard-pressed homicide detective who also happened to be a new mother separated from her baby for extended periods of time. Her husband wasn't too happy with the idea, either.

* * *

The days in Kansas were a whirlwind of activity. Pfeiffer interviewed women nurses at Irwin Army Hospital who worked with Jimmie Slaughter and knew him well from their shared hospital shifts. There were some nurses who knew him much better than that, the detective soon found out.

These women eventually talked to Pfeiffer about their intimate relationships and affairs with Slaughter. The detective also questioned Nicki Slaughter and made some startling discoveries about this former nurse.

Andrews was busy on similar interviews with the male witnesses. He also was the one who questioned Jimmie Slaughter. Everything they were learning about this large and smooth-talking psychiatric nurse was pointing to his disdain for women, if not an actual hatred, despite his successful romantic involvements.

Pfeiffer did not talk to him, which made her quite glad.

But in the candid interviews they had with Slaughter's coworkers, his lovers and ex-lovers, the detectives began to put together the profile of a sociopath and the bizarre story of how he entered the life of a naive, Christian-raised young woman who, it seemed, would have been the most unlikely target for his predatory ventures.

But then, all of the women that Jimmie Slaughter pursued and seduced were a particular type: shy women, unsure of themselves with men, who had low self-esteem and obvious physical and personality weaknesses; women who could be enslaved by Slaughter's early affection and devoted attention, and later would submit to his dominating control.

Pert and pretty, but often unsure of herself, perhaps because of the long battle with epilepsy, Melody Wuertz was indeed like a lamb being led to Jimmie Slaughter, who could read women like a book and turn their pages at will.

Chapter 10

Amid the lush farmlands and gentle sloping hills of Indiana during the 1960s and the 1970s, people lived their lives much like their ancestors had in earlier and less sophisticated times.

Godliness and family values still were the way of life among these quiet rural folk, who lived in the same place for many years, raised their children there, sent them to country schools, saw them off every morning on the school bus and welcomed them when they came home in the afternoon.

On Sunday the families were in church, singing the old-time hymns and listening to solid preaching on the gospel message of Jesus Christ. They enjoyed the fellowship after church; they had a big Sunday dinner at home or, as a special treat, a meal at the favorite restaurant in town.

Such was the life of Indiana small-town and rural people at a time when the rest of the country, especially the big cities, were going to hell in a handbasket. The flower children of the sexual revolution of the 1960s had as their loving creed: Do anything that feels good.

The old-fashioned lifestyle of loving God and country was the way Lyle and Susie Wuertz had grown up, and the way they raised their own children. Most of their thirty-eight years of marriage had been lived in the pleasant countryside some ten miles south of Washington, Indiana. Usually people had not heard of Washington, Indiana, unless they were native Hoosiers. The community of about 25,000 population is southwest of Indianapolis and closer to Bloomington.

The Wuertz family could have come from a Norman Rockwell painting of American life in those years when family and tradition and religious faith meant something.

From the time they started dating seriously, Lyle and Susie dreamed of someday, in their future married life, of having a baby girl with "a bright, sunshine smile." That dream came true on September 17, 1961, with the birth of their first daughter, Melody.

She was so named because she was a song in the hearts of her parents. Susie always remembered her as a "miracle baby," because Melody slipped into the world so easily as compared to the difficulties Susie had when Wesley, her oldest child was born. The smoothness of the birth for her mother seemed to herald a happy life for the little girl.

Besides the overflowing love of her parents, Melody was adored by her older brother, Wesley; they stuck together like twins.

Melody had been an energetic child, always smiling and laughing, making many friends, never having to be disciplined by her parents. It was a special Sunday when Melody was baptized at their church. Wesley was proud when he watched his little sister walk down the church aisle to accept Christ into her heart.

He was a faithful churchgoer himself and had decided at a young age that he had a calling to become a minister.

Melody had musical talent and was interested in drama. She and Wesley sang together in musical groups in school and church programs.

Melody was a thirteen-year-old eighth-grader when one day she suddenly collapsed, falling to the floor, her young body jerking convulsively as she slipped into unconsciousness. Wesley will never forget that dark day when he witnessed the frightening scene. The family listened with sinking hearts at the doctor's diagnosis. Melody had suffered an epileptic seizure. She could be treated with medication, but the unexpected seizures would be something that she must live with the rest of her life.

The Wuertz family members, in their strong faith, had learned to accept the tough times with the good. Melody adjusted best of all, patiently taking her required medication that helped to prevent and control the seizures, enduring them when they happened. But she never knew when the next seizure might send her reeling into unconsciousness. As her mother recalled later, "She dealt with it so well. Melody never let the threat of having a seizure keep her from doing anything."

Melody had plenty of courage. She refused to let her disability turn her life into one of "walking on eggs." She was spirited and determined, and had no patience with anyone cautioning her that she needed to be careful. It was a pattern that followed her through high school and into college and her later workday life. But she always bounced back from a seizure with more determination than ever, though it never was easy.

Her whole family felt pain from Melody's affliction. They were understanding enough, however, to realize it was a handicap that Melody had to handle herself without observing any demonstrated anxiety over her every moment by her family.

It was her family's wisdom and love and encouragement that helped Melody to get on with her life. Prayer and unquestioning faith had gotten them through many bad times. "Trust in the Lord" was a Bible scripture the Wuertzes had learned to live by.

Her grandpa Buddy, with whom Melody had a close childhood relationship, sat down one day and wrote in longhand an inspirational poem, hoping it would help his granddaughter through the struggles ahead.

It was entitled "Don't Quit," and was most appropriate during a time when Melody, then a major in Christian music at St. Louis Christian College, found herself with an identity problem, a growing feeling of low self-esteem and insecurity that made her want to drop out. The same problem had touched her life in high school, where her brother Wesley was an upperclassman. She was regularly referred to as "Wes's little sister."

Not a disparaging description at all—Wesley Wuertz was an achiever, much admired for his scholastic and extracurricular achievements. Melody and Wesley always had been close—her older brother always had been her hero.

Wesley had been proud when his sister decided to attend the same college where he was a ministerial student, St. Louis Christian College. Still, as much as she loved her older brother, Melody wanted to be recognized and liked for her own personality, abilities and talents.

During this period of discouragement, it was the counseling and encouragement of her father that kept Melody in school. She always drew strength from the telephone conversations she had with her mom and dad.

Her father was proud that she stayed in college and went on to graduate. He later said that he believed it was the difficult times in college that prepared her for the tough times later in life.

*   *   *

After finishing college, Melody decided to live in St. Louis, on her own. She went to work for a convenience store and soon advanced from clerk to assistant manager.

When she occasionally had car trouble, she phoned her dad for advice. Lyle admired his daughter's growing sense of independence. She rarely asked for help, and he was sorry it was not that easy to repair a car over the phone.

She still visited frequently with her parents, and with her brother and his wife, who were now living in Kentucky, where he was a minister.

In the summer of 1988, Melody joined Wesley on an unforgettable excursion in the Smoky Mountain National Park. At the time Wesley was director of a church camping program. That vacation in the Smokys was a time of fun and happiness for Melody and her brother; yet it would later haunt the older brother with heart-wrenching memories, to the point it would be many months before he could ever go back to the beautiful Smokys.

It was while working in St. Louis that Melody Wuertz became close friends with Dianna Angell and her husband. For a while, she dated Dianna's brother. During her days as an employee of a convenience store, Melody became a good friend of a co-worker with the improbable name of Jack Daniels.

When they first met in 1987, Wuertz and Daniels both were basic cashiers at a 7-Eleven Store. Both of them later were promoted to assistant store managers. Daniels was married, and his relationship with Wuertz was platonic. At work they shared laughs and problems, the usual things that people who work on the same job come to expect from one another. At first, Daniels was going to school during the day, and they worked different shifts. Later, they were on the same night shift. One time after getting off work at the store at 11 P.M., Daniels and Wuertz went to see a movie together. They had asked Jack's wife to go, too, but she had said she wasn't interested and told them to go ahead.

While still working at the convenience store, Wuertz also took a part-time job with the U. S. Department of Veterans Affairs Medical Center in St. Louis. Dianna Angell's husband was assistant chief of medical administration at the government hospital. Because of her own physical impairment and countless visits to doctors, Melody Wuertz already had an interest in the medical field. She was ambitious, and did well on both of her jobs. Her epilepsy never seemed to interfere. She was keeping it well under control with careful attention to taking her medication and avoiding stressful situations.

After Dianna's husband was transferred to the VA Medical Center at Oklahoma City, where the Angells moved in 1987, Wuertz seemed less ebullient when she and Dianna talked by phone. She admitted she missed them. Wuertz had decided she wanted another career other than the grocery business. She was enjoying her work at the Veterans Hospital in St. Louis and was interested in pursuing that type of work on a full-time basis, she told Dianna.

When Dianna notified her that a job was available at the Medical Center in Oklahoma City, Melody jumped at the chance, made a trip to Oklahoma City, and got the job.

It was a fateful decision.

Wuertz moved in October 1988. At first she lived with the Angells, paying them $25 a week. When she became more established and was assured that the job was permanent, she got her own apartment. And some time after she began work as a ward clerk at the Veteran hospital, she met Jimmie Ray Slaughter, who was a psychiatric nurse on the same fifth-floor unit.

Chapter 11

Dianna Angell wondered what was troubling Melody Wuertz, if it was anything more than maybe loneliness in her new surroundings. She knew that Wuertz had lived in St. Louis for a long time, had many friends there, had been in close proximity with her alma mater, St. Louis Christian College.

Wuertz had changed noticeably, Angell thought. She seemed to be withdrawn at times, didn't call as often as she had in the past, didn't come by for visits. Whenever Angell called her, she noticed that Wuertz was sleeping more often, staying in her apartment and watching television when she was off duty, hardly going out at all.

When Angell asked if anything was wrong, Wuertz agreed that she was missing her old friends and familiar surroundings, feeling homesick and a little lonely.

Dianna Angell's parents came from Illinois to visit in midsummer of 1989. Wuertz, who knew them well, came over for dinner.

Dianna was in the kitchen cooking when she heard her father casually ask Wuertz if she was seeing anyone special these days.

"Yes, I am," she replied.

Dianna was startled by the remark. It was the first time that Wuertz had mentioned having any kind of social life.

Dianna turned around from the stove. "Hey, I didn't know you were seeing somebody. Who is it, Melody?" The answer was like a slap in the face. "It's none of your business." The remark and the tone of voice were completely out of character for Wuertz.

It was a second before Dianna Angell recovered from the sharp and surprising response of her friend. Then she said softly, "Well, okay . . . pardon me for asking."

Wuertz had been dating Slaughter only a short time when she went home to Indiana to attend the tenth reunion of her high-school class. She was exuberant when she told her mom about the job at the Veterans Hospital in Oklahoma City.

Like she always did during their visits, Susie Wuertz asked Melody if she was dating anyone.

"I have had one date with this guy," Melody said. "He is a nurse where I work. He has been a big help to me at work."

She told her mother that Jimmie Slaughter was an older man, about fifteen years or so older than she was. He had been married and divorced three times, but he was really nice and always so interested in her, in helping her learn the new work and adjust to living in a new city.

Slaughter's marital history as recited by her unworldly daughter rang alarm bells with Susie. Later when she talked to her husband Lyle, neither of them was at all happy about the man whom Melody was dating. They were gravely concerned over this disclosure.

As Susie Wuertz would recall later, "Melody was twenty-eight at the time, and we never told our kids after they got older what they could do, you know, specifically.

"We made suggestions but when they were growing up, they were allowed to mostly make up their own minds and make their own choices, and at the age of twenty-eight, you certainly don't tell a child, when they are an adult, what they can do. But we did express our dislike of her dating a person of this type."

And Melody Wuertz, who had never talked back to her folks, had shrugged. "Don't worry about it, Mom. I can handle it," she replied.

Wuertz and her mother talked regularly in long-distance calls every Thursday and usually Saturday. Thursday was Melody's day off, a day when she had more time. During these conversations after her return to Edmond, Melody sometimes mentioned things that she and Jimmie Slaughter had done. Thursday was his day off, too, and that's when they were together. She seemed happy and upbeat about their relationship.

About the third week in October, Lyle and Susie Wuertz planned for a weekend visit with their daughter to cap off a vacation in Branson, Missouri, the entertainment capital for people who prefer family-type entertainment.

They were going to make the trip on Lyle's motorcycle! When they took off anywhere, Lyle drove and Susie hung on behind him. It was certainly more economical than automobile travel, and it was fun for both of them.

They scheduled the trip around their daughter's days off from the hospital, Thursday and Friday. They spent almost a week in Branson, then zipped off to Oklahoma City.

The motorcycle trip from Indiana to Missouri and on to Oklahoma was about a fourteen-hour journey.

Upon their arrival at Melody's apartment, they found a note on the door. It said that she had gone to the doctor to have her epilepsy medicine reevaluated and she would be back soon, but meanwhile Dianna Angell would let them into her apartment.

Angell showed up while they were reading the note, and Melody showed up fifteen minutes later.

After the embraces, she explained she had been having problems with the epilepsy medication and had gone to the doctor to check it out.

In retrospect, it was amazing how optimistically Melody Wuertz talked and routinely detailed the reason for her doctor's appointment. That was the day that she had found out she was pregnant.

The first day of her parents' visit, Wuertz mentioned that she and Slaughter were taking them out to supper at a nice place. The Wuertz family called the evening meal supper, instead of dinner. Dinner was the noon meal.

But later that day Melody received a call from Slaughter, saying that he would not be able to make it because of some things that had come up.

The Wuertzes were disappointed in a way—they wanted to meet this man that Melody was dating and talking about so much, and about whom they had so many doubts and questions. But they weren't that surprised that he had not kept the supper appointment.

Susie Wuertz was an attractive woman, still youthful in appearance. Looking at her, no one would realize that she had any health problems. But she had sugar diabetes and was on a well-regulated regime of proper diet, exercise and rest. She paid dearly if she overdid herself, or fell off her schedule. If she stayed up too late and didn't get her rest, it was as hard on her body as missing her three daily insulin shots or not eating properly.

But that night she wanted to talk with her daughter. The hour was getting late and Lyle had gone to bed. They fell into the subject of Slaughter easily enough.

Susie Wuertz expressed her concern about Melody dating the older, experienced man. She said that she and Melody's father were opposed to the relationship for the reasons of his past three marriages that ended in divorce.

Susie feared that the older man might try to talk Melody into things that she did not want to do, through his obviously persuasive manner. Melody earnestly defended Slaughter, saying she was convinced he was a good person who had had some bad breaks in his marriages.

Susie was beginning to feel the effects of staying up much later than usual. Melody noticed her mother was becoming tired, and she said, with a smile and reaching over to pat her mother, "Mom, you're so sleepy. You might as well go to bed. And don't worry, Mom, please, I can handle it."

The visit with their daughter and what she had told them about Jimmie Slaughter had left the Wuertzes uneasy of mind. And the motorcycle trip home didn't help, either. The wind was blowing hard in Oklahoma as they departed and stayed with them for many miles blowing against them, almost seeming to try and push them back.

The roaring wind in their faces only heightened the uneasiness and anxiety they were beginning to feel about Melody. The wind that sometimes threatened to blow them off the road had a depressing effect.

A few weeks later, Wuertz had changed her mind about not talking about her romantic relationship. When she phoned Angell she was close to tears.

"Dianna, I think I'm pregnant," Wuertz said, her voice

breaking. Now the words poured out, an emotional recounting of how she had become involved with this man whom she really knew nothing about.

As Dianna Angell recalled later: "Melody was very disappointed with herself. She said she had been raised with a different set of standards than this kind of conduct . . . she was very disappointed in her behavior. She was confused about her feelings toward the person she had been dating. She said she didn't know how she felt about him—she barely knew him."

She still didn't give his name.

Melody Wuertz had never felt this hopeless, this near the brink. Her lifelong struggle with epilepsy was nothing compared to the despondency, uncertainty, and mental turmoil that gripped her now.

The sense of guilt was worst of all. She could not even think at this point of telling her mom and dad. It overwhelmed all other feelings and thoughts. She was so mixed up in her emotions toward Jimmie Slaughter, the man who fathered her baby.

At the start he had been so understanding; he seemed to know her every need, her every emotion, her frequent feelings of no confidence. His soft-spoken words of encouragement always buoyed her up. She felt stronger when she was with him.

He was caring and comforting. He made her feel like such a complete person, feel like a woman more than she ever had before. There was still a lot of the little girl in Melody Wuertz, though she never would have admitted that to herself, much less anyone else. But it lurked far beneath the surface, this buried timidness. There was a part of her inner being that always needed tenderness and love and reassurance.

Even when she told him that she was pregnant, he didn't

panic or blow up. He said that if she wanted to have an abortion, he would pay for it. The mere suggestion was appalling to Wuertz. She was unquestionably pro-life. She hated herself for the sin she had committed, but she was not about to follow it with another one, an act that she considered to be murder. Slaughter also said that he would help her financially, or he would even take the baby and raise it himself. That idea was as distasteful to Wuertz as an abortion. She would raise her own baby—no way could she do otherwise.

However, she was full of anxiety. How would her epilepsy and her medication affect the tiny being that was growing inside of her? Could she even carry the baby to full term? And there was so much confusion about her future relationship with the father. She had begun to worry that he was married, although he had assured her when they started going out that he was a divorced man. He said his ex-wife had his two daughters, whom he saw regularly. She had seen his girls and thought they were very nice.

The possibility of paying for and raising the baby on her own meager income was frightening and beyond her capability. Besides, she was in love with Slaughter and wanted them to be happily married with their soon-to-be-born child.

But pushing aside all of the other worries, which swamped her mind, was the most disturbing one: How was she going to tell her mom and dad that she was pregnant? She had known that day when they were in Edmond, when she returned from the doctor visit purportedly made to reevaluate her medication. There had been no way to tell them.

Wuertz had always promised her father that she would not marry a man who would not first come to him and ask for her hand in marriage, as it had been done through the generations of the family. She could only imagine how he and her mom would feel and react about this.

* * *

Melody Wuertz, however, did not try to hide her continuing relationship with Slaughter. More than one time when Susie Wuertz made her regular call on Thursday, Melody would say something to the effect of, "Jim is here and we're getting ready to go eat and catch a movie."

When Melody did talk for a while, her mother sensed that Slaughter was there. She could hear his voice or his laugh occasionally in the background.

Early in 1990 the Wuertzes received a long letter from their daughter that confirmed their worst fears. They would never know the anguish she had suffered in bringing herself to write it, but time was running out. The letter that brought tears to their eyes announced that their daughter was pregnant.

The last portion of the letter said, "Mom, and Dad, don't call me right away. Give yourself a little time to think about this, and if you don't want to call me, that's all right. But think about it for a little while, and I need to know how you feel."

Susie, with Lyle at her side where he could talk, too, called Melody immediately, even though she already was at work. It was a tearful conversation. The Wuertzes assured the distressed Melody of their forgiveness and promised that they would support her all the way, no matter what had happened, and that they loved her very much and would always love her.

Susie later described her and Lyle's reaction: "The situation was distressing, but our daughter was not distressing to us."

The mother mentioned that they would start saving some money so that she could be with Melody when the baby was born.

But Melody Wuertz was already thinking practically. She said that Slaughter would be there with her when the baby was born, and if for some reason he could not be present, then her friend Dianna Angell would be.

"When I will really need you most, Mom, is after the baby comes."

Susie could see the logic of that statement. Melody had never had experience with the care of any infant. She already was living away from home when other youngsters in the family, her nieces and nephews, were born. Melody really had no idea of what taking care of a baby was all about.

In private, the Wuertzes' sadness was almost like a physical wound. The news of Melody's pregnancy by a man she was not married to was devastating. There had never been an unwanted or an out-of-wedlock pregnancy in their family as long back as could be remembered.

But it had happened, and now their daughter, feeling intense guilt and depression, needed more than ever their comfort and love and help.

They prayed for a long time that night.

Later, they learned that Slaughter had told their daughter that when she informed them of her pregnancy, they would tell her to have an abortion. His assumption, or more accurately his saying what he thought would help his own cause, could not have been further from the truth.

The Wuertzes lived the tenets of their Christian faith, and what they looked upon as murder by abortion violated everything that Christianity stood for, the value on human life and love being uppermost.

But over the next few weeks, it seemed that the parents' earlier apprehensions about Slaughter might have been misguided, based on what they now were hearing from their daughter.

She let them know that he was pledging his full support. After that first dismaying suggestion of abortion, he had even suggested, really insisted, that she move out of her apartment and into a house.

Melody said that Slaughter had set aside a down payment on a home, and she thought she could handle the payments as easily as she could pay rent.

Wuertz and Slaughter looked around for several weeks, and eventually found the modest but comfortable house at 216 West Seventh.

She brought it up and Slaughter agreed that with a new baby, she would have to have a washer and dryer. In those early stages of infant care, going to a Laundromat was out of the question.

Melody told her mother when she called one evening that Slaughter had told her to go ahead and get the best of appliances. But she was practical like her mom and said she didn't want to do that. She was going to shop for used appliances so that the payments would be more reasonable.

Melody said Slaughter was giving her the money for the down payment on the house and the washer and dryer, but he insisted all the purchases be in her name on the contracts. He did not want to put it on his charge account or sign any loan papers himself, but he would give her the money.

Slaughter's behavior served to raise Susie's initial concerns about this older and divorced man, who literally had swept Melody off her feet.

Susie Wuertz still felt antagonism toward Slaughter, as hard as she tried to fight against it. Later she regretted what she said to Melody: "Why don't you get brand-new ones, honey. If he's going to make the payments, let him make them on a new washer and dryer."

Melody didn't take offense, however. She said only, "No, Mom, I might wind up making the payments myself."

Her practical outlook always came through, her mother noted. And it sounded as if Melody herself wasn't all that confident of Slaughter's promises of financial help.

She knew that Melody lived in a similar manner to them—everything budgeted to the penny and to the availability of their income.

Melody only said, "I think I can handle it, Mom."

But Susie Wuertz was concerned. Melody had explained how she allotted so much for this and that, and when it all was added up, there was little left from her paycheck for anything that might suddenly be needed.

Melody never asked her parents for financial help, but her mother was working, and she saved what she could and sent some money each month to help out. It might not seem like much to some people, Susie said later, but $40 or $50 a month—the amount she tried to average— was to the Wuertzes a challenging sum of money to come up with.

Besides setting aside money for the plane trip she would make after the baby was born, Susie Wuertz also set aside $10 from each of her own paychecks for diapers because she promised her daughter, "I will keep the baby in diapers."

But there were more serious worries than finances for Melody and her parents. From the beginning Melody had expressed her concern about the possible effects of her epilepsy or the medication on the baby.

In fact, the doctor had said there could be no certainty at this stage that the baby had not already sustained damage.

Once again, her mother and dad reminded Melody that they must trust in the goodness of God.

Dianna Angell noticed that Melody Wuertz had become completely open about her relationship with Slaughter. Wuertz and Slaughter attended a Hanukkah party together at Angell's house. She noticed that they sat close together, talked and acted friendly like any normal couple. Several times she saw Wuertz smile and touch Slaughter.

Angell also saw that Slaughter was not wearing a wedding ring. She had heard, and believed, that Slaughter was *not* divorced. He was living with his wife and two daughters in the nearby town of Guthrie, the old and historic capital of the former Indian Territory, about ten miles from Oklahoma City.

Angell told Wuertz that she believed Slaughter was not telling the truth about not being married. She suggested Wuertz should do some checking at the courthouse to determine if there really had been a divorce. Wuertz said she did not think Jim would lie to her about his marital status. But she confided that she was worried about him. Something he had recently told her about his past life and frightened her.

Slaughter had said that several years ago he had been highly interested and involved in the occult and Satanic rituals. As a strong Christian, Wuertz could not imagine engaging in such terrible practices.

"This was years ago and he's not doing any of this stuff now," Wuertz said. "But he did say something that really scared me, and I know it is preposterous. He said that he still has two demons who do things for him. He told me he has seen these demons."

When she realized how serious Slaughter was about this matter of demons, all the black magic stuff he had talked about no longer seemed to be just some kind of far-out silliness. It seemed real scary.

Wuertz said that when she asked why he didn't get rid of these so-called demons, he replied he did not want to get rid of them. He could control them, and they still served him. They gave him money sometimes.

Could Wuertz actually believe that kind of malarkey, Angell wondered. She laughed and told Wuertz that surely Slaughter, a highly professional and competent psychiatric nurse and ex-Army major, could not have been serious. He must have been putting her on.

Angell recalled having watched a television program recently about people involved in Satanic worship. The program had revealed that some men deliberately had impregnated women so they could sacrifice the babies in Satanic ceremonies.

Wuertz's eyes grew wide, and Angell was sorry immediately that she had discussed the TV show.

Shaking her head negatively, confused about Slaughter's occult stories, Wuertz said she had no doubt that Slaughter was serious and meant every word. Besides leaving her shocked and scared, it only added to Wuertz's belief that he needed her as badly as she needed him in some aspects of his personal life.

They had discussions about good and evil, God and Satan. Wuertz said she was sure that Slaughter was really searching for God, and she could help him find the faith that had been the most important part of her life—that is, until she met and became involved with Slaughter.

At one point in their romantic affair, the conscience-stricken Wuertz had broken off with the Don Juan nurse. But she resumed seeing him after learning that she was pregnant. She would do everything in her power to assure that her baby had a father and a proper home.

Chapter 12

Melody Wuertz was eight months pregnant when she moved on May 30, 1990, from her apartment into the house on West Seventh. The gray, wood-frame, three-bedroom home with an open-style carport on the side was in a pleasant middle-income residential neighborhood not far from Edmond's downtown business section.

Dianna Angell and her husband, and another friend, moved Wuertz's things in a U-Haul trailer that Melody rented. Wuertz and Slaughter had intended to do the moving themselves, but they drove up at the new residence as the Angells and the other volunteer mover were finishing the last of the load from the U-Haul.

Melody Wuertz was excited with this first house of her own. She was glad that she had rejected a suggestion made by Dianna Angell during the dark period after the pregnancy was confirmed. Angell thought Wuertz should return to her parents in Indiana, or to Kentucky where her brother and his wife lived.

The idea of moving to be with her family had been

considered by Wuertz before her friend brought it up, but she decided against leaving Edmond. She wanted her baby to grow up knowing its father's family. Melody told Dianna that Slaughter's daughters seemed like pleasant children.

Slaughter had told Wuertz that he did not want his baby to grow up in an apartment and he would help her get a house.

Slaughter wanted her to find a house in Guthrie, where his two young daughters lived with their mother, but she opted for living in Edmond. Slaughter put a $2,000 down payment on the house she bought.

During their house-hunting, Wuertz felt sure that she and Slaughter would be married before much longer. Looking around for a home that would have a baby's room seemed like any old-married couple happily planning their life together after the baby arrived.

The first date that the doctor estimated for the arrival of the baby was June 19, which coincidentally was Susie Wuertz's birthday. The grandmother-to-be was elated with the possibility that her new grandbaby might be born on the same date.

But the weeks dragged by, and, ironically, it was Susie Wuertz who was getting desperate over nature's bad timing. She had quit her job to take a better paying one, prompted by her and her husband's desire to help out their daughter as much as they possibly could with their own limited income. She planned on taking a week off between jobs to help out during the first few days of her inexperienced daughter's indoctrination into motherhood.

But after three weeks Susie Wuertz had been confronted with a deadline from her new employer—start work the next week, or they would be forced to hire somebody else.

Susie phoned her daughter and told her, "Honey, I have to come this week or I can't come at all."

Melody replied, "Come on, Mom. It can't be much longer, the doctor is sure."

Susie Wuertz took a plane to Edmond via the Oklahoma City airport the next day. But when she arrived, her daughter seemed no closer to delivery. They took long walks together; Melody even took castor oil. They tried everything that was known to expedite a birth. Still nothing happened.

Melody Wuertz, at first, opposed a suggestion by her mother that she ask the doctor to do something to speed up the birth. She feared that trying to rush the natural birth process might harm the baby. The baby and its welfare were always foremost in her mind. But finally she agreed. The doctor told her to check into the hospital the next day, and if nothing happened on its own, he would break the water. The night before she was to go to the hospital, Wuertz and her mother prayed fervently that the baby might come naturally in the hours before the hospital appointment.

But no labor pains came, and on Sunday morning, July 7, 1990, the doctor kept his promise to intervene, and a baby girl was delivered at about 1 A.M. It was a difficult delivery, but the infant appeared to be normal and healthy in every way.

Jim Slaughter was not there, but Susie Wuertz and Dianna Angell both were in the birthing room. Melody named the beautiful baby Jessica Rae (the feminine spelling of Jim's middle name). The baby had curly blond hair.

Later, Wuertz told her mother, "Mom, I'm going to call Jim and tell him he has a healthy baby."

Susie left the room to give her daughter privacy for the call. Wuertz also phoned her brother, Wesley, in Kentucky to inform him he was an uncle.

The new mother was exhausted but happy. A nurse brought her a full meal, and she ate it hungrily, then slipped into peaceful sleep.

* * *

Jim Slaughter did not make an appearance to see his new daughter until the next Monday afternoon, when mother and child had gone home from the hospital.

Susie Wuertz was there when he dropped by the house on his way to work on the evening shift at the Veterans Hospital.

Susie kept her feelings about Slaughter concealed. She knew that her daughter hoped to marry the man soon, and she didn't want to say or do anything that would hamper Melody's future chance of happiness. She kept in the background.

She did say to Slaughter, as he and Melody sat on the couch with the newborn babe, "I hope you realize what a beautiful baby you have. It was not easy for Melody to bring Jessica into this world. She had a very hard time."

She was saying these things because she knew that Slaughter was the man responsible for the baby, and she wanted to hear him acknowledge his daughter. She felt that Melody needed to hear him say it, too.

And he did.

"She is a beautiful baby," Slaughter agreed with a smile. He said the usual things a new father should say, Susie remembered that later. Perhaps everything would be all right, after all, she thought.

But she had one more thing to tell the baby's father.

She said, "Jim, I want you to know that Melody and this little baby girl are the two most precious things in the world to me. Please take care of them."

Slaughter's answer would never be forgotten by Susie Wuertz. He said simply and quietly, in his usual soft tone, "Oh yes. I will."

* * *

Jim Slaughter had not wanted to sign any of the papers at the hospital when Jessica was born. He told Melody he would help her to support the child, but he did not want his name affixed to any legal documents. This seemed strange to her, and heightened her gnawing anxiety about the future of their relationship and the prospects of a marriage. She wondered if he really meant to marry her after all.

But ten days later, on July 17, 1990, she did persuade Slaughter to sign a paternity affidavit at the hospital that said he was the natural father of the baby. Wuertz was relieved. Thank God, Jessica had a legal name on the record. But everything started going bad between Wuertz and Slaughter after that.

All of Wuertz's coworkers at the hospital adored her new baby.

And knowing that she was having a hard time financially, some of the nurses chipped in regularly to help her buy new clothing and other items for Jessica.

One nurse, Cecelia Johnson, a heavy-set, plain-looking woman in her forties, had started buying infant clothing for the baby several weeks before Jessica was born. Johnson and Wuertz had become friends while working together on the unit, and they talked several times about the pending birth.

After the baby was born, the nurse spoke frequently of how she would like to have a beautiful baby like little Jessica for her own. She said she would be glad to adopt the pretty baby girl.

It wasn't just any baby the nurse wanted, and she made that clear. It was this one darling infant that, for some reason, she would love to legally adopt and raise as her own daughter. Johnson had a reason why she lavished such affection on the infant; it was because the baby's father was Slaughter. But Melody Wuertz had no idea at all of the true emotions behind Johnson's worshiping attitude toward Jessica.

Cecelia Johnson was childless, and her own ten-year marriage—one that had been a bad marriage, according to hospital gossip—ended in divorce. Johnson was a woman of sad bearing, a lonely person who obviously was short on self-esteem and moved through life seeking approval. Wuertz heard that Johnson had a miscarriage before her marriage dissolved, and she wondered if that had some influence on her wanting a baby with so much longing, particularly little Jessica.

The hospital workers noticed that Johnson and Slaughter talked together frequently in the hospital unit's break room, and there was conjecture that maybe they had something going, though no one could really understand how such mutual attraction might have developed.

But Wuertz didn't see anything like that in Slaughter and Johnson's on-the-job visiting and friendliness—to her, it was nothing more than cordiality between fellow employees.

And besides, she understood that Johnson and Slaughter's most recent wife, Nicki, the mother of his daughters, had been close friends ever since they worked together in the past when Nicki was a nurse at the same hospital.

Wuertz recalled Slaughter telling her it was during that time, too, that he had met Nicki.

Wuertz would have gone to pieces if she had known the true motivation behind Johnson's generous gifts to Jessica. Johnson and Slaughter were having an affair. In fact, Slaughter had gotten Johnson pregnant, and it had been his baby she was carrying when she suffered the miscarriage that left her so emotionally destroyed.

The hefty nurse and Slaughter were sexually involved at the time that Wuertz also became pregnant by the same man.

* * *

In addition to clothing gifts from Johnson, Wuertz told Dianna Angell that another female hospital employee also had given her a box of "very nice clothes" for Jessica. Wuertz was afraid to tell Slaughter about the generous gift because the woman was black and "Jim hates black people."

However, she did tell him about Cecelia Johnson's continuing generosity.

At first Slaughter had been partly true to his promise of helping to support Jessica. He gave Wuertz about $100 a month on the average, and he had bought various things for Jessica when Wuertz would express a need for them.

But there were limitations to his financial help: Wuertz had to make a request for money or a specific need, and Slaughter would consider it and give her the money or buy it if the request met his approval.

Jessica's baby bed had been one such purchase. Wuertz and Dianna Angell were shopping one day when they spotted the bed. Wuertz didn't have nearly enough money for it, but she had the bed put in layaway so that she could pay it out.

Later, when she told Slaughter about the bed that she wanted so much, he gave her the money for it.

Dianna Angell visited Wuertz frequently and was not surprised by what she saw in the new mother's home: Oh, how well Melody took care of baby Jessica; how neat and clean she kept the baby and her house. Anyone who visited Wuertz's place was impressed with her housekeeping.

But Angell noticed something else that worried her: Her friend was losing weight, not that she ever had that much to lose. She was a tiny woman, really, only five feet two inches tall and weighed 108 pounds. But she was losing weight now, looking skinny and almost sickly, Angell thought.

One day Angell said to her, "Melody, I don't think you are eating enough. You're looking so skinny, girl. Are you sure you're feeling all right?"

Wuertz said sometimes she could not afford even her regular epilepsy medicine, let alone groceries for herself. Anyway, she did not want to take the medication because she believed it would interfere with her breast-feeding of Jessica.

"Why are you still breast-feeding her?" Angell asked. Most of the women she knew discontinued breast-feeding after the first days of their baby's life and placed them on a baby formula. Most pediatricians considered baby formula more healthful anyway, especially in instances where the mother's own health might be impaired, or her health already was such that it was not good for the infant.

But Wuertz said she continued to breast-feed the baby because it was less expensive than baby formula. She just could not afford to buy the formula.

Occasionally when Wuertz asked Angell to get something from the kitchen or the refrigerator, Angell noticed that there was hardly any food inside. When she commented on the nearly empty larder, Wuertz dismissed the short supply with remarks that she had been dieting recently, or she had not been to the grocery store yet and was going shopping later.

Dianna Angell wasn't fooled by the cover-up, and Wuertz never asked for any money or food from her friend.

Nevertheless, Angell would take foodstuffs to her struggling friend, saying, "I didn't have room for this in my refrigerator or freezer, Melody. Can you use it?"

Melody usually would accept the contribution, but Dianna, well aware of Melody's strong sense of independence and pride, and her reluctance to ever seek help, felt it important to offer the casual explanation.

Angell was a frequent visitor at Melody's. She came over before Wuertz went to work in the midafternoon on her hospital shift. Angell sipped a cup of coffee or iced tea, and they talked while Wuertz went about her routine of getting Jessica and herself ready.

She noticed that Wuertz's routine hardly ever varied. Wuertz usually got up about 10:30 or 11 A. M. and switched on the TV. Before doing anything else, she had a playtime with Jessica after she took her from her small bed. They frolicked on the floor—Jessica making bubbly baby sounds, and her mother laughing and calling her pet names.

Next she would feed the baby, and then herself. Again she would play with Jessica on the floor or in the baby stroller. As the morning passed, she would bathe the baby and dress her.

Then Wuertz began getting herself ready. She dressed first before putting on makeup and doing her hair. She used an electrically heated curling iron to fix her hair. No way could she afford a visit to the beauty salon.

Scheduled to start her shift at 3:30 P. M., she first dropped Jessica by the house of Phyllis Davis, her baby-sitter, and would pick her up after getting off at midnight.

There were obvious signs when police investigators entered Melody Wuertz's home on that terrible day—still months away on July 2, 1991—that the hardworking mother had been in the midst of this daily routine when a monster struck.

Chapter 13

With Desert Shield escalating into Desert Storm in the Iraq-Kuwait turbulence in the Middle East during late summer of 1990, the life of Melody Wuertz was filled with more despair.

Jim Slaughter, who seldom came around anymore to visit Jessica, was more difficult to get in touch with every day.

Much-needed money to meet the bills was not forthcoming, either. Wuertz's monthly bills now exceeded by a large amount her ward clerk's meager income; payments on the house and the appliances and insurance and Jessica's barest needs left little for food or medicine.

It had been in late August that Slaughter told Wuertz that because of the intensifying crisis in the Middle East, he was going to be reactivated by the Army, in which he was a reservist. He had served in the Vietnam debacle. When she learned he was voluntarily going back into the service, Wuertz could not understand why he would do this when she and Jessica needed him so badly. It became more apparent with each slight of attentiveness to her and the baby that Slaughter had no intention of marrying her.

For many weeks, she had never doubted Slaughter's claim that he was divorced, or doubted anything else he told her; but now, she was wondering why she ever took him at his word.

Wuertz told Angell one day that she was going to find out for herself, and for sure, whether Slaughter was married or divorced. At first she had called the county clerk at the Oklahoma County Courthouse to see if there was a record of his divorce. Finding nothing there, it dawned on her that the divorce would have been filed in the county where he and his wife Nicki and their two daughters lived. Guthrie was the county seat. She could find no record of the divorce there, either.

Wuertz knew she could find out for sure from one source. Thoroughly exasperated, she called the residence of Slaughter's purported "ex-wife" during the late hours of November 1, 1990. When a woman answered, Wuertz asked who was speaking.

Nicki Slaughter identified herself. In answer to Melody's next question of "Who are you?" she replied that she was the wife of Jim Slaughter. Melody Wuertz was stunned, but then she managed to say that Slaughter was the father of her baby. After the call, Jim Slaughter stopped sending Melody any money at all.

Slaughter was developing a searing rage for the pert little hospital worker. All of a sudden she was trying to control his life, and if there was anything that characterized Jim Slaughter, it was that he had to be in control, of everything, all the time. Especially the women in his life.

As it would be learned later, the marriage of Jim and Nicki Slaughter had been one in name only for quite some time, with each partner more or less, leading separate lives.

Nicki Slaughter was of the Catholic faith. To her, divorce was out of the question. She was content to carry on with the outward appearance of being married while in reality having only the most casual relationship with her husband.

For one thing, as Slaughter told people, Nicki believed that marriage was for the purpose of procreation. Since they both had agreed they did not want additional children, sex was pushed into the background and, finally, all the way out.

The sex part did not bother Jim Slaughter in the slightest. He had abundant resources elsewhere, had them back in the days when Nicki might have been trying to be a wife.

Slaughter did, however, love his two daughters, self-admittedly the oldest girl best of all. He did not want to lose them, as well he might in the process of divorce. There was also the fact that his wife's folks were well off, and he liked that, too. Nicki Slaughter was paying her own way and sometimes part of his as their strange life together-but-apart continued.

When Nicki confronted Slaughter with, "This was what I was told by a woman on the phone," Slaughter had a ready comeback.

"That must have been my second wife. She's drunk, and she's trying to cause trouble."

Perhaps it only was a case of injured pride, but Nicki Slaughter at that time was calling his hand. She threw down a challenge to her wandering husband: "Well, you better clean up your act, or you don't need to bother coming back from Kansas."

Slaughter already had been assigned as an Army nurse with the rank of major at Irwin Army Hospital in Fort Riley, Kansas. He had left the VA Medical Center in Oklahoma City for his new assignment in September 1990.

Between then and Wuertz's phone call to Nicki, Slaughter had sent Wuertz small amounts of money, which he referred to as "patches for your leaky canoe." He never

offered regular support at a time when Melody Wuertz was
sinking under her financial obligations.

After the phone call to his wife, everything stopped,
including any response to Wuertz's pleas for help.

He did send her some letters, which were far from comforting and empty, of course, of cash. In one, he suggested
she could participate with him in the making of X-rated
videos for which they could make $40 an hour while
enjoying life's simple pleasures. To Wuertz, the obscene
idea was like a slap in the face when she already was cring-
ing in helplessness.

It was hard for her to believe that the man who fathered
her baby and once said such sweet things to her was capable
of such a revolting thought. It was almost as if Satan himself
was speaking from the mind of Jim Slaughter.

Melody Wuertz was ready to fight. Jim Slaughter had
underestimated the gumption of the small, naive woman
he had been able to control like a yo-yo on a string. Jessica
was entitled to help from her father, every bit as much as
his other children. Wuertz told her friends and her family
that she intended to see that the baby got it.

In one of her weekly telephone conversations with her
mother, Wuertz said that she was considering filing a formal paternity and child-support lawsuit against Slaughter.

She had talked to counselors at the hospital and to her
friends who knew something about the legal procedures.
She had learned she could get the assistance of the Oklahoma Department of Human Services (DHS) to force
Slaughter to submit to a paternity blood test. Upon determination that he was undeniably the father of Jessica, he
would be required to pay regular child support in amounts
to be set by a district-court judge.

Her parents and her friends encouraged Wuertz to go
ahead with the court action. Less than two weeks after

she had confirmed her worst fears that Slaughter still was married, Melody Wuertz went to the Department of Human Services Child Support Enforcement Division office in Oklahoma City and picked up an application for child support. She returned the completed form on December 12, 1990.

Wuertz did not think she would have any trouble getting the financial support from Slaughter since he already had signed the hospital affidavit declaring he was the natural father of Jessica. Her optimism would be short lived. The child-support agency sent a routine letter to Slaughter at Fort Riley informing him that, according to the preliminary information given to the DHS, he was legally responsible for helping with financial support for the child.

Jim Slaughter exploded when he learned Wuertz had begun the legal steps to force him to contribute to the upkeep of Jessica. In a rage, he scribbled a long-hand letter to the DHS responding to the letter from the agency.

It was an antagonistic letter in which he denied being the father, and lambasted the DHS as incompetent bureaucrats for even suggesting that he pay support for a baby with which he had no "biological affiliation."

The next time Wuertz visited the DHS office, the investigator handling her case showed her Slaughter's letter. The usually quiet and reserved ward clerk was furious about Slaughter's claim of having no "biological affiliation" with Jessica. She could not believe that Slaughter so blatantly denied being her baby's father. He knew that she had been with no one else, and he had signed the affidavit at the hospital, Wuertz reminded the caseworker.

When Wuertz phoned her friend Angell that evening, she said, "Dianna, you'll never guess what happened. I was at the DHS office today and I read a letter that Jim had written them about the paternity suit." She sounded like she was crying.

"I can't believe that he denied being Jessica's father.

He knows as well as I do that I have never been with anyone else but him. I'm hurt and I'm so mad, too, Dianna. I'm going to push this all the way now, and let the blood test prove that he's the father."

Angell could sense the tension in her friend's voice.

Wuertz said, "You know, I believed all along that Jim was being honest with me about being divorced, and that he really cared for Jessica and me. Now, I just don't know . . . if he can deceive me like that, I don't know what he's capable of."

The remark puzzled Angell. "What do you mean by that, Melody?"

"I'm not sure. I'm not sure how far he would go. I'm beginning to worry about him hurting me or the baby. I'm scared, Dianna."

As Wuertz described it to her mother in one of their phone talks, she was "boiling mad" when she read Slaughter's arrogantly worded reply to the DHS. If ever she had any doubt of going through with the paternity lawsuit, it was gone now. She was going to have a showdown.

At the same time, she felt a twinge of real fear with the realization that Slaughter would go bananas in the face of her stubborn opposition. He had always demanded control of everything in their relationship.

It was March 22, 1991, when an attorney for the DHS filed a petition in Oklahoma County District Court "for the determination of paternity and establishment of child support," on behalf of Jessica Rae Wuertz, a minor child, by Melody Sue Wuertz, mother.

The petition alleged that Jimmie R. Slaughter "is the father of Jessica Rae Wuertz, born July 7, 1990."

The lawsuit further claimed that "the plaintiff [Melody] had furnished said child articles necessary for her support and plaintiff is entitled to judgment."

The petition sought $2,790 for "support expenses expended" from July 1990 through the date the legal action was filed, "plus additional amounts expended to the date of the court's order."

The suit also asked $310 a month child support from Slaughter, whom it described as "an abled-bodied man capable of earning $2,500 a month." The $310-a-month figure was arrived at by totaling the combined monthly wages of Slaughter and Wuertz—$2,500 for him and $659 for her, and dividing the combined sum of $3159 on a ratio of eighty percent for him and twenty percent for her.

Thus, Slaughter would pay $310 a month and Wuertz $77 a month for Jessica's support, based on this computation.

Further, the petition stated, "the child requires medical insurance and support, and that defendant should provide such health and medical support as is reasonable."

Slaughter got himself an attorney, surprisingly a woman lawyer, and filed an answer denying that he was the baby's father.

Attorney Kathy Christensen, who specialized in family litigation, was the lawyer Slaughter contacted, and they agreed on a meeting that would be after hours because Christensen had been about to leave for the day. Probably the reason he called Christensen was that she had been the attorney who represented Cecelia Johnson in her divorce action.

But those who knew Slaughter best said later they wondered why he went to a woman for legal help, considering his often-repeated remark that he really "hated women" in spite of his romantic involvements with a goodly number of them.

As Slaughter sat across from Christensen, the lawyer was aware that this man was really angry—mad at Melody Wuertz, mad at the State of Oklahoma, mad at the whole legal procedure he found himself in.

As she went over the legal forms and explained the

judge's order to appear in court on May 7, 1991, Slaughter's face reddened.

Christensen was explaining that the State of Oklahoma did have the power to order someone to appear for a hearing, order him to submit to a blood test for determining paternity and, if that was determined, had the power to order payment of child support for as long as the court might decide.

As she enumerated the state's authority in such a case, Slaughter slammed his fist into the palm of his hand, and his voice rose in obvious anger.

He raved against any order forcing him to pay child support. "I have been helping her voluntarily. I don't like this idea of a court telling me that I have to pay a certain amount of money on a certain day," he shouted.

At this point, the attorney excused herself momentarily. She went into the office of another lawyer who shared the suite with her, and asked him not to leave until she was finished with the interview.

For the first time in her career, Christensen realized, she had to admit that she feared for her safety because of the temper display shown by her client. She had been cautious before—frequently asked for someone to watch as she walked to her car in the parking lot if it was dark—but that merely was being careful. This request had been prompted by actual fear of what she deemed imminent danger.

She was afraid to be alone with Slaughter in the office. She was grateful that her law partner still was in his office and agreed to stick around.

Then, as she continued to outline the child-support law, Slaughter calmed somewhat. He asked a practical question. It concerned the factor of timing in his having to come to Oklahoma some 300 miles from Fort Riley, where he was assigned at Irwin Army Hospital.

Christensen said that situation could be worked out easily enough by the court; Slaughter could undergo the required blood test at a center in Kansas.

She tried to explain to Slaughter where he stood in the case. In doing so, she chose her words carefully. She quietly related that his control in the support matter was going to be removed, that he would no longer be able to pay how much he wanted and when he wanted to do it.

"She obviously does not want to be at your mercy," Christensen said. "She obviously doesn't want anything to do with you anymore, Mr. Slaughter."

Slaughter rose suddenly and started pounding his fist into his palm again, yelling as he protested against the idea of his losing control of the support payments. Christensen resisted an impulse to shove her chair back and retreat, but she knew her partner would intercede if the client turned physically violent.

A few minutes later, after they agreed to meet shortly before the scheduled May 7 hearing, Slaughter, still seething, left the office.

Kathy Christensen could not help feeling pity for the mother in the child-support case, the object of her client's wrath, though it would be a feeling that would not affect her representation of Slaughter in the matter.

When Dianna Angell came to Melody's house one day in late spring of 1991, she saw that the inside wooden door was closed.

She tried the storm door and found it to be locked. Before her visit, she had phoned Wuertz to let her know she was coming by.

Suddenly Angell was apprehensive.

She knocked on the door. A few seconds later she heard Wuertz ask, without opening the door, "Who is it?"

Angell sighed with relief. "Melody, it's me."

Wuertz opened the door and then relocked it after

Angell entered. She also slammed the dead-bolt lock into place.

"What in the world is the matter, honey?" Angell asked. "You're locked in here like the money in a bank's vault." In the past, Wuertz might have the outer glass screen locked, but the inside wooden door would be standing open.

"Dianna, I'm really frightened. I never hear from Jim at all, and I have this feeling about his brooding, him getting so mad. The hearing is set for May 7, and the DHS says that the judge probably will order him to take a blood test. I know it has to be done, but it's going to make him furious."

Wuertz said the thing that really bothered her was that Slaughter still had keys to the front-door locks. Every night when she came home after work, she was afraid that he might be inside, waiting for her.

"Why don't you get the locks changed?" Angell suggested.

Wuertz said she didn't have the money to do that right now.

Not only did the judge order Slaughter to submit to a blood test; it turned out that May 7, 1991, the day of the hearing, also was a blood-drawing day for the DHS. Slaughter had to let his blood sample be taken after the hearing.

Slaughter was told he would be notified of the results when the blood-test report was completed.

Melody Wuertz's fears only grew worse. She remembered now, with such clarity, what Slaughter had told her about his divorces from his former wives. Slaughter bragged that he never had to pay anything to the divorced wives. He was adamant when talking about it, saying that he would never pay anything to an ex-wife, that he always got out of it someway. He said the power that women had in such matters burned him up.

Susie and Lyle Wuertz were overjoyed in May when Melody and Jessica paid a surprise visit home to be with them on Mother's Day. Melody wanted her parents to see how much Jessica had grown, what a beautiful little child she was becoming.

She did not mention it, but there was another reason for coming to Indiana—her fear of Slaughter. His silence was worst of all. Melody had no idea what he was doing, what he was thinking. The suspense of the unknown can be scarier than reality itself, Melody thought.

But in Washington, Indiana, in the comfort of the cozy home and the peaceful surroundings where she had grown up, Melody did manage to relax and enjoy herself. The days were full of pleasures for the grandparents. Susie and Lyle basked in the delights of helping with Jessica. They gave her baths, rocked her to sleep in their arms, fed her, played with her, showed her the interesting sights around their rural home.

They beamed over the happy baby girl with the blonde hair like an angel's halo, her joyous laugh, her radiant smile, the words she was starting to form, and the biggest event of all: Jessica taking her first steps.

It was almost as if Melody was a baby again because Jessica was a carbon copy of her mother at that age. Susie wished they could always be this happy, together with Melody and Jessica. And Melody was laughing and cheerful for the first time in a long time.

Susie Wuertz's only regret of the wonderful visit was that she had not taken off work to be with the baby and Melody more hours of the day. Susie had decided to go ahead and work because Melody and the rest of the family were planning a really big get-together on July 7, Jessica's first birthday. Her daughter and grandbaby would make a special trip back for that event. Susie worked her regular hours so that she could get ahead and spend full-time with Melody and Jessica during the planned July visit.

The parents and daughter discussed how wonderful it would be if Melody could move back to Indiana or Kentucky, where Wesley and his wife lived. The Wuertzes realized it would be hard for Melody alone to raise Jessica without a father. There was a Veterans Administration Hospital at Louisville, Kentucky. Perhaps Melody could get a job there, she was doing so well in the field. Only recently Melody had received a promotion and had been honored with several awards since she first began work at the hospital in Oklahoma City.

The Wuertzes dreamed of the day that Melody could meet and marry a good Christian man who would love her and Jessica, and give them the kind of home they deserved. Lyle thought it would be a chance finally for a big wedding for his daughter; maybe Jessica could be a flower girl.

The last night before Melody and Jessica would return to Edmond was filled with happiness for the grandparents. Melody and Susie gave Jessica a bath and then brought the baby to her grandpa's waiting arms. He watched her close her eyes and drift into sleep as he rocked her in his favorite rocking chair. As he looked upon her tiny face, he thought to himself how blessed he was to have this precious angel asleep in his arms.

The next day, the visit ended all too soon when Melody flew back to Oklahoma with Jessica to face what she knew would be trying times when the blood-test report was received by Slaughter. That could be anytime now, the DHS had said. Tears flowed as the Wuertz family said goodbyes at the Indianapolis airport.

It was their last time together.

Chapter 14

On Memorial Day, 1991, Melody Wuertz answered the ringing phone in her home. The caller made what sounded like a kissing sound over the phone.

"Is this Jim?" Wuertz asked, almost breathlessly.

"No, this isn't Jim," a male voice answered.

There were a few seconds of silence, then Wuertz said, with a stronger sound to her voice, "Well, this must be Jack." And she laughed.

Jack Daniels, her old friend from working together at the convenience store in St. Louis, identified himself.

The kissing sound he had made on the phone was a holdover of an inside joke. During their late-night shifts at 7-Eleven store, they sometimes received rude prank phone calls. The mildest ones consisted of someone making a kissing sound, then hanging up. The store employees themselves had adopted the prank, making a kissing sound when they phoned the store for some reason.

Now, Daniels explained, he and his wife had been divorced for about a month, and he was trying to renew old friendships among people he had been good friends with—to form kind of a support group, he said. With the problems and unhappy times he was having, he wanted some old friends to talk to.

He had contacted friends from his high-school and college days, and then he thought of Melody and the good times they had at the store in St. Louis while working together.

In that phone conversation on Memorial Day, Daniels and Wuertz brought their lives up to date for each other. They discussed what they had been doing since Melody left St. Louis to come to Oklahoma City; talked about her different job changes and her new career. But the biggest surprise came when Wuertz told Daniels that she had a baby girl, who was nearing her first birthday.

Jack Daniels was working at a large drug store in St. Louis, Missouri, when he found himself with a week of vacation time coming. He had an idea. He liked to travel, to go to new places, see new country, visit historic sites.

On the Friday following his first call on Memorial Day, he phoned Melody Wuertz again.

"Hey, I've got a vacation coming up. I've never been to Oklahoma City. What's worth seeing in that area, besides you?" he asked.

They discussed things there were to do and see in the old Indian Territory region. Daniels talked to Wuertz three more times before he loaded up his 1991 blue-and-white Chevrolet pickup. He left St. Louis about 11 P.M. and drove straight through, except stopping for a short roadside nap near Tulsa, and arrived in Oklahoma City about 8:20 A.M. the next day. He looked at his watch as he drove into the driveway of the house on West Seventh on June 21, 1991. He walked to the front door and knocked. He could hear the clicking of what sounded like a dead-bolt lock before

Melody opened the wood door, unlocked the outside storm-door screen and let him in. She had been feeding her baby.

Daniels wondered about all the locks on the doors, everything locked and bolted at this time of the morning, broad daylight in a small quiet town where probably nothing much ever happened in the way of crime.

"What are you scared of . . . me?" Daniels said jokingly as he walked inside.

"Oh, it's nothing. . . . How have you been, Jack?"

While Wuertz was taking care of the baby, she and Daniels talked about old times and what had happened to them since. About eleven o'clock they phoned in an order for a pizza from an Edmond pizza parlor and ate it for lunch.

Daniels was dog-tired from his all-night drive. After lunch, he took a nap on the living-room couch. Wuertz started getting ready to go to work at the Veterans Hospital.

Wuertz left for work, and Daniels went shopping in one of the malls and came back to the house between 5:30 and 6 P.M. He used a key Melody had given him to get in. He still was sleepy and he hit the couch again. Several phone calls awakened him during the evening. One was from a man, who did not say who he was, asking for Melody.

Daniels was sleeping soundly when Wuertz and Jessica came home. He mentioned the phone calls, one from some guy who asked for her but didn't give his name. Melody wondered if it had been Slaughter.

After Jessica was put to bed, Wuertz and Daniels watched a movie, *Look Who's Talking*, on TV. They sat up talking until about 3:30 A.M., when they retired to their respective beds. Jack again on the couch and Melody in her bedroom. It was strictly a platonic friendship between the two.

When Daniels got up at 8:30 A.M., he found that Wuertz was already up and feeding the baby. She got up about 7:30, she told him.

"How can you get up this early after working so late the night before?" he asked. She said she always got up early because Jessica had to be fed at 7:30 A.M. Wuertz had a definite daily routine that was dictated by Jessica and her own hospital job.

That day, between Melody getting the baby and herself ready, they managed to visit the 45th Infantry Museum during the morning and the Kirkpatrick Center in the afternoon. After Wuertz went to work, Daniels headed back to St. Louis about 6:45 that evening. It had been a short but enjoyable visit.

Daniels wondered about Wuertz and her baby and the child's father. She had mentioned the father several times, never by name, just "Jessica's daddy," but she did not go into much detail about him.

Jack Daniels kept in touch with Wuertz after he returned to St. Louis. On June 28 he talked to her on the phone about seeing her again when she had a layover in St. Louis of about fifty minutes in her scheduled plane trip to see her parents in Indiana on July 3. Wuertz would have another two-hour layover on the return trip to Oklahoma on July 12. Daniels said he would meet her at the airport during both stopovers.

On June 30 Melody phoned Jack at 8:20 P.M. As telephone company records revealed later, they talked for over 3½ hours. Melody was upset because she had talked to Jim Slaughter that morning, and he had told her "there was no way the baby was his and he was not paying anything for it."

She was highly upset by Slaughter's denial again of being Jessica's father. Now he was claiming that he had signed the affidavit at the hospital when Jessica was born only so that she would have a legal name. Wuertz again spoke of her concern that Slaughter still had keys to the house.

"Well, Melody, why don't you have those locks changed?" Daniels asked.

She said she planned to do just that the next day because she was frightened when she came home after midnight.

"I'm afraid Jim might be in the house, and I'm not sure anymore what he might do."

Daniels had one more telephone conversation with Wuertz on Monday, July 1, 1991. She called and awakened him at a late hour, around 11 P.M. When the phone rang, Jack thought it was the security firm calling about the burglar alarm at the drug store where he worked. The alarm had been sounding recently for no reason, and the regional vice president of the drug firm had asked him to keep records of the times the alarm malfunctioned so they could be matched with the alarm-company reports.

That's why he looked at the clock, expecting the call would summon him to the drug store to reset the alarm.

Though still groggy from the disruption of his sleep, Daniels could tell that Wuertz was agitated. It was the way she was speaking—talking in a low tone, words spewing out in bursts of short and incomplete sentences. And she was crying or about to, he thought.

He remembered another time when she had sounded this way. It was while she was still living in St. Louis. She had called him then shortly after midnight and said a young man she was dating had shot himself with a .22 pistol at her apartment while she was at work. That time she seemed near hysteria. Jack and his wife had invited her to spend the rest of the night with them, and she had.

Now, on this July 1, 1991, she was talking with the same emotional jumble of words. She said she was calling on the watts line from the Veterans Hospital. He guessed that's why she was talking so low that he could hardly hear her. At first they discussed trivial subjects. But there was an undercurrent that Daniels noticed.

"What's wrong, Melody? What's bothering you?" he asked.

"Nothing, nothing," she said.

"You sound like something is bothering you."

"No, nothing. Nothing is bothering me."

When he asked her a third time, Wuertz said, "Well, I got—I can't talk about it here. There're too many people around. I'll tell you about it when I get to St. Louis."

Daniels persisted. "Well, is it bad?"

"Well, it's not real good."

"When you get home tonight and if you feel like you want to talk about it, go ahead and call me back. If not, we'll talk about it when you get here Wednesday."

Daniels asked if she had the front-door locks changed, as he had advised earlier.

"No, I didn't have time. I've been so busy getting ready for the trip, but I'm going to have them changed tomorrow."

"You need to do it, Melody, if for nothing else just for your peace of mind, so you don't have to worry about the house."

Earlier on that same evening, Susie Wuertz also had received a phone call from her daughter. Melody said she was calling from work to verify that she and Jessica would be there Wednesday, the day after tomorrow.

She said that she would leave Oklahoma City on a TWA flight at 2:38 P.M. on Wednesday and arrive at the Indianapolis airport at 5:33 P.M.

"I haven't even started packing yet, but I'll get it done after work tomorrow night," Wuertz said.

She was not elated over the plane trip because it was such a big job gathering up everything and getting ready to fly with Jessica. But she was happy over the prospect of the visit with her folks.

"I've got tons of stuff to do, Mom. But I sure will be glad to see you and Dad," she said.

Wuertz called Diana Angell that July 1, to ask if she could take her and Jessica to the airport. Angell said she would, and Wuertz gave her the time of the Wednesday-afternoon departure flight from Will Rogers International Airport in Oklahoma City.

These were the last times that Susie Wuertz, Jack Daniels, and Dianna Angell would ever talk with Melody.

She and Jessica were found brutally murdered the next day in her home.

Chapter 15

There was a sheriff's department patrol car at her house when Susie Wuertz arrived home from work at 9 P.M. on Tuesday, July 2, 1991.

With her heart pounding and a feeling of apprehension sweeping over her, Wuertz was followed inside by a deputy sheriff, who had been waiting in the car.

"Ma'am, I'm sorry but I have to tell you that there's been a homicide." Wuertz started shaking and she was cold all over, as if from a frigid blast of winter wind.

"It's your daughter, Mrs. Wuertz. We got a call from Oklahoma that she has been killed."

She gasped, and the deputy saw that her face turned white. He thought for an instant she would faint. Tears were streaming down her face.

"What about Jessica, where is the baby?" The barely audible words came out automatically as she struggled to get herself under control, but Susie Wuertz felt like she was outside herself somehow, floating and looking at this unreal scene through a red haze of growing agony. The deputy said he did not know.

He borrowed the phone and made several phone calls. He looked grave as he hung up the phone. Little Jessica was dead, too. Melody and Jessica both dead in their house, five days before the gala birthday party that was being planned.

Both murdered.

Susie and Lyle Wuertz were overcome by despair. Their lives caved in and never would be the same.

Wesley Wuertz was at church camp in the mountains when he received the telephone call from his wife at 11:30 P.M. on July 2. She was sobbing hysterically. He barely could understand the soul-crushing message she delivered: Melody and her baby had been murdered in Oklahoma. His father Lyle had called.

Wesley called his father. He was crying and it was difficult to understand what he said, but Lyle Wuertz gave all of the details he knew. Wesley went into shock and bitter denial.

This could not be true. It was some cruel misunderstanding. The God he knew and loved and served would not permit this to happen.

Wesley was sick enough to vomit, and the blood in his temples was pounding: Melody dead, murdered, horribly murdered, little Jessica, too, killed in the house with her mother. His little niece whom he had seen only one time briefly on a very short visit to Oklahoma. Jessica, the tiny toddler to whom Wesley had hoped he could serve as a father figure.

Wesley Wuertz, the faithful minister who had counseled so many people in their times of affliction and pain and personal sorrow, could not help himself now. It would take several days of counseling by minister friends before Wesley could come out of the black emotional cloud of deep shock.

His grandfather (his mother's father) had died in May, less than two months earlier, and that wound was still fresh in Wesley's mind. But there could be no comparison in the death of his granddad and that of his beloved sister and her baby. In the timetable of life, it was time for his grandfather to go, though it still was no easier on those left behind. But Melody was in the prime of her life, and Jessica was barely into the cycle of life.

Wesley and Melody had talked frequently about the years ahead. They would grow old together, take care of their parents in the years of old age, decide what to do with the old home place so dear in their lives, so full of happy memories. All of these plans to be done together.

Wesley Wuertz might as well have died with his sister, so deep was his unrelenting grief. For months he would be paralyzed in his role as a minister. He knew he was on the brink of a black abyss: possible loss of his lifelong faith.

As time dragged on, his state of helplessness, his deep hurt and overwhelming rebellion against what had been unquestioning faith, threatened his will to survive.

The second worst week was still ahead. There was no way he could ever describe those few days in September 1991 when he and his parents would go to Edmond to pack Melody's belongings. To put into only a few cardboard boxes 29 years of his sister's life.

Jack Daniels's phone was ringing again, jarring him from sound sleep. Out of habit, he glanced at the clock. It was 1:30 A.M. on Wednesday, July 3. The day he would see Melody Wuertz again at the airport on her stopover.

When he answered, a man, who said his name was Robert Macy of the District Attorney's Office in Oklahoma City, informed him that Melody and Jessica Wuertz had been killed.

Daniels's reaction in his sleep-fogged mind was that some crazy prankster was playing a crude joke on him. He made several disparaging remarks to the caller and slammed down the receiver. But he slept fitfully, wondering if the call possibly had been authentic. By 7 A.M. he decided to check it out.

He dialed information and asked for the phone number of the police department in Edmond, Oklahoma. He told the police dispatcher who answered that he needed to talk to someone about a strange phone call he received claiming a good friend, Melody Wuertz, and her baby had been killed.

The dispatcher switched him to a woman who identified herself as Det. Theresa Pfeiffer. It was then Daniels learned what he at first thought to have been a heartless-kind of prank was instead the most horrible of nightmarish tragedies. He would find himself in the spot of answering many questions about his friendly visit in Wuertz's home several weeks before the heinous murders.

Medical students who become doctors start learning their science from the bottom up. So it is with homicide detectives investigating murders, who are hard-pressed for a denouement to a complicated case.

Like the medical students seeking the expertise of learned men of their profession, homicide detectives often turn to the established experts in the science of murder and murder investigation—The FBI's National Center for the Analyses of Violent Crime in the Investigative Support Unit at Quantico, Virginia.

The novel and movie *Silence of the Lambs* made this FBI unit known to all America. But long before the movie made the FBI's murder scientists into a national legend,

almost any homicide investigator in the United States
worth his salt knew of, and often turned to, the FBI's
wonder unit.

The behavioral experts in this FBI special branch have
dissected the nasty elements of murder and classified them
into specific types of killing that a human being can do.
From the profilers who can characterize and paint a fact-
based verbal picture of a particular type of murderer, to
the forensic scientists who literally give the dead a voice
to speak out against their killer, the FBI's crime analysts
make Sherlock Holmes look like an amateur detective in
a Bobbsey Twins book.

From their years of studying everything they can find
out about practicing killers, the specialists have broken
down murder into categories and subcategories.

For the FBI, sex crimes in general are referred to as
"interpersonal violence." A sex murder is a "lust murder."
The general classification of "personal cause" homicide,
says the FBI, is "one motivated by interpersonal aggression
that results in the death of somebody who may or may not
be known to the offender."

The "authority" killing, commonly referred to by the
media as "workplace violence," is one in which the victim
represents some type of authority figure to the killer, a
supervisor killed by an angry subordinate, for instance.

Edmond Police Criminalist Rockie Yardley knew a lot
about that type, having worked the Edmond Post Office
mass killings several years earlier.

Another personal cause murder is the argument-conflict
type; still another is the domestic homicide, an argument-
conflict defined by the relationship of the victim to the
offender, says the FBI, i.e., husband-wife.

The erotomania personal cause slaying is one such as the
murder of John Lennon, where the killer had an unusual
interest in a certain personality; stalking murders fall into
this grouping.

Other personal cause homicides include the extremist killing, based on a body of ideas.

Also in the personal cause category: the hostage kill, which speaks for itself, and the mercy-hero murder, in which there is a killer trying to be merciful in his own peculiar way, i.e., a nurse who overdoses a suffering patient.

In the opinion of the FBI behavioral experts called upon by the Edmond police investigators, the murders of Melody and Jessica Wuertz were personal cause homicides of a specific brand known as the staged domestic homicide.

In simplest terms, they were murders of specifically targeted victims done in a manner involving the planting of false clues meant to divert suspicion from the killer.

Special Agent David C. Gomez of the behavioral unit reviewed the crime-scene photos, investigative reports, autopsy and forensic findings, the background of the victims (known technically as "victimology") and came to this conclusion:

The crime scene had been purposely altered in order to mislead the police by suggesting a false motive for the murders and pointing to a perpetrator who might be traced by phony forensic evidence left at the crime scene.

Rockie Yardley and his investigative cohorts who worked the scene could not have agreed more completely.

After contacting Detective Pfeiffer at the Edmond Police Department, Jack Daniels made a long statement about his friendship with Melody Wuertz and his short visit to her Edmond home the month before she and her baby were slain.

As other friends and relatives of Melody had told the investigators, Daniels recalled Melody had expressed fear of the man who was the father of her baby, and this fright had soared after she filed the paternity suit against Jimmie Ray Slaughter.

Daniels, like others, had urged Wuertz to change the locks on her doors after she said Slaughter still had keys to the house, he said.

It did not take long to eliminate Daniels as a possible suspect. Witnesses where he worked in St. Louis and other people who knew him verified Daniels's presence in St. Louis during the time period Melody and Jessica were thought to have been killed—noon to 12:45 P.M. It also had been obvious that Daniels was personally devastated by the violent deaths.

Meanwhile, the Edmond investigators located Mason Hollinger, the former boyfriend of Melody Wuertz. He confirmed breaking off his relationship with Wuertz several weeks ago. But he denied there had been a violent argument, as had been described to the officers.

He had an alibi for the time frame in which the slayings were thought to have happened. When the detectives checked out the alibi, it held up. During the time that he had been at work, there was no period that he could have driven to and from Wuertz's house and done the murders. Detective Ferling made several runs in his car to check the driving time.

Nothing was found that would suggest he had a motive. After talking to Hollinger and interviewing coworkers and other witnesses who supported his story of what he had been doing and where he was during the vital time period, the investigators were almost sure that he was in the clear. The veracity of the witnesses who backed up Hollinger's alibi was strengthened by the fact they were impartial witnesses, not close friends of the young man.

The sleuths also had followed up Jimmie Slaughter's story to Detective Meador and Sergeant Griffin that a black man had been prowling the West Seventh neighborhood, an "agile sucker who jumped over fences" and disturbed the neighborhood dogs, as Slaughter put it.

Detectives canvassed the area for several blocks around the victims' neighborhood and failed to locate any resident who recalled such an incident, other than Melody's next-door neighbor who had reported her dog barking at the estimated time of the killings.

The investigators also combed through police radio logs for the past several weeks, concentrating on the period of time from when Melody moved to that address in May 1990 up to the date of the murders. There had been no reports of a black man prowling around houses, jumping over fences, and causing dogs to bark in that section of town.

The homicide investigators continued to punch holes in Slaughter's account. When detectives asked Melody's close friends if she had dated or ever expressed a preference for relationships with black men, they scoffed at such an idea. The only black people that Wuertz knew were those she worked with at the Veterans Hospital, and none of them had ever visited in her home or socialized with her off the job, the friends said. At work she was friendly toward the black employees, the same as she was with all of her fellow workers.

More and more, Slaughter's suggestion to check out Melody's "black acquaintances" and a black prowler, who had been jumping fences in her neighborhood, left the officers wondering why he alone, of all the people they questioned, would bring up these possibilities. Slaughter's remark to look for black suspects only served to raise the detectives speculation about Slaughter himself.

Was it only a coincidence that the male nurse had stressed the "black acquaintances" and that evidence apparently planted at the crime scene by the murderer seemed also to point to a black killer? If the killer of Melody and her baby had staged the scene to incriminate an unknown black perpetrator, what would be more logical than to enhance this fakery with stories such as Slaughter had volunteered when he was quizzed at Fort Riley?

Chapter 16

Jimmie Slaughter was emerging as the prime suspect in the deaths of Melody and Jessica Wuertz. But to clear a murder, the investigators need to prove motive, means, opportunity, and physical evidence.

It had been established early in the probe that Slaughter had been off duty on the day of the murders, had finished his last shift at Irwin Army Hospital about 7 A.M. on July 1, and had not been on duty again until 7 P.M. on July 2. Slaughter recently had changed from the day shift to night duty at the hospital.

Detectives knew that he would have had to drive 304 miles from Fort Riley to Edmond to commit the murders, an automobile trip of about 4½ hours each way, if driven at the maximum legal speed.

It was vital to learn what time on July 2—before the murders—was Slaughter last seen by reliable witnesses in Kansas, and the first time he was seen and where after the estimated time of the crime.

So far, Major Slaughter seemingly had an alibi—he had

been shopping with his family in Kansas during the time
the murders were committed.

As related by the male nurse during two periods of questioning by the Edmond officers, his wife Nicki and the
two girls had arrived at Fort Riley from their Guthrie,
Oklahoma, home on Sunday, June 30, 1991, for a visit that
had been planned three or four weeks earlier.

Monday had been spent in routine family activities—
watching TV in his officers' quarters in Carr Hall, later
going to Manhattan, Kansas for dinner at a Mexican restaurant and an evening movie before returning to the base.

On Tuesday, July 2, the day of the murders, the Slaughter
family had slept late and left the base shortly before noon
to eat lunch at a restaurant in Junction City. Following
lunch, they took a driving tour around nearby Milford
Lake, a short way north of Junction City, then went shopping at a large discount store and later at a mall in Topeka.

Finishing the shopping, they attended a movie in the
mall, returned to Fort Riley after 10:30 P.M., and retired
for the night.

Slaughter's account of the day's activities was supported
by his wife, who said they all were together most of the
time except for a few minutes when Slaughter and his
daughters shopped in another part of the large mall.

When first quizzed, Slaughter said they had made the
trip in his wife's car, but in a later interview he remembered
they had gone in his Dodge Shadow. It was later that he
also remembered they had driven around Milford Lake
for a while.

"Looks like he needed the lake trip to cover part of the
time that wasn't covered the first time we talked to him,"
said the detective who conducted the interview.

While shopping, Slaughter had bought his oldest daughter
a Timex watch, and the younger girl a small denim purse,
among other items purchased, the major and his wife said.

On the surface, at least, it would appear that Slaughter

could account for his whereabouts during the time span in which Melody and her baby had met their violent deaths. But it was odd, the investigators thought, that a man would have trouble recalling which car was taken on the shopping trip. And it remained for the Slaughter family version of the day to be checked out with sales clerks, restaurant and theater employees, sales slips and any other source that might confirm or reject the nurse's alibi.

During the time they spent in Kansas, Larry Andrews and Det. Theresa Pfeiffer visited the business places specified by the Slaughters as where they had spent their time on July 2.

After hours of questioning employees and examining sales records and receipts that bore the time and the date of various transactions, the detectives concluded that only his wife completely supported Slaughter's recounting of where he had been, and at what time, on that fateful day.

Employees questioned in the restaurant and the stores were generally indefinite on recalling Slaughter's presence or identifying him. They did remember Nicki Slaughter and the children in most instances.

At the restaurant in Junction City, where Slaughter said they had lunch, he could not remember which waitress served them, but he mentioned that he had eaten at the same restaurant a number of times previously, probably thirty or forty times.

Shown a photograph of Nicki Slaughter and her daughters, the nineteen-year-old waitress who served the food remembered and identified them. She did not identify Slaughter. Nicki looked like the mom of one of the waitress's friends, and that's why she remembered her so well, she said. She remembered, too, that Nicki did most of the ordering. She thought there might have been a man with the woman and girls, but she was not certain.

The only impartial witness who could definitely identify

Jimmie Slaughter was the clerk from whom Slaughter had
bought a Jockey T-shirt at 5:14 P.M. on July 2, according
to the sales records. The item had been purchased at one
of the large department stores in the mall.

Though it was a positive identification, the time of the
purchase was well after the slayings in Edmond, with plenty
of time for Slaughter to have made the 4½-hour drive back
to Kansas, the detectives noted.

But Slaughter also claimed he had bought a Timex watch
for his oldest daughter before buying the T-shirt, which
would have placed him in Kansas even earlier. The investigators tended to discount this statement about the watch
because no receipt for such a watch had been found in
the wastebasket in Slaughter's quarters, where cash-register
slips for other items they purchased had been recovered
the morning of July 3. If such a purchase had been made
by Slaughter, it was suspected that he did it several days
after July 2, a theory that would not be substantiated—at
least partly—until several months later.

The investigators believed that Slaughter easily could
have driven from Fort Riley the morning of July 2, killed
the mother and child, and driven back to buy the T-shirt
at the department store in the mall at 5:14 P.M.

A clerk in a specialty store in the mall remembered
Slaughter, after viewing his picture, as a man who came
into the store about 5:30 P.M. Among the store's merchandise was a collection of knives, and the man had sat down
and discussed knives with him, the clerk recalled.

Nicki's presence at the large mall was confirmed by a
small shop where she had bought a T-shirt for Slaughter.
She had paid for it with her Visa card, which showed the
transaction occurring at 6:35 P.M. on July 2.

Recalling the electric clock in Wuertz's bedroom that
was flashing on and off with the time stalled at two o'clock,

the detectives theorized that the killer had adjusted the clock to make it appear it had been knocked off onto the floor or otherwise disturbed at the time of the killings.

If the murders had taken place at two o'clock, it would be impossible for the killer to have been at a Topeka department store buying a T-shirt only three hours and fourteen minutes later, the sleuths realized.

More staging, they thought, done with the finesse of a playwright giving precise, minute-by-minute stage directions in a detailed script.

"Cherchez la femme"—Look for the woman.

Some Frenchman said it, but homicide investigators know the truth of the words. Someone said that if you want to know a man, talk to the women in his life. There had been two former wives in Jimmie Slaughter's life, his present wife, and innumerable girlfriends and mistresses— this was the story Detective Pfeiffer and D.A.'s investigator Larry Andrews and Det. Richard Ferling and several OSBI agents were hearing as they quizzed coworkers of the male nurse at the VA Medical Center in Oklahoma City and Irwin Army Hospital at Fort Riley.

From what the detectives were learning, Slaughter went through marriages and affairs with the regularity that a public library's most avid patron checked out books. The male detectives couldn't help but wonder about the guy's secret formula: At best he was average-looking, having a high forehead, a double chin, and little hair on top of his head. Sometimes he wore black-rimmed glasses.

He was big for sure—six feet two inches and weighing 240. He spoke softly, but some women said he occasionally was uncouth and given to suggestive remarks. He obviously had a high IQ, and he was competent in his work as a psychiatric nurse. This meant he had to know people well,

understood what made them tick from mental and emotional standpoints.

Those who knew him well said Slaughter studied women
as he might a new patient. He would habitually seek relationships with women of certain personalities and character,
usually women of low esteem with apparent physical, emotional or mental weaknesses and flaws. By supplying the balm
of his pleasant personality and well-aimed compliments and
understanding, he quickly bent a woman to his will.

As time would tell, it was a strong and dominating will.
Jimmie Slaughter had to be in control in all personal and
even professional relationships.

Was he the world's greatest lover, a Don Juan of the
hospital wards? During the long investigation into Slaughter, Detective Pfeiffer became curious enough to ask
Slaughter's women if he was some sort of sexual athlete
or bedroom maestro. Not at all, came the usual answer.
Just an average type lover, maybe even a little below par
in some opinions.

Luckily, not all women fell under his spell of certain
charm. One nurse with a will of her own once asked her
colleagues around the nursing desk after Slaughter had
made a few remarks and walked away, "Who is that obnox-
ious ass?" But reactions like that were the exception in
the circle of women Slaughter surrounded himself with.

It was not unusual for him to have as many as a half-dozen
affairs going at the same time. Usually he had Thursday and
Friday off. Thursdays were devoted to his extramarital love
life. Fridays he spent with his family, unless something
special came up.

Look for the woman. As Pfeiffer and her colleagues
followed this truism, it was like leafing through a copy of
a true-confession magazine, with a tad of horror fiction
thrown in. Slaughter in action with his assorted women
over the years was a piece of work.

Chapter 17

When Dr. Beatrice Alexander began her residency at the Veterans Affairs Medical Center's psychiatric unit, she was looking forward to helping the patients with their assorted problems. It was a fertile field for the psychiatrist. Here were some of the emotionally- and mentally-damaged castoffs from the Vietnam Conflict.

The huge, red-brick hospital at N.E. 13th and Kelley on Oklahoma City's north side, is not far out of the central downtown section. Many of the ex-servicemen had landed in the alcohol- and chemical-addiction and dependency unit, a part of the psychiatric division, victims of the combat horrors that drove so many of them into chemical abuse and addiction.

It was not among Dr. Alexander's professional expectations that she would encounter her most devastating experience not from any of the troubled patients but in the form of a male psychiatric nurse, a former Army nurse major named Jimmie Ray Slaughter.

She first met Slaughter when she came to the hospital

in 1979. The following year they both were assigned to the psychiatric unit, and not long after that their on-the-job relationship turned into a torrid romantic affair. When they first started dating, Slaughter told Alexander that he was not married—though he candidly admitted to having two former wives and a daughter by one of them.

If Dr. Freud had been around, he might have cautioned the new psychiatrist to be wary along her road of romance, which was littered with two past mishaps in the life of her charming nurse boyfriend. Jim Slaughter was a Vietnam veteran himself, and as such, well qualified to deal with the patients under his care. As Dr. Alexander would learn, the ex-Army major had "been there, did that" in some of the darker action against the Vietcong.

It was just as well that in the early stage of their love affair he did not tell many personal war stories. When he did, it would be as shocking in some respects as the electroshock procedure that psychiatrists use in treatment programs.

Their professional intercourse developed into an intimate sexual relationship that would last for eight years, one of the longer of Slaughter's assorted flings. There was a good reason: He was deeply enamored with this intelligent woman who was immersed in the challenging task of sorting out patterns of the human mind.

They had not been romantically involved very long when Slaughter told Alexander he had lied. He admitted he was married, though not happily married. He had to fess up to his true marital status because of what he called a sudden "crisis" in his life—one he was afraid might end their relationship, Slaughter told her with a pleading look in his eyes.

While Dr. Alexander had been expecting to be married to Slaughter at any time, he announced that Beatrice, his wife Nicki, and himself were about to have a baby.

Immediately she wondered about his arithmetic in this proclamation.

"You and Nicki and I will be delivering a baby before long," he boasted. The biggest question in the psychiatrist's mind was how the three together were going to be involved in this event.

Slaughter had a ready explanation. She had become such an integral part of his life, his love for her was so intense, that anything that happened in his life was a part of Beatrice Alexander's life automatically, he said.

Beatrice knew well the frailties of humankind. People count things up differently. But it probably was the strangest tale she ever had heard outside the range of the psychiatrist's office couch.

Yet, Jim Slaughter had such a way about him that his interpretation of the triage of childbirth did not seem that far out to her at the time.

Alexander felt sorry for Slaughter after hearing his version of married life with Nicki. In spite of his deception about not being married, she continued in the relationship with him. Slaughter assured her that as soon as the expected child got through its key developmental years, and would understand such things, he would leave Nicki and live with Beatrice in bliss. There was a time in the future when they would marry, he promised.

During their first four years of love-making, Beatrice Alexander became pregnant three times by Slaughter. This was due mostly to the failure of Slaughter's preferred method of averting pregnancy: the practice of withdrawal. Consequently, Dr. Alexander underwent three abortions.

She eventually confronted Slaughter on his lack of assuming any responsibility in the failure of his contraception plan. Slaughter's only response was to get into a huff about her criticism and he showed a bad flare of temper.

Alexander initiated contraceptive procedures of her own, which did work, and there were no more pregnancies to be aborted, though the frequency of chances was unchanged.

When the new baby girl, whom Alexander had "delivered" with Slaughter and his wife, was old enough, the libidinous nurse frequently brought the child to his mistress's apartment for visits.

The doctor also visited Slaughter and his wife and their daughter at the house in Guthrie. If Nicki Slaughter knew anything was going on between the doctor and her husband, she did not show it, or did not care. And Alexander did not think that Nicki, a former nurse whom Jim had met at the VA Medical Center, was dense.

Later on, Slaughter told Alexander he would not bring the toddler to visit anymore because she was repeating words to her mother like "We love Bee, don't we, Daddy."

Bee was Beatrice's nickname. Slaughter decided his daughter was "too confused" about his and Bee's relationship to keep exposing her to the situation.

During visits to Slaughter's house Alexander saw signs that seemed to support his contention that it was an "open marriage," one lacking in love and intimacy, maintained for convenience. It was apparent to Alexander that the couple slept in separate bedrooms.

Slaughter frequently criticized his wife to Dr. Alexander, complaining of her coldness, her unwifely attitudes. He and the doctor discussed his getting a divorce, but he worried about Nicki keeping their daughter, whom he did love very much, even though Nicki was not a negligent mother. He said he wished his wife would get a boyfriend, "get a life," get herself out of his life.

Once, he mentioned the idea of killing her and making it look like a natural death. Alexander was horrified at such thinking. Slaughter seemed serious when he said a drug regularly used as a muscle relaxant in electroshock treatments would leave no trace of murder. It was a short-acting medication that would paralyze the muscles, including those necessary for breathing, and in the proper dosage could be fatal. He said the drug would not leave any trace in the body.

The doctor thought Slaughter was daydreaming, and did not take his murderous ramblings seriously. Much later, when she analyzed her feelings, she realized that Slaughter said and did things that she downplayed in her mind, a bad mistake on her part but not uncommon for someone in love.

And he talked about other things that made her wonder about the man, whether he was the "quiet hero" that she envisioned and wanted to believe, or an entirely different personality along the Jekyll-Hyde classification.

His war stories upset her when he started telling them. He claimed to have been a member of Special Forces when he served in Vietnam. Under the guise of furnishing dental care to the Vietnamese, his real assignment was to ferret out suspected Vietcong or sympathizers, and personally eliminate them, he said.

Slaughter said his favorite weapon had been the garrote, although he told other hospital colleagues that he often enjoyed using a knife, savored the mutilation it could produce. He remembered his senses as extremely sharp during the act of killing, all of his physical faculties functioning at their highest level, he said.

In simple language, if his stories were to be believed, he plainly had enjoyed his wartime killing. This was obvious to Beatrice Alexander and the other hospital workers. "He had positive feelings about killing," was the refined way she described it later.

He put it in more crude terminology when discussing his Vietnam "mission" with some of the female nurses at the hospital. They found his rumination distasteful. At least two of his coworkers later would recall Slaughter telling them he "got a hard-on" when killing Vietnamese, especially when cutting their throats.

Dr. Alexander became aware that Slaughter knew a great deal about knives and guns. During their shopping trips together, the hulking male nurse talked very knowledgeably with clerks in the stores that sold guns and knives. He talked the language as he thumbed through the catalogues and looked over the displays. The lovers visited the specialty shops before eating dinner and taking in a movie— their usual routine that preceded sex on Slaughter's Thursdays off.

Alexander recalled later that Slaughter told her she should have a gun for protection against housebreakers, and he helped her to select and buy one. He taught her how to clean the weapon and how to use it in target practice on his Guthrie property.

Slaughter gave her another gift, too, a knife that he said had special sentimental meaning to him. He told Alexander that the knife originally had belonged to one of his girlfriends in El Paso, Texas, who had killed herself with an overdose of drugs in her home fifteen years ago. He said he had been very much in love with her.

Slaughter had given the woman, Nancy Gilliland, the knife and also a small pendant. After her death, he had gone to her parents and asked if he could have the knife and the pendant back, in remembrance of Nancy.

The knife sheath bore a stylized symbol in which Slaughter worked his initials into the unusual design. To look at the symbol, you would not immediately recognize the design as one made with his initials.

He told some coworkers about the woman's suicide and said he had removed some of his personal effects from the house before the police arrived because he was worried they might think he was linked in some way to her death.

Love's rites of passage can be painful and tedious. To Dr. Beatrice Alexander, her relationship with Jimmie Ray Slaughter was becoming painfully tedious.

Or, as she later phrased it in her professional words, their affair had become "increasingly superficial."

"We were just doing the same thing week after week. Just going to movies and going out to eat. I had expected we would be getting married at some time, but I was beginning to wonder if that was any more real than when I thought to begin with that he wasn't married.

"I was wondering if instead of him being this quiet hero that I thought of him as, that maybe he wasn't any more responsible or realistic than he had been about my having become pregnant earlier."

She tried to talk with him about some of her doubts, but he brushed her off by changing the subject.

She told him that she wanted "more out of life than going to the movies," so the next week they went to the horse races instead.

When Alexander told Slaughter that the horse races were not what she had in mind about changing their routine, he answered that he liked to be entertained.

Sitting on the love seat in the living room of her apartment, the doctor once again brought up Slaughter's failure to take any share of responsibility in the series of pregnancies and abortions.

Standing over her now, his face flushed and his voice rising, Slaughter made a statement that hit her like a pitcher of ice water in the face. Slaughter said sternly, his face somber, "I get power from killing babies."

For a minute she wondered if she had heard him correctly. He never before had indicated any thinking along these shocking lines. It was at this moment that Alexander realized that she had misunderstood him completely during their lengthy affair. Where would he even have come up with such a belief?

"I'll bring some things by tomorrow that will help explain what I'm talking about," Slaughter said as he walked to the door and left without further words.

She sat stunned on the love seat. What in God's name was this man, with whom she had made love so many times, thinking about to come up with a statement of getting power from killing babies? This very man who had been so gentle and loving with his own small daughter.

The material Slaughter brought turned out to be books on the occult, something that Dr. Alexander had no idea he had ever been interested in. She glanced through the books. They were about beliefs in the occult, the supernatural, witchcraft, but she found nothing about power from killing babies.

But presumably his purpose in giving her the weird reading material was to bring out into the open his own thinking on this stuff that she relegated to crackpots and so-called cultists.

She recalled some letters that Slaughter had written to her in the past about sending "spirit watchers" to guard her, and that she might notice glowing eyes in darkened rooms. He had used phrases like "focal point of power," she remembered.

She had decided then that Slaughter must be watching too much TV or reading too many horror novels when things were quiet on the hospital ward. Either that or the psychiatric nurse, who always had seemed such a normal, ordinary type with a tendency to tell wild stories, was rapidly becoming a candidate for psychiatric treatment himself.

* * *

Dr. Alexander told Slaughter that she was ending the relationship. Later, he came by her apartment and picked up his personal belongings. She was remembering more things he had talked about or done that did not fit her perception of him as a "kind, wonderful person"—the statements such as wishing his wife were dead, even thinking of ways to accomplish that, the claim of feeling an erotic thrill when he killed in Vietnam.

Love is blind. Her strong desire for a loving marriage had overwhelmed the dark and undesirable undercurrents in the life of Jim Slaughter. She had chosen to ignore, to minimize them in her mind, and think instead on the good points of their relationship. Wishful thinking by a trained psychiatrist with a pragmatic understanding of life. How could she have been so misled, a medical professional whose job was to sort out the mixed-up minds of people?

Dr. Beatrice Alexander had had her whole concept of Jimmie Ray Slaughter yanked rudely from her life, pulling the plug on the long relationship.

Slaughter dropped by her apartment one more time. His visit was unexpected, and when he rang the bell and identified himself on the other side of the door, she refused to admit him. She felt actual fear as she stood there and calmly told him she did not want to talk to him.

All of a sudden there was a feeling she had never experienced, a stark fear of someone she had known so intimately and so well, a pulse racing fear in which she admitted to herself that she did not know what Jimmie Ray Slaughter was capable of doing. The most frightening thought of all was that he still had a key to her apartment, though he did not try to use it when she turned him away.

*   *   *

But Jimmie Slaughter did indeed return. He obviously had entered the psychiatrist's Oklahoma City apartment while she and a female friend, who was visiting over the weekend, were away.

Her friend was the first to return to the apartment. She noticed immediately something was wrong. The door they always were careful to lock was unlocked. And when she walked inside, the friend saw that several of her things were missing: a radio, a small clock, and a typewriter.

When Dr. Alexander came home and was told what had happened, she was sure it must have been Jimmie Slaughter. But why he would take her friend's things was a mystery. She could think of a few possible reasons: spite, and to show her that he had been there, could walk in when he pleased.

After their breakup, Slaughter had written a letter to Alexander, blaming her woman friend for influencing her to end the relationship with him. It was not true, of course.

It was wounded pride—and that was something that Slaughter had a lot of—or perhaps false pride and certainly an overblown ego. Her ending of the affair undoubtedly had been an affront to Slaughter's arrogant attitude, an intense desire that he always must control all situations and the people around him, especially the women. That had been another source of trouble between them: Slaughter tried not to show it sometimes, but he was a male chauvinist in every way and thought.

It could have been no one else who entered the apartment. Professional or even amateur burglars would have taken the more valuable things such as the TV, some expensive jewelry and similar items. An expensive watch of the doctor's still was on top of the TV.

As she looked around, it suddenly dawned on Beatrice that the knife in the sheath with the odd symbol on it, and a ring given to her by Slaughter who said it was his late mother's ring, were missing.

No one but Slaughter would have taken those two items. Again she felt the chill of fear.

She did not want to be alone in the apartment ever again. She would not even report the thefts to the police. Something in her mind told her she did not want to antagonize Slaughter. She knew of cases in which people of Slaughter's mental makeup had, by even small affronts, been pushed over the edge.

Chapter 18

Things settled down in the alcohol- and drug-dependency unit at VA Medical Center as the 3:30 P.M. to midnight shift moves into the late-evening hours. After the Alcoholics Anonymous meeting which all patients are required to attend before they return to their rooms for the night, the halls grow quieter as the psychiatric unit settles into another night.

Phones ring occasionally at the nurses' stations, or a lab technician's cart rattles along the corridors. The floor nurses stay busy at the nurses' station, finishing up reports for the next shift. Once in a while, they are called to the room of a patient who is beset by the night horrors of his mind.

When Annabelle Roberts, a petite and attractive young pharmacist's technician, came by the desk delivering medications, she had caught the eye of Jimmie Slaughter. He had smiled at her, and said, "Hi."

Roberts had not been working this shift very long and she did not know many people. She had returned the nurse's friendly greeting and started sorting the deliveries from the pharmacy.

"I know somebody else short like you," Slaughter had said, still smiling. "Pardon me for saying this, but you're really cute."

The other "short person" he knew, Melody Wuertz, had not been working that night.

Roberts had not replied. For one thing, she did not like people commenting on her short stature. She bristled if anyone even jokingly called her "shorty." She guessed it was part of her inferior feelings about herself, the low self-esteem she had. Ever since the bust-up of her terrible marriage, she had felt this way—unwanted, undesirable, a no-count who couldn't do anything right, at least from a man's standpoint, especially a mean SOB like her ex-husband had been.

After that first brief encounter, Slaughter, if he wasn't busy, would exchange small talk with Roberts when she came on the floor. She had decided he was just a big, friendly guy. She was too cautious and reserved and withdrawn these days, she knew that. But even now, she tried to figure out why Slaughter would like her.

Coming out of the marriage where she had been mentally and physically abused, she was jumpy around men and their overtures. She made a point to concentrate on her job and the two kids left to her to raise as a single mom.

But Jimmie Slaughter seemed to be a really nice guy, maybe a little lonesome like herself. He wasn't good-looking, not one of those guys that can't keep from looking in the mirror. She had begun to feel more at ease during their brief chats.

She was working in the pharmacy one evening when the phone had rung and it was Slaughter.

"Hey, Annabelle, this is Jimmie. How would you like to go out for coffee after the shift? I would like to get to know

you. I think you're a nice person." He had the routine
down pat. He felt like he already knew Annabelle Roberts
and the chinks in her fragile being.

She had hesitated. "Well, I don't know. When do you
have in mind? I have to get home pretty quick to my kids."

"How about tonight?"

"Okay, I guess so, I can't stay very long, though." They
had agreed to meet at The Kettle, an all-night restaurant
on Interstate 35 out by Frontier City. It was a popular spot
with the hospital workers and other night-shift people from
nearby. Usually the cops were around drinking coffee, too,
so it was a safe-enough place for single women.

As they sat in a booth, Roberts and Slaughter learned
that both of them had grown up in Tulsa. They talked
about their old high schools. Roberts, as she grew more
relaxed, asked the nurse if he was married and he said he
wasn't. She noticed he was not wearing a ring.

But that didn't mean anything, she had thought to herself. Lots of guys don't wear rings and you find out later
they're married. Since she had become single again, she
had learned a lot. She had told Slaughter she wasn't interested in knowing someone who was married, in any way
except as a friend. But Slaughter seemed open enough
about his life.

He told her he had been divorced twice, had two pretty
young daughters at home—he and his ex-wife had joint
custody—that was more than her old man had even asked
for. He had another older daughter by another marriage
living elsewhere.

Jimmie Ray Slaughter was quiet in speech, smiled a lot,
took an interest in Annabelle that she was not accustomed
to. He really appeared to be interested in her and her life
and what she thought about things and her job and her
kids and the busted marriage.

When she learned he had been in Vietnam, she had

asked a bunch of questions. She wanted to hear about how the war had been. It must have been awful.

"You know, Jim, I think there were a lot of innocent children and women killed over there," she had remarked.

"Yes, I'm afraid that's probably true," he had said.

She bet he knew, but he wasn't talking about it, probably couldn't. It made her like him more.

"I don't understand how anybody can kill someone, even in a war. It seems like it would really be difficult to do something like that."

He had looked somber. "Well, you get used to it."

He hadn't expanded any, not saying he had done it or gone into any details. He'd seemed pretty reserved, and Roberts had felt glad to know a guy like Slaughter.

It had been the first of their coffee breaks after work. He hadn't tried to get out of line and he'd struck her as a lonely guy wanting to talk.

She worked up the nerve to ask him if he had a relationship with somebody now. He mentioned he had a girlfriend in Texas a few years back when he was stationed in El Paso but that she had died. He'd acted like he had thought lots of her.

Recently he had been involved with a lady doctor. "But she wanted more than I could give her and we quit seeing each other," he said quietly.

They had talked about getting together sometime, maybe having dinner or going to a movie. She asked him if he had a home-phone number. She knew that guys usually don't give out their phone number if they are married.

Slaughter had given her his number right off, telling her to call anytime. When he wasn't working, he was around the house in Guthrie, usually with his kids those times he had them. Thursday and Friday were his days off.

After that, she did call him a few times after she went home. They talked about everything. It became pretty regu-

Melody Wuertz, 29, and her six-month-old daughter Jessica, on January 13, 1991, six months before they were murdered.

Jessica Wuertz at nine months.

A pregnant Melody Wuertz poses for the camera.

Jimmie Ray Slaughter at the time of his arrest on January 7, 1992. *(Photo courtesy of Edmond, Oklahoma Police Department)*

The bodies of Melody and Jessica Wuertz being removed from their home. (*Photo courtesy of* Edmond Evening Sun)

The .22 caliber revolver Slaughter used was never found. The prosecution introduced Eley ammunition and guns similar to the suspected murder weapon during the trial.

Artist's rendering of Medical Examiner's diagram of symbol carved into Melody Wuertz's abdomen. (*Courtesy of Louis Malcangi*)

Former home of Melody and Jessica Wuertz in Edmond, Oklahoma.

The U.S. Department of Veterans Affairs Medical Center in Oklahoma City where both Wuertz and Slaughter worked.

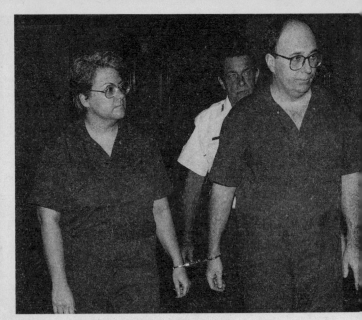

Nicki and Jimmie Ray Slaughter being escorted to their preliminary hearing. All charges against Nicki Slaughter were dismissed and Jim Slaughter was bound over for trial on the murder charge and denied bail. *(Photo © 1992, Oklahoma Publishing Company. From the July 3, 1992 issue of The Daily Oklahoman.)*

Slaughter leaving courtroom during his murder trial. *(Photo courtesy of Edmond Evening Sun)*

Edmond, Oklahoma Police Detectives Theresa Pfeiffer and
Richard Ferling. *(Photo courtesy of Rockie J. Yardley)*

Detective Captain Ron Cavin (left) and evidence technician
Rockie J. Yardley.

District Attorney Robert Macy, the nation's leading death penalty prosecutor. (*Photo courtesy of the District Attorney's Office of Oklahoma County, Oklahoma*)

District Attorney's Office investigator Larry W. Andrews.

lar when she made her rounds on the shift. Slaughter
would ask, "You want to meet after work for coffee?" It
became more or less a set deal, their having coffee or tea
at the end of the shift.

Annabelle Roberts now felt like she really had a friend.
He always seemed to understand her problems and her
feelings, and was willing to listen and talk about them.

He was a nice guy, older than she was, but maybe that
was why he was considerate where so many guys weren't
these days she had decided.

One evening at the hospital Slaughter said he needed
to talk to her about something important, and they agreed
to meet at The Kettle after work. When she sat down in
the booth, Slaughter asked, "Do you know Melody Wuertz,
the ward clerk on our floor?"

He described her and, with a grin, said she was the
one he mentioned that time who was short and cute like
Annabelle. Roberts had seen her around but was not personally acquainted, she said.

Slaughter had a serious look on his face when he said,
"I've got to tell you something, I need to tell somebody."

He looked worried. She felt sorry for him and hoped
she could help him someway to feel better, the way he
helped her when she had troubles.

"She is pregnant, and it's my child she is carrying,"
Slaughter said slowly. "I wanted you to hear it from me
and not the hospital grapevine. You know how rumors are
rampant in a hospital."

With unconcealed disappointment in her voice, she
asked if it was a serious relationship, and he replied, "No,
no, nothing like you might think. Believe it or not, she
just wanted a baby, and that's what I gave her, a child, and
there are no ties, no relationship."

To Roberts his description of the episode did not ring true, but she did not push it.

"I hope it works out okay," she said.

Slaughter was a funny guy in some ways, Roberts sometimes thought. Funny, as in strange. Like talking about that knife all the time. She knew he liked knives and guns, but he always was bringing up this one certain knife. He had told Roberts he had given it to his girlfriend in Texas, the one who killed herself.

After she died, he'd asked her folks if he could have it for sentimental reasons. But later on, when he had this thing with the woman doctor, darned if he hadn't given her the same knife. Most guys give jewelry to women. Roberts knew that she would rather have a ring than some old knife.

Once on a pretty night after work, they were driving around in his car, just sipping on Cokes and talking. Out of the blue he had asked her, "Would you mind going over to a friend's house?"

When she had asked who he said it was Beatrice Alexander the woman doctor he had had the long affair with. Roberts had thought bringing her up was sort of rude, especially asking her to go with him to see her. But all Roberts had said was, "Is she home?"

"Well, no she isn't, but I need to pick up something, that knife I was telling you about."

Roberts was beginning to think Slaughter was an Indian giver. She was getting tired of hearing about the Texas girlfriend and the doctor and that knife.

"I don't care to go," she had said. "I don't go to somebody's house when they haven't invited me. You better just take me back to my car."

Slaughter had driven her to the hospital parking lot.

When she had gotten out, she asked him if he was going to get the knife. He nodded.

"If she's not home, how are you going to get in?"

"I still have her key," he said, pointing to the key ring in the ignition of his car.

It was about 1:30 A.M., not a time, Roberts had felt to be getting things out of peoples' houses, without their being home.

"How can you go over this time of morning and the neighbors not notice you and call the police?"

"Don't worry about it, they know my car," he said, patting her hand lightly. "I'll see you tomorrow."

Apparently that was the time that Slaughter went to Dr. Alexander's apartment and took back his favorite knife, as well as a few other items belonging to her friend.

It was becoming a habit for Slaughter to visit the house of someone who was not there. The subject came up again when Roberts was with him at the end of their night shift.

As they had left the hospital and walked to his car, he stopped suddenly and said: "We can go over to Melody's house. I've got her keys, and we can talk or watch a movie, or whatever."

It was July 1990. Melody Wuertz was in the hospital, having her baby or about to have it. The suggestion by Slaughter that they use her house as a rendezvous point startled Roberts. The more she thought about his suggestion, the madder she got.

Every time she was around Jim Slaughter she was realizing more and more that he had a negative side. He had won her over with his glib talk and free-flowing compliments; and he was warm and friendly at a time when she needed it in the worst way. She had been so lonely and down, and having a difficult time coping with work, her children, and the divorce aftermath.

Now he was no longer the same guy she initially knew. For one thing, he was coming on strong, just like all the other guys she had known. Here he was suggesting that they go to the house of the woman whose baby he had fathered, and who might even be going through the pain of childbirth at this very moment. He said he felt free to do it because he had given Melody Wuertz the money for the down payment on the house and had bought the washer and dryer and other stuff.

How Wuertz might feel if she knew that the man she once thought she loved and a female coworker were using her home for a cozy get-together apparently didn't even cross Slaughter's mind. He obviously didn't intend for Melody Wuertz to know, or if she found out he didn't care.

Roberts knew full well what he meant by "or whatever" in his list of things they could do in the privacy of Wuertz's home. The whole thing was starting to make Roberts a little sick to her stomach.

Slaughter had started talking recently about their going to bed together. He had suggested they go to a motel, and once he said he knew of an empty room at the hospital they could use! Or why not go to Roberts's house, to which she had responded she didn't do that sort of thing at home where her children were. Slaughter should understand that; he had said his two daughters were at his house in Guthrie.

Until now, Roberts and Slaughter had refrained from sexual intimacy. There had been moments of affection, some hugging and kissing in the car, but that was it. Not that Slaughter hadn't kept trying to go all the way.

One Thursday night when he was off from work and she was on duty, he had called and asked if she would like to meet him at a motel after her shift. She had finally given in.

They agreed to meet at 12:30 A.M. at a motel in Edmond. However, during the evening, the on-duty pharmacist asked if anyone would like to go home early since there was an abundance of workers available that shift.

She had accepted the offer and driven home. There she decided to call Slaughter and let him know she had gotten off early. When she had dialed his number, a woman answered the phone.

Slaughter had mentioned that there were occasions when his ex-wife came to Guthrie with his daughters, and sometimes his mother visited, too. Was this his mom?

"Is this Mrs. Slaughter?" she asked.

"Yes, it is." Annabelle still wasn't sure which Mrs. Slaughter she was talking to.

"Are you his wife?" she asked.

"Yes, I am. Do you want to leave a message?"

The woman had not said she was his former wife.

"No, I'll call back," Annabelle had said and quickly hung up.

Slaughter had lied to her after all.

Depression was setting in when she drove to the motel and sat in her car until Slaughter showed up. When they were in the room, he asked, "How was your day?"

She had let him run on for a few minutes before interrupting. "By the way, I called your house." The calmness of her voice surprised her.

"You did?" He didn't seem surprised or upset. "Well, I wasn't there, I guess you found out."

"Yes, I know. But your wife is."

"She is?"

"You lied to me, Jim. Why didn't you tell me you're married?"

"It's not a big deal, really. You'll understand when I explain how it is with me and my wife. Like I told you, I don't really have a wife."

"Well, it's a big deal to me. I don't get involved with

married guys. I told you that when we went out the first time."

"I was going to tell you," he said.

"Yeah, when?"

"Later, after we knew each other better, when I could tell you how it is with Nicki and me. I didn't want to lose you. You're so different than her, honey, so sweet and caring and understanding about things. I was scared you would stop seeing me."

He told her about the bad marriage he had, an "open marriage where we both do what we want to do, and live our own lives."

For the sake of convenience and for the kids, they remained man and wife in name only. He said his wife had stopped having sex with him long ago.

"We both decided we did not want any more children, and Nicki is a Catholic. She always believed that sex was only for procreation. She's very cold in bed. I need you, Annabelle. I'm really a very lonely person, as you say you are. We need each other, and that's why I didn't tell you the truth."

If Slaughter was anything, he was a convincing talker—and a remarkably patient man. For him, that turned out to be a virtue. They had talked for over an hour, and then they had gone to bed.

Why had she consented to having sex that night? Roberts wondered about that long afterward. She decided it was what Slaughter had done for her feelings of low esteem and for her long-deflated ego.

"Jim could take something that would be totally wrong in my mind, what I knew was morally wrong, and he would make it look right for me. Jim made me feel like a million dollars, not a loose woman at all. I guess I did it that night because I needed to know that someone could still care for me. I wanted so badly to believe everything that he said, and I did that night."

But the next day, she had been deeply depressed. Roberts told Slaughter that she did not want to see him again, except when she had to at work. Their relationship was over.

And he was never able to persuade her to make love again, though he tried persistently. Later, even after he had left Oklahoma for reactivation with the Army at Fort Riley, he had called her and tried to get her to come to Kansas. He offered to pay for her trip.

But there was no way for Roberts. Her brief and wonderful romance was over. Regretfully, it had become a one-night stand that would always haunt her conscience.

Although it was the only time they would be sexually intimate, it was not the last time Roberts and Slaughter would talk together in private. The terrible murders of Melody and Jessica Wuertz changed everything.

Roberts was stunned when she read about them in the newspaper on July 4, 1991. Less than two months after Melody and her baby had been slain, Jim Slaughter was discharged from active duty and returned to the VA Medical Center in Oklahoma City as a nurse in the psychiatric unit.

It was known that Slaughter had been questioned as a suspect in the dastardly murders, and his daily presence in the hospital made many of his coworkers highly nervous.

Some of them felt certain Slaughter was the killer. Not unexpectedly, many of the hospital employees were afraid.

They were reluctant to talk to the detectives who came to question them about what they might know about Jim Slaughter, might have heard him say when he worked there before the murders, might have noticed how he acted in relation to Melody Wuertz before the violent demise of the well-liked young mother and her pretty, smiling baby girl.

Some of the hospital employees had seen and heard quite a bit, as a matter of fact. Getting them to talk about it was another thing. Eventually it would take a special session of the Oklahoma County grand jury, called by District Attorney Robert Macy, to dislodge much-needed information—although a few of the hospital workers had begun to tell some things they knew to the persevering investigators.

It was awkward for Roberts the first time she ran into Slaughter after he was back to work at the hospital. Their conversation was stiff. She told him how sorry and sad she was about the deaths of Melody and Jessica.

And she added, "I don't see how anyone could kill a little innocent baby. I mean, killing an adult is bad, but taking a baby's life would take a cold-blooded person to do that."

Slaughter said nothing. He showed no emotion whatever,. Roberts noticed. That was unusual, she thought, because people around the hospital still were crying when they talked about the awful deaths.

She encountered him one day while making her medication deliveries. Slaughter looked somber when he said he would like to meet and talk. With some apprehension and reluctance, Annabelle agreed to have coffee with him after the shift. They met at the Split Pea Restaurant.

Slaughter said the police had harassed him after the murders. He said emphatically he had not done it.

"I wish they would leave me alone and start looking for the one who did it," he said. Slaughter told her that he thought a black transient had killed them. He said some evidence was found in the house that indicated that. And he said that Melody "had been seeing someone."

"I told them over and over that I did not do it, and they

needed to be looking for the person who did," Slaughter said. He told her that Melody had talked about having a preference for black men.

According to Slaughter, he and Melody had talked about her finding a husband, someone to help raise the baby. He said he had told Melody he would have no objection to that, as long as the man was not black. Roberts had not been aware of Slaughter's racist attitude.

During their talk, Roberts began to get upset when Slaughter started criticizing Melody, his voice rising as he spoke.

"Nothing I did was ever enough. She was nickle and diming me to death. She wanted more and more and more.

"If she hadn't been so greedy, she wouldn't be where she is today."

That remark shocked Annabelle. Suddenly she felt nervous and wanted to end the talk promptly. She rose from her chair and said, "I've got to get home. I've got to be at work in a few hours."

She saw that it was raining hard.

Slaughter said, "My car is close to the door. Come on, I'll drive you to your car. It's pouring out there."

As she scooted into the front seat, she saw a knife in a leather sheath stuck behind the visor. She wondered if that was the knife she had heard so much about. It had a gold handle and a blade she later estimated at six to eight inches long. It looked like a hunting knife.

She was glad when he pulled up beside her car. As she got out, he asked her, "Are you working with the police? Are you wired?"

"No, I'm not. Good night," she said and got into her car and locked the door.

She guessed when he asked about her being "wired" he meant was she wearing a tape-recording device. It was apparent that Slaughter was worried. He was concerned about people he knew who might be cooperating with the cops in the intensive investigation under way within the Veterans Administration Hospital. That was the last time that Jimmie Slaughter and Annabelle Roberts talked together.

Chapter 19

By mid-July 1991 the Wuertz murder investigation had taken on mammoth proportions. It had become evident there would be no early break in the case.

Homicide investigators have learned from painful experience if a murder is not solved within the first twenty-four hours—forty-eight hours at the maximum—they are in trouble. The longer a homicide probe drags on, the less chance there is of arriving at a solution.

Evidence is destroyed or lost. Witnesses forget information or move away or even die. Each passing day, week and month lowers the chances of solving any murder, just like winter weather lowers the mercury in a thermometer. After a long time, it's mostly a matter of luck if the killer is caught. Either that, or somebody decides to tell something, or once in a while, a killer confesses.

There are cases on record where investigative persistence has paid off after years, but those cases are few in number. Thankfully, there are dedicated detectives who never give up on a murder investigation.

To the men and women assigned to the Wuertz murders, the case no longer was just a job to be done—it was a mission. From District Attorney Bob Macy on down the ranks of the investigative team, enough hours could not be worked to bring down this particular killer.

The scope of the investigation, as indicated already by the growing number of witnesses questioned, prompted the formation of a task force composed of the Edmond Police Department, the Oklahoma State Bureau of Investigation and the Oklahoma County District Attorney's Office.

With headquarters first at the Edmond Police Department, then later in the OSBI offices in Oklahoma City, and finally in the District Attorney's office, members of the task force would put in hundreds of hours, travel thousands of miles, and question and take statements from scores of witnesses.

Sometimes the sleuths would face delays that seemed to take forever to overcome. There were countless witnesses at two large hospitals operated by the United States government—the Veterans Affairs Medical Center in Oklahoma City and the Irwin Army Hospital at Fort Riley.

The phalanx of smothering rules and regulations barring outside intrusion across bureaucratic boundaries was not easily cracked. Going through the legal guardians of those potential witnesses sometimes left the investigators highly frustrated.

Uncle Sam can be dutifully and jealously protective of those who work for him, the detectives would conclude over the long span of the murder probe. Cooperation was forthcoming, but at times slowly.

The bizarre and brutal murders had occurred on property within city jurisdiction, but those whom the detectives believed knew the most about the murder scheme unfortunately were located within federal jurisdiction—the two big hospitals where Jimmie Ray Slaughter worked and was well known.

The task force included Detectives Pfeiffer and Ferling, who drew the assignment of lead investigators for the Edmond Police Department; supervisor Lt. Terry Gregg, the initial director and coordinator of the probe; Det. Capt. Ron Cavin, boss of the Criminal Investigation Division; Det. Sgt. Mike Meador, Det. Ray Gehrig and Det. Dennis Dill. Actually, everyone in the Edmond Police Department was working to some extent on the double homicide.

OSBI agents on the case included Tom Jordan, Lonnie Rickey, Lydia Williams and Jackie Johnson, among others.

The criminalist who was the primary evidence technician was Rockie J. Yardley, working with numerous forensic lab technicians of the OSBI. There were blood-spatter and crime-scene analysts, such as Det. Capt. Tom Bevel from the Oklahoma City Police Department, who contributed their technical skills to the investigation, plus the highly professional supportive work of the FBI's special violent-crime units.

From the D.A.'s office, then-chief investigator Larry Andrews would figure prominently in the probe from the first day of his assignment given by District Attorney Macy. He spent hours like all the other detectives, seeking and quizzing witnesses and hunting possible evidence.

When the task force was moved to the D.A.'s office in the County Office Building in Oklahoma City, Andrews would assume supervision of the case as it headed toward the courtroom.

Overall, it would be one of the most massive local murder investigations in Oklahoma's history, to be superceded in scope only when the devastating Federal Building bomb explosion rocked Oklahoma City, and the entire nation, in April 1995.

                          *   *   *

Two separate telephone calls on the early morning of
Sunday, June 30, 1991, drew the avid interest of the investigators. In their interviews of coworkers and friends of Melody Wuertz, the detectives turned up information that
Wuertz had received a phone call from Jimmie Slaughter
shortly after midnight on Sunday, June 30, 1991, that left
her emotionally upset.

She had told Jack Daniels and other friends about it.
The call had come only two days before she and her baby
were murdered.

There was a watts-type long-distance phone system available at military bases for free use by service members.
Known as AUTOVON, it enables military and other govern-
mental personnel from all around the globe to keep in
touch with their families. Calls are relayed from base to
base, and from a base out into civilian communities.

Agent Lonnie Rickey of the OSBI contacted the chief
operator at Tinker Air Force Base at Oklahoma City to
obtain the name of the AUTOVON operator on duty at
midnight on June 30. He learned it was "Operator 10,"
Paulette Thornton Hollis.

Hollis remembered, and her notebook confirmed, an
AUTOVON call that had been placed a few minutes past
midnight on June 30 by a "Mr. Slaughter" in Kansas to
an Edmond, Oklahoma, residence.

There was a good reason for her remembering the call:
The last four digits of the number had been identical to
the last four in her own daughter's telephone number.
The coincidence had stuck in her mind, and it was easy
for her to come up with the details.

The number called in Edmond proved to be Melody
Wuertz's number!

Hollis recalled she had been on duty only a few minutes and was doing some book work at her switchboard when a man identifying himself as "Slaughter" called from Kansas.

There was a reason for her remembering him, too. He had asked her name several times, persisting after she told him it was against the rules for her to give her name. She recalled he also inquired about the weather in Oklahoma while the call was being processed.

"Excuse me, I don't think I caught your name," he said. Hollis replied her name was "Operator 10," and said again that policy prohibited an operator from revealing her name.

She said Slaughter gave her the number to call on the AUTOVON line and asked if she would please remain on the line long enough to make sure the call had gone through.

"He said he had tried two times previously, but there was line trouble and the call was not completed," Hollis said later.

She wrote out a ticket, dialed the number but had trouble with the line, not getting a ring until her second try. She hit the release button after the call was answered, but the line did not release.

When she plugged in again, she heard voices and stayed on to confirm the connection. She listened long enough to hear a woman answer and say, "Hold on a minute," and a child crying in the background. She presumed the woman must have had to quiet the child before talking.

When she returned to the line to make sure Slaughter still was connected, it sounded like voices were being raised, but she unplugged before hearing enough to know what was said, she told the OSBI agent.

Detectives knew that Slaughter had received the report on the DHS blood test in mid- or late-June, which identified him positively as the father of Melody Wuertz's baby. They surmised the call had been the one in which he told Wuertz he would not pay child support, blood-test results or not, and may have threatened her—causing her to be so upset when she told her friends about the post-midnight call.

This had been Slaughter's first move in a carefully planned series of events ending two days later with the murders, including setting up an alibi that he was shopping in Kansas with his wife and children when the mother and her baby were slain, the detectives believed.

Making a search of AUTOVON and phone-company records for other calls to or from Jimmie Slaughter on that same date, investigators found a call that was made from a pay phone in Oklahoma City to a ward phone on Ward 4-B of Irwin Army Hospital at Fort Riley.

Slaughter had been on duty on the ward at the time of the call, it was determined; in fact, he had just hung up on his call to Melody Wuertz a few minutes earlier.

The call to the Irwin Army Hospital ward number was at 12:25 A.M. The records revealed it lasted for 215 minutes and cost the caller $26. The call had been charged to the credit card of Cecelia Johnson. Johnson had been on duty at the VA Medical Center in Oklahoma City during that time period, and the call apparently came from a pay phone there, further checking revealed.

The telephone numbers as reflected on a copy of Cecelia Johnson's phone bill indicated that the nurse had phoned someone at Irwin Army Hospital, thought to be Slaughter.

Investigators already had learned of the affair between Slaughter and Johnson, but they wondered what had been important enough to talk for 3½ hours.

Statements that the sleuths obtained later from nurses who worked in the same unit with Cecelia Johnson threw some light on the question. Further along in the probe, when detectives learned the source of evidence recovered at the murder scene—specifically the pair of men's Jockey shorts and the foreign hairs on the shorts, in the man's comb and on Melody Wuertz's body—they would have a definite theory about the possible subject of the marathon phone call from Cecelia Johnson to Jimmie Slaughter.

From nurses and others who worked on the same unit with Johnson, Detectives Ferling and Pfeiffer and Agent Tom Jordan were hearing reports that Johnson undoubtedly had fallen under the spell of Jimmie Slaughter, and was having an affair with him.

No one on the psychiatric unit could understand why Slaughter had become romantically involved with the unattractive nurse, but then, he wasn't any prize himself in the looks department. It was surprising, too, because Cecelia was a good friend of Slaughter's wife, Nicki. They had worked together as nurses.

Johnson often visited in the Slaughters' home at Guthrie, participated in family activities. She seemed the least likely candidate for a sexual affair with Slaughter, although her own marriage was falling apart. But Slaughter had been working on Johnson for several weeks, and their friendship obviously had developed into a sexual relationship. Johnson's introverted and self-conscious personality changed, as had her usual amiability with other unit workers. Now she seemed critical of everybody and everything. Her coworkers could hear and see Slaughter in how she talked and acted.

"You could hear Jimmie speaking when she talked," said one nurse. "It was amazing how she reflected his ideas and actions."

The nurse said it almost was as if Cecelia Johnson were a robot that had been programmed by Jimmie Slaughter. She had been so overwhelmed by her devotion toward

Slaughter as to remark one day that she would do anything for him, would gladly kill somebody for him.

Cecelia Johnson was quoted as having said to Elmo Meredith, a psychiatric assistant on the unit, "I like Jim. Jim is the best friend I have. Jim and I think a lot alike. I would help him kill. I would help him kill or I would do it for him if he asked me."

It was the strangest thing anyone had ever heard come from the mouth of the backward, shy and withdrawn nurse, whose affections mainly had been directed at baby Jessica Wuertz for several weeks.

And there was a time when Cecelia Johnson and Melody Wuertz had become almost like sisters in their warmth toward each other, the unit staff remembered.

The remark of being so worshipful of Jim Slaughter that she "would kill" for him would be regretted by Cecelia Johnson for the rest of her short life.

Johnson's infatuation for Jimmie Slaughter spilled over into her work on the unit. He now was at Irwin Army Hospital after being voluntarily reactivated. She spent so much time on the telephone talking to him that it was interfering with the routine on the psychiatric unit.

One nurse, who recently had been assigned to the unit, confronted Johnson one day about her habit of absenting herself from the nurses' station and not letting the nurse know where she was.

The new nurse said, "I remember my anxiety was high because Cecelia would go off somewhere and not tell me. Finally I just said, 'Hey, I'm new here. I need to know where you are in case I need help.'"

Johnson responded, "Well, I'm in Joyce's office, using the phone." The office was around the corner from the nurses' station.

"If you need to make a call, use the phone here at the nurses' station—I'm usually out on the floor anyway," the new nurse told her.

"No, I can't do that," Johnson said. "These are personal, private calls."

One time, the same nurse accidentally punched the button for the phone line Johnson used, and heard herself being bad-mouthed by the hefty nurse to someone she called "Jim."

Chapter 20

The Edmond Police Department received an unsigned postcard suggesting that the police should talk to Cecelia Johnson and another worker on the unit, Elmo Meredith, about information they might have relative to the Wuertz murders.

The police also should take a look at the phone calls on the hospital watts line that were logged from an office near the psychiatric-unit nurses' station, the writer of the card said.

Later, when detectives reviewed the hospital phone records, the log showed numerous telephone calls to Fort Riley, between midnight and 4 A.M., when Cecelia Johnson was on duty.

Elmo Meredith was older than most of the unit employees. He was a good worker whom everyone liked and confided in, and strangely enough, he seemed to get along well even with Jimmie Slaughter.

In light of Slaughter's often expressed racial bias, the amiable working relationship between Meredith and Slaughter might be thought of as unusual, as Meredith was black.

On the other hand, there never had been any question of Slaughter's professionalism. He was competent and had a good work record, except for sometimes bad-mouthing, a patient in discussions with other employees. But he never got out of line with a patient, coworkers said.

In the late summer and fall of 1991, Meredith was in a fearful dilemma. He had heard some things from people on his unit that he knew he should pass along to the police. But he was fearful for the welfare of his family, particularly for his wife who was alone at their house when he worked the night shifts at the hospital.

There was a killer loose out there, the killer of Melody and Jessica Wuertz. As far as Meredith was concerned, people who talked to the police might be next—or their family. He was not alone in his apprehensions.

An atmosphere of fear was beginning to envelop the Medical Center's psychiatric unit. Fear of the unknown, of possible retaliation for having a loose tongue. Even with the mentally and emotionally unstable patients who filled the rooms, the less illuminated areas of the corridors had never before seemed so dark and threatening to the nurses and assistants. Still, Meredith knew that he should tell the cops some things.

Detectives had been questioning employees in the unit about Melody Wuertz and Jimmie Slaughter and even Cecelia Johnson. The cops had talked to Meredith, too; apparently some of the other employees had mentioned he might know something. That was the trouble, he already had talked too much to some of his coworkers.

Meredith had answered some questions the cops asked,

but he had not let it all hang out—the nagging fear of a killer still free out there in the night was too much of a block.

Meredith had seen a lot of life, and he was a keen observer of human conduct and misconduct. Having been employed at the Veterans Hospital since 1985, he may have been one of the first psychiatric-unit workers to notice that Jimmie Slaughter and Melody Wuertz seemed to be "interactive," as he put it, which some people thought was a pretty highfalutin word for screwing around.

He noticed that the pretty little lady held Slaughter's hand. They would have lunch together in the report room. When Meredith walked in and out, she might be holding Slaughter's arm, smiling at him.

It was in the spring of 1990 that Meredith noticed a big change, literally, in Wuertz's appearance. He had been on vacation and he noticed her physical difference immediately when she came in. Her face was flushed and her figure was full. Also she was wearing maternity clothes, which cinched it.

Meredith and Slaughter were friendly enough for Meredith to make a remark about it. He asked Slaughter if Wuertz was pregnant. Slaughter smiled but did not answer.

After that, Slaughter talked to Meredith about Wuertz and her condition and Slaughter said he would like Wuertz to farm the baby out for adoption.

Slaughter mentioned that one of the nurses, Joanne Contreras, was looking for a baby to adopt. The expectant father said he was going to talk to Wuertz and see if she wouldn't let Contreras adopt the baby.

Later, Meredith told Cecelia Johnson that Slaughter had said Joanne Contreras wanted to adopt Melody's baby.

Cecelia's face flushed, and she said firmly, "If Melody is going to adopt the baby out, I want to adopt the baby."

Elmo's opinion that Slaughter and Cecelia were "interacting" was more or less confirmed one evening when Slaughter walked behind the desk, sighed and said, "Well, Elmo, I finally got to old Cecelia."

One thing for sure, Slaughter seemed to be a ladies' man, and he wasn't a good-looking guy, either. Slaughter had talked to him about still another woman friend, a lady psychiatrist, who worked in the hospital doing her residency. He told Meredith that he had been dating her for a long time and that she had asked him to divorce his wife and marry her.

"I told her I could divorce my wife, but I could not divorce my kids," Slaughter said to Meredith.

Slaughter said he had been divorced before, and that wife had taken him for everything. "If I divorced Nicki, she would take everything, including the kids, and I couldn't stand that. And if she tries to divorce me, I'll have to take out a contract on her."

Meredith guessed he meant "contract" like a hit, hire a professional hit man to kill her. It was a shocking thing to say, if Slaughter was really serious in saying it. But Elmo Meredith already had noticed that Slaughter seemed to have some tendency toward violence.

One evening they had been watching one of those Arnold Schwarzenegger movies on TV, in which the actor was butchering people all over the place, using a knife and a machete. Meredith recalled Slaughter had remarked to nobody in particular, "There's nothing to that. I could mutilate a sleazeball like that and he wouldn't be recognized."

Slaughter's comment surprised Elmo. He had always had a higher opinion of nurses, believing nurses took care of people and didn't have the urge or ability to kill people, except maybe doctors sometimes.

Once when a patient griped at Slaughter about not getting his medicine, Slaughter had responded in a cool and professional manner. But as Slaughter turned away, Meredith had seen that his face was flushed red and he was scowling. He'd told Meredith, "That guy's the type of sleazeball I could kill and mutilate."

After Slaughter volunteered to be reactivated and was going to Fort Riley, Meredith thought that he seemed depressed. He thought it was because Slaughter was heading into war.

"Are you worried about getting into the war, Jim?" he asked.

"Not really, Elmo. I'll be glad to get away from these damn pushy women, especially Melody. If she keeps pushing me, I'll have to kill her."

Violent talk again, Meredith thought about killing another one of his women. First his wife, now his girlfriend.

Slaughter already had gone to Fort Riley when Meredith had a conversation with Melody Wuertz in September 1990. She came into the TV room where Elmo was watching a movie with some patients.

She hesitated a minute, then said, "Elmo, I need to know something. Do you know if Jim is married?"

"Of course, everybody around here knows that, Melody."

She looked surprised and quickly walked away. He thought there were tears coming down her cheeks.

The last time that Elmo Meredith talked with Melody Wuertz was on the Friday before she and her baby were killed the following Tuesday. It was about 10:30 P.M. when she approached him behind the desk, checking to see if any doctors' orders had to be removed, and said, "You're the very person I'm looking for. Have you heard anything from Jim?"

He shook his head. "He wouldn't contact me, Melody. Check with Cecelia. She may have heard from him, be more likely to hear from him than me."

He noticed Wuertz looked upset. She was pale, and her face was drawn.

"What's the problem, Melody?" Meredith asked sympathetically.

Her eyes wide behind her glasses, almost in tears now, she said, "I'm real scared, Elmo. I filed this paternity suit against Jim, and I haven't heard from him at all. It frightens me. I don't know what he will do."

Meredith paused, then he said quietly, "Melody, you need not to push Jim too far. He could be dangerous." He was remembering what Slaughter had said before leaving for the Army, that he would have to kill Wuertz if she kept after him.

Meredith came to work about 3:30 P.M. on Tuesday, July 2, 1991. When he came into the unit office, the ward coordinator was standing in front of the computer.

She turned around, and he saw she was pale. Something is wrong, he knew before she spoke.

"Did you know that Melody and Jessica were killed?"

Her question did not register immediately—he already had started writing the names of patients on the duty board. Suddenly he stopped and turned back to the ward coordinator.

"What did you say?" he asked incredulously as her words sunk in, wanting to be sure he had heard right.

"I said that Melody and Jessica have been killed."

"Oh, my God," Meredith responded. He thought immediately of Jim Slaughter's statement.

About two hours later, Cecelia Johnson, who was standing near him, reached out and grabbed his hand.

"Come on, I have something I need to talk to you about." She pulled him toward the report office.

Her face was white and she was shaking, and her eyes were darting around. She said breathlessly, her voice pitched low, "I have not talked to you about Melody or Jim at any time, you understand what I'm saying?"

Meredith remembered the remark that Cecelia had made to him one day on the unit, that she thought so much of Jim Slaughter that she could help him kill somebody, or even kill somebody for him.

All he could think to answer was, "Why?"

"Well, that's just the way it is," she said and walked away.

When Meredith had first seen Johnson when he came to work, she had been acting normally. But when the news of Melody and Jessica's murders swept through the ward, she had fallen apart completely. He understood from her stressful statement to him that she did not want him repeating anything she had said about Slaughter or Wuertz to anyone, especially the police. It was the beginning of Elmo Meredith's dilemma.

When the detectives came to the hospital and started asking everybody questions, he did not tell all he had heard from Slaughter and from Johnson. He presumed that some of the people on the ward had told the cops that he had mentioned to them in past weeks some unusual statements made by Johnson and Slaughter.

He guessed Detectives Richard Ferling and Ray Gehrig knew he was holding back. But he had to think about it, about his family and the danger his wife might face being alone at night. A man has to think of his family first, doesn't he?

Finally, Meredith went to his church pastor and discussed the problem. He also talked it over with his wife and other family members. All of them, the preacher and his family, agreed. He should tell the police everything he knew. So he phoned Agent Tom Jordan of the OSBI, and said he was ready to come in and talk to him about it.

Jordan asked if Meredith would be willing to do that with the district attorney present, and he said yes. He knew it was the thing to do. A man has to be right with his God before he can be right with himself.

Chapter 21

It was September 18, 1990, and the group of reactivated reservist nurses was being processed on their arrival at Fort Riley, where they would be assigned to the Irwin Army Hospital.

The hospital and the base were not new to Major Slaughter. In the past he had served here during his regular two weeks of reserve duty. It was all new to First Lt. Darlene Ellis.

Although they knew they could be involved in a war in the Middle East at any time, the nurses were feeling sentiments almost like the first day of college. The processing was a day of introductions, backslapping, handshaking, and hugging.

For a short while Ellis and Slaughter lived in adjoining but separate barracks. Then she moved into Carr Hall, an officers'-quarters dormitory. Slaughter moved there a few days later. She saw him struggling painfully with his belongings and went to help. He said he had injured his back recently in a fall.

Slaughter had been her night supervisor at the hospital, but he was taken off that job because of the painful back injury.

Now living in the same dormitory, Ellis and Slaughter found themselves together much of the time—working on the same hospital ward and residing in the same dormitory. One day when going off duty, she put on her coat and felt a piece of paper in her pocket.

It was a note from Slaughter: "Maybe we could go out to dinner some night. You seem like a really nice person." It was signed Jim.

However, the healthy-looking, robust male nurse was about to become a patient. He would undergo back surgery—an operation for a ruptured disk—at Fitzsimons Army Medical Center in Aurora, Colorado, he told Darlene on Thanksgiving night during a gathering at the head nurse's house.

She and Slaughter washed and dried the dishes after the meal. It was a festive evening, with much joking and laughing.

Slaughter said he was going home the next day on a ten day pass, and after that, he would check in at Fitzsimons Army Medical Center for the back surgery.

It was the beginning of their close friendship, which would later take off like a rocket to become a hot love affair.

After several weeks, when they did become sexually intimate, there were some serious conversations about Slaughter's marital status. Darlene Ellis was not married, but Slaughter admitted that he was married and had two girls by his wife, Nicki.

Ellis reacted with anger. "Hey, buster, you know I don't need a wife coming after me with a shotgun!"

But he soon convinced Darlene—as he had his other girlfriends—that it was only a marriage of convenience in which love and sex had ended long ago.

He emphasized they no longer slept together, they had separate bedrooms, and they stayed together only for the children. He said that from almost the start the marriage had not turned out the way he thought it would.

Slaughter told Ellis that his wife's family was wealthy, and when he and Nicki got married he thought the family's money would help him greatly. But he was still having to work and to pay half of everything, he complained.

Ellis, who bristled at the self-acclaimed superiority of most males, wondered what the world was coming to when men didn't think they should earn a living for their wife and kids.

Slaughter said that his main reason for staying married was their oldest daughter. She was his favorite child, and she in turn worshiped him, he said. It crushed his daughter Betsy if he even raised his voice to her. He loved the younger girl, of course, but he said she was more like her mother, whiney, really a brat. The admission of child favoritism did not sit well with Ellis, either.

Slaughter went on to say that he believed Nicki would take the girls from him if they divorced. So, he stuck it out, and he and Nicki went their separate ways. It was an "open marriage" in which they both did what they wanted with no attempt of concealment.

Nicki even had her car registered in the name of both her mother and herself. He gave her some money, which she put into her own bank account. They were just friendly enemies. Darlene did not have to worry about a wrathful wife coming after her, Slaughter said.

Ellis still did not feel right about it, but she had to admit that their sexual activity was wonderful.

* * *

Ellis was concerned about Slaughter having his surgery in the Colorado hospital. He had said none of his family would be there, meaning, of course, his wife. She thought that was terrible, to be alone when having such major and painful surgery.

After the operation she called him several times. Once when she called he came to the phone breathless and hurting. There was no phone in his ward and he said he had walked a long corridor to take the call.

He was worried about getting back to Fort Riley. He had left his car at the Wichita airport, and he hoped it would start when he returned. No one should have to crank up a car in the bitter cold after having surgery, Darlene thought. She offered to meet him, but later, he said an old friend, Sandy, another nurse, would pick him up. He explained Sandy and he once had been lovers, but they only had a platonic friendship now.

Ellis had to live with that explanation. She also found out that another nurse, one from the VA Medical Center at Oklahoma City where he had worked, had been to the Denver-area Army hospital to visit Slaughter. Her name was Cecelia Johnson.

Back at Fort Riley, Slaughter was recovering rapidly and regaining his strength. He soon was back on duty, and he and Ellis picked up where they had left off in their steamy sexual togetherness.

Slaughter exercised to get back into shape. Even when driving, he had a contraption with strong springs which he squeezed with one hand and then the other to strengthen his hands. They had not been touched in the surgery, but he used them occasionally in his work to restrain a patient.

* * *

Ellis and Slaughter were looking at some pictures in his apartment one night, photos of Slaughter's two girls with Nicki and another older girl by a former marriage.

Darlene saw a picture of one of the cutest babies she had ever seen. The baby was laughing as she opened a present. It must have been taken at Christmas. With a darling little bow on a headband, the happy baby did not look even a year old and was already sitting up by herself.

"Who is this, Jim? She's precious," Ellis asked.

"Yeah, that's my baby, too," he said.

Ellis was puzzled. Slaughter had always mentioned the older children by two wives. Now suddenly here was a picture of a baby only several months old. What's the deal, she wanted to know.

She commented on how cute the bow was, but he snapped angrily that the bow was the dumbest thing he ever saw. She dropped the subject, but brought it up again later when they were out for dinner at a restaurant in the nearby little town of Junction City.

"Doesn't this new baby cause a problem with your wife?" she asked.

No, he said there was no problem at all. Nicki knew he had this baby by a young woman at the VA Medical Center in Oklahoma City, where he worked before being reactivated. He had fathered the baby, but neither the mother nor the baby was a problem. He said he helped the woman financially.

He explained there had not been a love relationship involved. He said that the young woman had come to work at the hospital as a ward clerk. She was new in town and didn't know her way around, and he became friendly and tried to help her.

Their relationship had been one of two adults who had consensual sex, and that was it. He said that on one occasion the young woman had said she was grateful for all of his help and that she offered to have sex.

He had accepted, but that was it, no big deal. Except she had gotten pregnant, and he did not want the baby. He did not need another baby. He already had enough babies, he said.

He had suggested an abortion, but she wanted the baby.

So he helped her to get a place to live and had paid the hospital costs when the baby was born. He also bought her furniture and other things because he felt responsible, even though she wasn't holding him responsible or asking for his help.

It sounded pretty brutal to Ellis. She could not understand any woman agreeing to a deal like that, unless she was very young and completely taken in by the man involved. Darlene Ellis would always have the picture of that beautiful little baby in her mind.

Chapter 22

It was like a bad dream, a nightmare in which she found herself trapped on a clattering roller coaster hurtling toward the brink . . . of what? Thrills or destruction? Or madness?

As a nurse therapist frequently immersed in the weird mechanisms of the human mind, Ellis began to wonder how in hell she would counsel herself in this predicament. About the time she would catch her breath from the last dizzying plunge, she would be moving upward on a crest of excitement, which could only end in still another screaming dive taking her breath away.

And that could describe either the roller-coaster effects of Slaughter's strange revelations to her, or the exciting sex of their relationship, which she later would refer to as "wonderful." In retrospect, the sex may be one of the few things that Slaughter might agree Darlene was right about.

As an intelligent, highly trained practitioner of psychiatry, Darlene Ellis found herself on the defense. She was in a state of denial over what she was hearing and experiencing with a fellow professional, who knew all the rules and seemed intent on breaking them.

In her mind Jimmie Slaughter was rapidly becoming one combat veteran for whom she could prescribe no helpful therapy, not that he thought he needed it. As far as he was concerned, there was nothing amiss in the weird conceptions he held in matters of human relations, or his terrifying beliefs in the spirit world.

His reaction was patronizing when she asked so many questions. Instead of answering, he would laugh, as if amused at how naive she was.

Ellis had seen patients hallucinating, but Slaughter was not suffering from that malady. He was dead serious, perhaps deadly serious, about the weird things he told her.

That damn business of the Druids was the first thing that really shook up Ellis. Then the spooks he called his "Protectors," like something from a Stephen King or Dean Koontz horror novel.

And the knowledge he had at his fingertips on how to kill.

And his control over women, his eventual control of her, something she never thought could be accomplished by any man.

Slaughter had to control every facet of his life, and hers, and everyone else's he encountered, or he would go bananas—and she had seen him do that after he got that letter about paying child support for that cute little baby that he admitted was his child.

They talked about a lot of different things when they were in the car driving from the Army base to Junction City for dinner. Slaughter realized that Darlene Ellis had an inquisitive nature.

And sometimes, knowing he knew this, she thought he was probably baiting her.

They talked about religion, and she said she was raised a Catholic. When she asked about his religion, he said, with all seriousness, "I'm a Druid."

Darlene Ellis wasn't sure what a Druid was, but she thought it had something to do with an ancient religion. She did some research, and the next time they were together, she told Slaughter she understood that Druidism was an old Celtic religion practiced by people in Gaul, Ireland and England. They were people who had a great respect for nature, particularly trees and the earth, as if these things had a spirit. Real environmentalists, she said.

He seemed amused. He smiled and said, "Yes, but there is a lot more to it than that. I'll give you a tape I have and you'll understand better."

Slaughter loaned her an audiotape of a talk given by a man who claimed to be an ex-Druid, and who now was a born-again Christian preaching about the Druids at conventions and church meetings, telling what kind of terrible things exist in this world.

The preacher said it was a cult, a Satanic-worship that included human sacrifices. The human-sacrifice part left Ellis dumbfounded because the tape and Slaughter's own description did not come anywhere close to what the encyclopedia said about Druidism.

When Ellis asked if Druids held Sunday services, he laughed. Slaughter confirmed that Druids believed in human sacrifice as a ritual, adding that women were the most bloodthirsty of all Druids. "They can't wait to get their first kill," he said.

Ellis recalled later that part of her was denying all this. It just didn't jive. Slaughter said victims were available anywhere, like hitchhikers who would never be missed.

A group of Druids—he called them a coven—had met in a field on his farm in Oklahoma, Slaughter claimed.

The members all were women, except him, and he was the leader, the Grand Druid dude.

It figured, Ellis thought, that Slaughter's coven would be all females. He said his wife Nicki and the nurse friend who had visited him when he had the back surgery were members, too.

He said the other members didn't like Nicki, but they had to accept her because she was his wife.

Slaughter boasted that all of the women in the coven would have liked to be impregnated by him and have his babies. Except maybe Nicki, Ellis thought.

Once when Jim Slaughter and Darlene Ellis were out driving around the countryside, he spotted a large boulder in a field near the road. Slaughter slowed down to get a better look at the big rock, which was about six feet long, three feet wide and flat on top.

Slaughter thought the rock was beautiful and wished he could get it back to his Oklahoma farm. "God, it would make a great altar," he said.

She guessed the rock would about fit a human sacrifice. Slaughter never appeared to be joking when he talked about the coven. To her, it was so much baloney, but Slaughter was insistent that he believed these things.

He said his daughters went to a Catholic school. The girls were not Druids, but he thought it would be a hoot if the nuns and priests ever found out the Slaughter kids came from a Druid family.

Again in his apartment in Carr Hall, there was another episode that gave Ellis an eerie feeling. Slaughter talked about two spiritual "Protectors," who were with him all the time. They were present now and kept him from getting hurt. They must have had a day off when he hurt his back, she thought, but she didn't dare say it.

No, they were not guardian angels. They were spirits, but they could materialize, and Slaughter said when he saw them once they were so "gory, distorted and ghastly" that it scared even him. Sometimes you could see their eyes glowing in a dark room, he said.

More B.S., Ellis told herself. But it made her nervous when he talked so seriously about this stuff in the semidark apartment.

The "Protectors" also kept him in money, he said, remembering one morning when he got up and money had been stuffed in his briefcase. It had not been there the night before.

Jim Slaughter's making a disciple of Darlene Ellis escalated after he had loaned her the tape about Druidism and she had started asking questions. He seemed eager to tutor Ellis in the dark byways of mysticism. And to her surprise after hours of listening to Slaughter in his role of mentor, she was changing. Absorbing Slaughter's subtle innuendos about his powers and intelligence and superiority, she began to question her own integrity.

She wondered if she was so smart after all. Never before had she had a problem with self-esteem, nor ever felt herself a victim. But as the lectures went on, her own confidence faded. She was a willing target of manipulation. She could not explain what was happening. He was taking charge of her very being.

Maybe Slaughter does know all these things, she thought. Because she had not been exposed to the world to the extent that he had, maybe he did have all the answers, and she should just ease back, listen, agree, and comply.

Slaughter was pleased with her new attitude of interest, listening, and subjugation. And his reaction, his new bearing toward her of "now you're a good kid," was like a pat on the back.

Gone was the bluster, the self-assurance of a woman of the New Age, a feminist who could hold her own with a man in private or professional life. Now she was feeling dumb, inferior, unable to compete. She was agreeing that the man should be in charge of a woman's life, of everything.

Slaughter had been talking about getting a new tattoo. He already had one on his left lower arm, near the wrist. To Ellis it looked like two big Roman numerals I placed together. It did not appear to be a professional tattoo job.

When she asked about it, Slaughter said it was something that he had done when he was young and was a member of a brotherhood or something. He told her once that the tattoo symbol was "the gates of power."

"You mean the gates of Hell?" she asked.

He laughed, and replied, "No, they represent the Gates of Power." The way he stressed it, he capitalized Gates and Power.

Later they went to a tattoo parlor in Topeka where he looked through what seemed like thousands of tattoo designs before he found the one he wanted. First he had wanted a tree to be put on his left chest, but he changed his mind and started looking at dragon tattoos.

There were all kinds of dragons. After looking through page after page, Slaughter said, "This is the one I want. See the difference. The dragon has a cloven hoof. A cloven-hoof dragon is the symbol of Satan. It's in the Bible, that's how Satan is described in the Bible, as having a cloven hoof."

It was a large multicolored tattoo with a great deal of

blue in it, she noticed. It was about six inches high. He had it put on. They had joked about her getting a flower, a magnolia, tattooed on her buttocks, but she didn't go through with it. She didn't want any needle artist making sketches on her fanny.

Chapter 23

They were on the couch in his living room, watching television. Darlene Ellis was on the outside, her head nestled in the crook of Slaughter's arm. It was cozy inside the apartment on a winter night.

Suddenly she was feeling confused, a dizzy, half-conscious feeling like just before fainting. Although she did not realize it, she actually was regaining consciousness at the time she became aware of the topsy-turvy feeling.

She heard Slaughter laughing.

"What's wrong? What's wrong with me?" she murmured. The light was coming back and she knew where she was.

"You should have seen your little head, it was just jerking around. You were having a seizure, hon."

"I don't have seizures. What's going on?" She sat up quickly. Her head was clear now. But her heart was pounding. What in hell was going on?

Still laughing, Slaughter explained there were certain

pressure points on the neck that could be squeezed to "put a person out and cause them to have seizures."

He had tightened his arm around her neck as she lay there unaware of what he was doing. The blood flow to her carotid artery, which supplies blood to the brain, had been cut off for seconds, dumping her off the edge of an abyss into the unconscious.

Slaughter had stacks of magazines having to do with knives and guns piled in the living room. Ellis knew he was an avid weapons collector; he had shown her guns and knives, commenting at length on their various merits. But she discovered one night that he had a strange affinity to the knives and books at an odd time.

He kept most of the magazines and catalogues in the living room, but he had a stack on a bed stand in the bedroom. He always had a knife close by, too.

After they had engaged in sex and were still naked, and Ellis was getting sleepy, Slaughter switched on the light and started looking at the knife magazines. He brought one big knife over to the bed to show her. He ran his finger along the blade. It was almost like a loving gesture, Ellis thought as she lay there, now wide-eyed and wondering what the devil he might come up with next. She wouldn't have been surprised if he had drooled when looking at the knives and magazine pictures of them.

As he thumbed through the magazines, pointing out various knives, he mentioned he had ordered a special handmade knife. Slaughter's switching on the light and having to look at and talk about these books and knives before he could fall asleep after making love made Ellis uncomfortable.

* * *

Ellis was working at the desk when Slaughter strode angrily into the nurses' station, waving a piece of paper in his hand. She never had seen him so livid.

Ellis put down the report. "Jim, what's the matter? What in the world is going on?"

He was pacing back and forth in the small area of the nurses' station. He tossed the paper and a tablet on the desk. He was pounding his fist into his hand, exclaiming so loudly she was afraid it might shake up the patients.

"She can't do this to me! They can't even prove it's my baby! Ths damn bunch of bureaucrats, they can't tell me what to do!" Slaughter exclaimed.

The letter was from the Department of Human Services in Oklahoma City telling him he had to start paying child support for the baby, he ranted.

Ellis didn't ask what baby. She knew—he had talked enough about it. And she couldn't understand why he was making such a big deal of helping support that cute little baby whose picture she had seen. She never had heard its name. But he admitted it was his baby, told other people it was his baby; he had paid for a house, furniture and stuff, why was he going on like this now, Ellis asked him.

Her comments only made him madder. "The bitch can't do this! Why would she betray me, go to this bunch of government idiots! They can't make me pay for that baby! They can't prove anything!" Picking up the tablet, he said, "I'm going to write and tell them what I think about their damn letter!"

Ellis put her hand on his arm. Trying to calm him down, she said, "Jim, don't do this, please. At least wait until you calm down before you write them any letter. Wait and think it through. It will only make things worse for you if you write that letter while you're this upset."

"Or write it, but don't mail it until you've had a chance to cool off," she suggested. They did this in therapy— asked a patient who is very upset and angry with somebody,

somebody even deceased, to write a letter and get it off
their chest, throw in everything he wants to say, everything
he can think of. It serves as a catharsis. Putting it all down
in writing, letting it all hang out, can be very therapeutic.

But Slaughter kept pacing from side to side, slamming
his fist into his hand, raving on. It was his worst fit of
temper she had ever seen, and she had seen a few. But
usually, he was a gentle and soft-spoken man.

"I'll get a lawyer! I'll fight them all the way!"

He was almost out of control with rage. The first time
ever that Ellis heard him call the baby's mother a bitch.

Previously he had told her that he had been paying the
mother some support on his own initiative, but it was how
much he wanted to pay and when he wanted to do it. He
had admitted he had not been sending much money since
he came to Fort Riley. But it made him especially furious
that some bureaucratic agency would try and tell him what
he had to do.

In fact, Ellis got the impression it was not the money at
all that set him off, but the idea of someone telling him
what he had to do. She knew that Slaughter had a problem
with anybody telling him what to do. He had to always be
in control.

Once he got mad at the nursing supervisor when she
told him to do his reports differently. "She's the same
rank as me, a major, so she doesn't have any business
giving me orders," Slaughter said.

He refused to change how he was making reports. He
didn't say it, but Ellis knew he was thinking that the supervisor especially did not have any authority over him because
she was a woman.

Slaughter was a bigot—always using words like "nigger,
fag, queer," terms that Ellis told Slaughter belittled him.
He was a male chauvinist, too—all the way.

Now, still fuming, flush-faced and sweating, he sat down
and wrote on the tablet, scribbling furiously his reply to

the DHS. It was the arrogantly worded letter that prompted Melody Wuertz to file a paternity suit against him, and to tell her family and friends she was not about to back down.

What was keeping Slaughter, Darlene Ellis wondered, glancing out the window again. He was supposed to pick her up to go to dinner. He already was thirty minutes late.

She tried to call his apartment, but the line was busy. Five minutes later it still was busy. Every time she dialed, she got a busy signal.

She wondered if the line was out of order. Slaughter did not like to talk on the phone for long periods of time— he made that clear to her one time.

It wasn't like him to be this late, so she slipped into her coat and walked over to his apartment, which was located in the same building. She knocked on the door.

When Slaughter opened it, he still had the telephone in his hand, stretching the line across the room to open the door. He motioned for her to come in, with the phone receiver still to his ear.

She walked to the other side of the room to give him privacy while he finished the conversation. He hung up in a few minutes and was shaking his head back and forth. He apologized for being late. He said he had been talking to the nurse he had worked with in Oklahoma, the same one that was a member of the Druid coven, and he couldn't get her off the line.

Slaughter was speaking in kind of a monologue, almost like talking to himself and not looking at her. "I'm having a terrible time with this woman," he said. "She is very mad at the mother of that baby I'm having all the trouble over. She wants to do something—I'm trying to talk her out of it. She wants to take care of the baby's mother for me. She will do anything to help me, anything for me." He said

the nurse was really a good friend, always had been supportive—"We're very close."

"She said she would kill her for me, wants to do it for
me. Maybe I should let her go ahead and kill the bitch.
Maybe she needs to be killed."

"Hey, Jim, am I hearing you right? This can't be true,
what you're thinking and saying, or what that nurse is
saying. This doesn't make sense at all. You're not just talking about some woman who's giving you trouble. That
woman has a sweet little baby, your baby, you said."

"The baby's not a problem. This friend would take the
baby, would love to have the baby," Slaughter said. He
seemed to be talking to himself.

"Sure, so someone dies, is killed, and then this friend
of yours shows up with her baby. Even if it wasn't so completely wrong, so crazy, that wouldn't make any sense at
all."

"She says she would leave the country with the baby,"
Slaughter said. "She would do anything for me, anything
in the world to make me happier."

They went to dinner, but Ellis couldn't think about anything except that crazy telephone conversation.

What had she become to even be listening to something
like that, and then going out with him, Ellis wondered.

Walking in on that phone conversation was the beginning of the end of their relationship, she knew that.

She did not know why women do what they do sometimes
in a relationship like this one; things they would never do
in any other kind of relationship; things that she never
had done before, and would never do again.

To have put up with things, kept her mouth shut about
things, played games with her own head—when part of
her was saying, "Come on, baby, get the hell out of here!"
And another part of her was saying, "Don't pay any attention, it is not real."

It was apparent now: There was an air of danger, real

danger, around Jim Slaughter. That time on the couch when he squeezed her neck until she passed out. He could have killed her. And at the time it only had intrigued her somehow.

But she felt the danger now, almost terror.

Ellis did not want to suddenly end her affair with Jim Slaughter while she was working on the same hospital ward with him, more or less alone at times in the same ward and building. Quite honestly, she was afraid of retaliation on his part. She did not want anything unpleasant, and she was starting to see how he could be very unpleasant to other people.

Ellis wanted to keep everything smooth and nice until she left, which she was going to do. After that, there would come a time when everything between them would ease off and it would be over.

After Ellis went back to Georgia in April 1991, Slaughter still kept in touch. He did not like to use the phone much, but he wrote letters, fairly long letters. In these he usually complained about the same things: the baby and her mother's paternity suit, and the Department of Human Services forcing him to submit to a blood test to determine paternity.

He had gone to a lawyer, but he still would have to take the blood test, he said during a phone conversation they had when she called him, something she had not intended to do.

"No one can be forced to take a blood test," Ellis said. "They can't even make you take a blood test for driving drunk. How can they make you take a blood test for paternity?"

Slaughter said his lawyer had said they could, and they had.

* * *

The last letter Darlene Ellis received from Slaughter was dated June 24, 1991. It was different from his other letters. They had been lengthy and always critical in tone.

This letter was shorter, all on one page, and with a positive message she had never known Slaughter could write. He spoke kindly of his wife, Nicki, which he never did in person or when writing or talking on the phone.

But in this letter, he said that Nicki and their two girls were coming to Fort Riley for a visit during the Fourth of July holidays. This would be nice, he wrote, a real family holiday.

One thing that Darlene Ellis remembered: Slaughter always had said that Nicki did not like bringing the children to visit. She wondered about the sudden change of attitude in both Jim Slaughter and his wife.

Chapter 24

Larry Andrews had learned about people, all kinds of people. He knew the various sides they present in public, as compared to how they really are. During his earlier years as a policeman with the Oklahoma City Police Department, he had been a patrol-car officer and a motorcycle jockey riding an old Harley-Davidson in the traffic squad. And, lastly, he worked as a homicide detective.

Eventually, listening to hundreds of people in all sorts of situations, he would feel a small inner alarm going off when they started lying. Call it gut instinct or whatever, all the good cops have it, and it's not learned in the training academies.

When Andrews first went to Fort Riley in July 1991, he spent hours in a room talking with Jimmie Ray Slaughter. In that time he gained some insight into the hulking, soft-spoken man peering from behind his glasses. With his balding head, glasses and neatly trimmed mustache, he could have been a bookkeeper or insurance salesman, as far as outward appearance was concerned.

Slaughter looked like anything but a cold-blooded killer, as Andrews and the other investigators increasingly were suspecting him to be. "If you didn't know anything about him, had just met him, you probably couldn't help liking him," Andrews recalled.

"It was real interesting being in that room with him. I'd find myself listening to him, and knew he's lying but at the same time, it's like you're almost liking him, the easygoing way about him, like just an ordinary guy talking about last night's football game on TV."

No doubt Slaughter was a professional when it came to dealing with people. That had been what he studied and trained for, and worked at, for more than twenty years—a psychiatric nurse whose job was to read and know people's minds and emotions, and help them with their problems.

It was an ability he used to his advantage. It explained, partly at least, why he could gain the confidence and the intimacy of so many different women by playing to their weak points. Knowing that, the investigators concentrated on the women whom Slaughter had snowed so well, feeling they held the key to bringing a case against the suspect.

The investigators learned that it was to his various partners in his illicit affairs that Slaughter talked most candidly of his real self and dark thoughts, desires, and sordid interests. He told them how killing and mutilating the Vietnamese gave him a thrill greater than a sexual orgasm.

He displayed his strange erotic relation to his many knives and knife books, which he loved to read with his women while naked in bed after sex. He spoke of his participation in the occult and stressed his dominance over all women, which they had to learn to accept.

It was his women who learned that Jimmie Ray Slaughter had the makings of a monster, and was an evil-hearted man. Slaughter claimed to be guarded by two spirit "protectors," who—when they actually materialized—were so ghastly in appearance that they scared him out of his wits. He told this to one of his women, Darlene Ellis.

The investigators were looking for Ellis, a former Army nurse in the reserves. She had been reactivated during Desert Shield and arrived at Fort Riley about the same time as Jimmie Slaughter did in September 1990.

Slaughter and Ellis had worked together on the same ward in Irwin Army Hospital for several months. The officers found out the two nurses' professional friendship developed into an intense romantic affair.

At Irwin Army Hospital the detectives were told Ellis had returned to civilian life in April 1991. She had gone to Atlanta, Georgia, her former hospital supervisor said. She supplied Darlene's Atlanta address.

Detective Richard Ferling did his best to find her in Atlanta, but she apparently had left town and her new address was not known. Ferling later found out she had moved to Tuskegee, Alabama, and was working at the Veterans Administration Hospital there.

As a registered nurse with a master's degree in counseling, Ellis worked as a therapist to help combat post-traumatic stress disorder among veterans who wanted to readjust their lives for a return to society.

Now, Ellis did not want to become involved in anything having to do with her past, and most certainly not Jimmie Ray Slaughter, who was a suspect in two murders. She had a brand-new marriage, a new home, a new life—she did not want anything to mess this up.

Darlene Ellis had been told about the murders of Slaughter's girlfriend and her baby when she phoned her former nurse supervisor at Irwin Army Hospital to let her friends there know about her marriage. The tragic news made her very sad because she remembered seeing a picture of the baby with a cute little bow in her hair and laughing so happily as she opened a wrapped present. Sheer delight had been written all over her innocent little face.

The hospital supervisor told Ellis that Oklahoma detectives had been there, talking to everybody who ever knew Slaughter, and she wanted Ellis to know that she had given the officers her name and address in Atlanta.

After that, Darlene Ellis found out from former coworkers in Atlanta that Detective Ferling was looking for her. He had left his phone number. When she tried to call she could not reach him. She was glad and did not try again.

But one day as she sat in her office at the Tuskegee Veterans Administration Hospital, her secretary said over the intercom that Det. Richard Ferling was here to see her.

He knocked on her door and then came in carrying a tape recorder. After introducing himself, Ferling said he needed to ask some questions about a suspect in two murders, the nurse she had worked with named Jimmie Slaughter. The interview lasted four hours.

Darlene Ellis felt the detective probably knew she was lying, but he was a quiet and courteous man who did not hassle her. She didn't tell her husband about the detective's visit.

It was later that Ellis received a subpoena as a witness in a court hearing in Oklahoma City in reference to Jimmie Slaughter and the murder case. She broke down and told her husband about the policeman's visit several months earlier.

"What am I going to do?" she asked. "I can't get up there under oath and testify after lying about it all when he talked to me."

Her husband said she must get in touch with Ferling immediately and tell him what happened. She was grateful that her husband was so supportive.

Ellis still had the detective's card and she placed a call to him at the Edmond Police Department. A woman answered. She said Ferling was out.

"I'm Detective Pfeiffer. I'm his partner. Can I help you."

Telling Pfeiffer about the earlier interview, Ellis said, "I lied like a dog when he talked to me. I have a subpoena in my hand. If I'm going to have to go to court and testify under oath, I can't do it this way, with this hanging over my head. I have to tell the truth."

Ellis told Pfeiffer she had denied everything, denied she and Slaughter ever had a relationship, had not been truthful about anything she told Detective Ferling.

"I did everything I could think to do to keep him from thinking I was anyway involved. I'm ashamed of that now, but that's what I did."

"I was afraid. I was afraid that if he thought for one minute that I was in any way connected to Major Slaughter, the least that would happen is that I would be hurt in my job here, now. I did not want anyone to know, including Major Slaughter, to even know that I was in Alabama. I did not want anything to do with it.

"Somebody needs to come back and let me tell the truth, Detective Pfeiffer, so I don't walk in the courtroom with this hanging over my head."

Pfeiffer told the upset witness that she had done the right thing by calling and admitting her mistake, and promised that another interview would be arranged immediately.

Pfeiffer and Larry Andrews came to Tuskegee, Alabama, to question Ellis again. It was an intriguing story she told, one with a familiar ring, and similar to the accounts of other women whom Jimmie Slaughter had conned and courted.

In the last days of her relationship with Jimmie Slaughter, Darlene Ellis was not the same confident and feminist woman she had been at the beginning. The voluptuous brunette nurse, formerly of sprite manner and assured and inquisitive bearing, was now pliant and unsure of herself. She believed that she was inferior and less intelligent than this man with whom she had such an overpowering romance.

Not only had she undergone this remarkable metamorphosis in the relatively short span of their relationship, she was afraid. She was like a helpless fly entangled in the sticky, unyielding web of a devouring spider. Her current state of mind was a shocking reversal of those first days at Fort Riley when she met Major Jimmie Ray Slaughter. Those had been days of excitement and merriment, happy, fulfilling times.

Chapter 25

The long days and late nights were paying off for members of the task force.

Everyone was putting in more hours than they could keep track of. The primary investigators for the Edmond Police Department were good examples of the around-the-clock drive to get the killer of Melody and Jessica Wuertz. New mother Theresa Pfeiffer, who had been away in Kansas during that first week, did not fare much better back in Edmond.

It was always long after midnight before she checked off duty and headed home. And, of course, her baby was asleep then.

She noticed, too, that her husband, a city fireman who had taken a few days of vacation in the beginning to look after the two kids, was growing restless about her extended hours. For one thing, he could not boil water, much less cook, Pfeiffer joked. The baby and their older daughter were in day care during the day, but he had them after 6 P.M.

Detective Richard Ferling also was working long after he went off duty. Frequently he finished up his investigative reports on his personal computer at home, hunched over the PC far into the night. He also had to miss a few of his teenage son's baseball games.

But the massive probe that had spread in many directions was beginning to focus sharply on Jimmie Ray Slaughter as the prime suspect in the murders. Statements taken from numerous witnesses were indicating that Slaughter had the motive, the capability, and the opportunity to have killed the mother and baby.

Two of the three boys who were walking along the street around noon on July 2 had identified Slaughter as the "bald old doober" they had seen sitting in a car a half block from the murder scene. They had picked his photograph from a group of photos shown to them. The other boy with them had not been close enough to get a good look at the man.

Slaughter's alibi that he was with his wife and daughters in Kansas, shopping at stores in Topeka, also was springing holes. At this point, it appeared that the only witness who could positively identify Slaughter was a clerk at a department store at the large Topeka mall where Slaughter had bought a T-shirt at 5:14 P.M. on the day of the murders. Other than his wife, no other witnesses could definitely place the suspect in Kansas during the estimated time of the murders. He could easily have driven back there by 5:14 P.M. after committing the slayings, which were thought to have occurred no later than 12:45 P.M.

The investigators had made a new and pertinent discovery that added to the increasing suspicion of the male nurse. Slaughter had accompanied his nurse friend Sandy, with whom he at one time had an affair, to Topeka where they visited and walked through the same two shopping malls and some of the stores that were pinpointed by

Slaughter and his wife in their accounts of their activities on July 2.

Slaughter ostensibly had made the trip only to accompany Sandy. But during that time, on June 28—only three days before the murders—Slaughter had visited the same stores that were key places upon which his alibi turned.

The detectives learned that he went to a jewelry counter in the Hypermart, where he bought Sandy a $1,200 ring, the same location which he later claimed as part of his alibi. They also went to Westridge Mall. The investigators believed that Slaughter had been laying the groundwork for his alibi.

But none of this information would put Slaughter inside the murder house on West Seventh in Edmond, Oklahoma. The only way to positively link the suspect to the murders would be to tie him to the false evidence at the crime scene. Mainly, this included the foreign hair found on Melody Wuertz's body, and the hair bunched in the comb and on the pair of men's shorts recovered near her body. Additionally, investigators needed to trace the four .22 bullets that had been fired into the victims—two recovered from the carpet at the spot where Jessica had been executed, and two slugs taken from Melody Wuertz's spinal cord and head—to Jimmie Slaughter.

It was known the hair certainly was not his. His connection, if one existed, would lie in the origin of the strange hair and the man's underwear, and if Slaughter might have had access to the evidence thought to have been planted at the scene.

To further complicate the progress of the murder probe, no murder weapon had been found—neither the gun nor the knife used by the killer. Faced with this absence of a weapon, the detectives' hopes for a definite link to the killer now lay in the four .22 projectiles, and whether they might in some manner be tracked to Jimmie Slaughter.

Without this much-needed positive physical evidence, there was no case against the prime suspect.

No one was more aware of this need for a key evidentiary break than Rockie Yardley, the Edmond PD's expert evidence technician.

With the hair looming as vital evidence, Yardley had obtained the contents of Wuertz's vacuum cleaner for analysis, and during the initial crime-scene check had vacuumed the carpets for other possible hair, fiber, or dirt samples.

He also had collected hair samples from every police investigator, a fireman and others who had been at the scene so that they might be eliminated as the source of any of the hairs under study.

After obtaining the two slugs taken from Melody Wuertz's body during the autopsy, Yardley took them, and the two found where Jessica was shot, to Ronald Jones, firearms examiner and forensic expert with the OSBI in Oklahoma City.

The four death slugs were identified as .22 long-rifle hollow points of the Eley brand, a brand not sold as commonly as other less-expensive manufactured .22 ammunition such as Winchester, Stinger and CCI.

Under the comparison microscope, Jones looked at the badly damaged slugs along with similar ammunition fired from guns that had been found in Slaughter's Fort Riley quarters and his home in Guthrie.

When a bullet leaves a gun under high velocity, it is marked with striations from the rifling in the gun barrel. If there is a matchup of the bullet markings with the gun-barrel riflings, the ballistic experts have a positive identification of the gun that fired the bullet.

But in the case of the four slugs from the murder scene, they were so smashed that such an identification would be impossible, even if the gun used in the murders was tested.

The Guthrie residence had been searched on July 6 using the waiver that had been signed by Slaughter and his wife before they were questioned at Fort Riley the day after the murders. Several guns, including two .22-caliber revolvers and boxes of .22 ammunition, had been found in a gun vault and elsewhere in the Guthrie house by Detective Ferling.

Jones concluded the killer had made a wise choice in the type of ammunition used. A .22-caliber long-rifle bullet gives an examiner far less chance to make a definite identification than many other types of ammunition would. That type of bullet is left badly distorted after being fired, rendering it useless for ballistic comparisons.

When Jones examined the two pillows taken from the scene, he found evidence that they might have been used by the gunman to muffle the sound of at least two of the shots—the second bullet fired into Jessica's head, and the final slug into Melody's head after she had been dragged into the bedroom.

The crime-scene analysts who had reconstructed the sequence of events as indicated by various evidence in the Wuertz home had said that, in their opinion, the two pillows were not used when each victim was first shot because the killer needed his other hand free to control the victims.

But he had obviously wrapped the pillows around the barrel of the gun to serve as homemade silencers when the last shots were fired.

Referring to the purple pillow found near the bathroom door where the baby was shot the first time, Jones said, "There was some slight tearing and blackening in an area

on the pillow, and some additional blackening a little farther down on the pillow."

He said he found the same type of gunpowder evidence
on the white pillow found in the master bedroom where
Melody Wuertz was shot the second time.

Jones had observed this evidence during a visual examination of the pillows, but he also performed chemical
tests that revealed some nitrates and lead residue in the
blackened areas. Gunpowder had left the blackened patterns on the pillows.

From the type of markings on the pillows, Jones was
convinced that a revolver had been the death weapon. The
blackened areas would be left if the pillow was wrapped
around the barrel of a revolver. He concluded from the
spacing between the black spots that the gun barrel was
four to six inches long. The reason for wrapping the pillows
around the gun barrel, of course, would be to muffle the
sound of the shots, Jones said.

Jones also examined the black comb with the hair
jammed into the teeth. The investigators had learned similar combs were available in both the Irwin Army Hospital
at Fort Riley, Kansas, and the VA Medical Center in Oklahoma City.

The combs were identified as having been manufactured
by New World Imports of Nashville, Tennessee, which sells
the combs to distributors throughout the United States
for institutional usage. The combs generally are not available for regular retail sale. In their search of Slaughter's
living quarters, the investigators found a box of these
combs.

Much later along in the investigation, after his initial
examination of the death bullets, Jones asked Ferling if
there were any non-lubaloy bullets among the ammo police

had found in Slaughter's house, and now stored under strict security in the police property room.

Non-lubaloy bullets are plain lead bullets not having a thin copper coating on the projectile as do the less-expensive and widely sold .22 ammunition. The ammunition stored in the property room included boxes of RWS, Federal Lightning, Federal Power Flight and Eley brands.

Ferling did not know what Jones meant by lubaloy bullets, and the firearms specialist explained those were bullets with a certain copper-looking coating.

After checking in the property room, Ferling turned over to Jones boxes of .22 long-rifle hollow-point bullets of both RWS and Eley brands—all being non-lubaloy long hollow points that Jones especially was interested in checking.

In addition to the box of Eley bullets in the gun vault in the Slaughter residence, the search also had turned up a .22 revolver loaded with six of the same type of Eley bullets.

Jones, the OSBI firearms expert, had decided to seek another way to possibly link the Eley long hollow point death bullets with the boxes of Eley ammunition found in Slaughter's gun vault, and in the loaded .22 revolver in his home.

It might be done by analysis of the composition of the bullets that killed the victims and those live rounds retrieved from Slaughter's home. And to learn more about the ammunition in Slaughter's possession would involve tracing the sales of Eley ammunition in the United States over a period of time by its manufacturer.

The FBI had laboratory experts who could analyze and match bullet composition, Jones knew from long experience. Checking out the volume and geographical scope of sales of the Eley ammunition, actually a specialty type of bullets, would be an endeavor also requiring some special help.

Agent Tom Jordan of the OSBI knew where to go for that special assistance to learn all they could about the Eley bullets. He got on the phone to George Kass, the owner of a company called Forensic Ammunition Service.

Jordan had known Kass and dealt with him previously when Jordan worked in the OSBI lab as a firearms examiner before becoming an investigative agent. The OSBI agent knew that Kass undoubtedly was the foremost expert on ammunition, where and when it was manufactured, the type of ammunition, its composition, capabilities, limitations, where it was sold, all anyone ever wanted to know about the making and distribution of every kind of bullet under the sun.

Kass's company supplied police crime laboratories worldwide with ammunition, test equipment, whatever the firearms sections of the labs needed. He also was a technical advisor to the crime labs on head-stamp identification, company identification, the works.

As for the importance of crime labs to have access to ammunition-providing services, Kass explains:

"In a shooting case where the bullet is recovered and the weapon is recovered they match the striations. (That is when the bullet goes through the barrel there are marks left on the bullet from the barrel.)

"To match those under the microscope, they would need to use the same identical ammunition in test-firing so that the markings will be the same. If one company makes their bullets a little bit harder, they don't get as many marks and they are not as deep.

"If it is softer they get more marks and they are deeper. As a result, they are hard to call on a positive identification."

He said it was important, too, to use identical ammunition in making comparisons in the case of determining how far the gun was from the victim when it was fired.

Different companies use different gunpowders; so the residue left around a wound at fairly close range will differ. The exact type of ammunition must be used for comparative purposes.

Kass collected data on ammunition the way a philatelist collects background on postage stamps. In the files of his ammunition company is information on 8,000 ammunition manufacturers who are licensed in the United States, plus the importing companies from almost every country in the world.

One of Kass's main services is helping law-enforcement officers to find ammunition of the same brand and type as was used in a crime scene. When President Reagan was shot, Kass received a call from the FBI that evening requesting background information. The ammunition used by the gunman who shot the president was called a .22 Devastator.

The FBI wanted background on who made it, when it was made, what it contained and how it was marketed. Kass knew immediately what question to ask the FBI in order to answer their questions: which caliber of .22 were they interested in—.22 short, .22 long rifle, or 221 Magnum?

When the FBI said it was a .22 long rifle, he wanted to know which one: the first type is identifiable by the hollow point inside being silver color; the entire nose of the second type of bullet is painted yellow.

Kass had been collecting ammunition samples since 1960 or 1961. He has over 7,000 single specimens of rimfire ammunition, and over 7,000 different ammo boxes. In his library are over 10,000 books, catalogues, brochures, documents, and related patents on ammunition. He visits most of the ammunition factories and has access to factory drawings and all the literature they publish on their products.

When Prime Minister Olof Palme of Sweden was assassinated several years ago, Kass was called by the Swedish National Police about one week after the slaying. They were seeking to verify the identification they had made of the fatal round. It was an American-produced bullet no longer on the commercial market or for sale to law-enforcement organizations.

The Swedish police were having difficulty obtaining a supply of the bullets for testing. The FBI had given them one box of the scarce ammunition. They wanted a larger supply of the bullets, because they did not know how many suspect firearms they might get over a period of time for testing.

Within seventy-two hours after being contacted, Kass located forty boxes of the now rare ammunition for the Swedes.

Kass was asked by Agent Jordan for all available information on the lead hollow-point .22 long-rifle bullet manufactured by Eley, a small speciality company in England. Eley makes match-grade and high-quality limited-use ammunition that is much more expensive than the common-run of .22 ammunition sold in the United States. Eley brand is not generally available in gun stores across the United States; Jordan knew that from his own previous experience in tracing ammunition.

An interesting characteristic of the Eley .22-caliber long-rifle hollow point is that it is a subsonic bullet, meaning that it travels at a speed lower than the sound barrier when it leaves a gun barrel. Because of this lower speed, the sound when it is fired is lower than that of a supersonic bullet, the usual type on the U.S. market.

By its very nature, the Eley subsonic bullet is excellent

for committing a murder. For someone knowledgeable in ammunition and guns, the subsonic bullet would be preferable over the noisier supersonic slug.

The supersonic bullet makes a much louder report as it passes through the sound barrier, and also because of the gunpowder in it. The supersonic bullet is coated with a silver- or copper-colored coating; the thin coating helps to maintain some of the bullet's formation when it is fired. The supersonic does not distort as badly as the subsonic bullet does, a bad disadvantage to the killer wanting to leave as little identifiable ballistic evidence as possible at a murder scene.

Eley advertises its .22-caliber subsonic hollow-point long-rifle bullet as extra deadly and quiet and excellent for hunting. Eley's advertising emphasized that "when silence is of major importance, your best choice is Eley subsonic hollow point. It has silent performance, target-standard accuracy, and lethal effect."

When the Oklahoma investigators explained their needs, Kass not only was familiar with the ammunition, he knew the personnel at Eley, who were able to provide the information he wanted only 1½ hours after he contacted them. And it was enlightening details for the task-force investigators.

The Eley sales figures relayed to Kass showed that importation of the .22-caliber long-rifle subsonic hollow-point bullet to the United States dropped by 5,100 boxes in 1991.

This worked out to the figure of only one-tenth of one percent of that specific type ammunition having been distributed in the United States in 1991.

Ronald Jones submitted the four death bullets from the Wuertz crime scene, along with some thirty similar type bullets that were found in Slaughter's home, to the FBI laboratory in Washington, D.C., for an analysis of composition of the live rounds and the death slugs.

Special Agent E. Roger Peele, assigned to the firearms section of the FBI lab, made the all-important tests on the bullets. Samples from the bullets that killed the victims, and from the other bullets from Slaughter's residence, were sliced off the bullets and their composition analyzed.

The findings were that all of the samples examined were basically indistinguishable in elemental composition, which meant that the death bullets and the bullets from Slaughter's house all originated from the same larger source of ammunition produced by Eley.

From the standpoint of composition, the murder bullets and the other bullets possessed by Slaughter were indistinguishable. They all had come from the same production batch of bullets turned out at the Eley factory in England. In all probability, according to the FBI lab findings, all of the examined bullets had come from the same box found in Slaughter's gun safe. And the special subsonic bullets were rare to start with the United States, and not that accessible to the general buying public.

The expert drew a comparison between two slices of bread from the same loaf, which would be indistinguishable in composition. But comparing a slice from one loaf with another loaf baked at a different time, the slices would be different in composition, even if only by a few grains of salt.

The findings meant that the detectives now had the forensic evidence to link Jimmie Slaughter to the shooting deaths of Jessica and Melody Wuertz, although no murder weapon had been recovered. The rarity and the indistinguishable composition of the Eley bullets pointed an accusing finger at Jimmie Slaughter as the killer.

Chapter 26

In September and October of 1991, the searing heat of Oklahoma's summers was giving way to the cooling of autumn, leaving the countryside splashed with the red and yellow hues of changing tree leaves. At times, in the early morning before the sun was up, there was a chill in the air, reminding that winter's cold was imminent.

There was a definite chill in the working atmosphere of the drug-alcohol-addiction and dependency ward of the psychiatric unit at the Veterans Affairs Medical Center in Oklahoma City.

Jimmie Slaughter was back among them, having been deactivated from Army service in late August. And with his return to civilian duty in the large Oklahoma City hospital came feelings of nervousness and even fear by some of the unit's nurses, technicians, and clerks.

They tried to retain normalcy in their contacts with Slaughter. But doubt and suspicion and fear hung over the ward where the husky male nurse was back on the evening shift.

With Slaughter's return, there was a growing reluctance by the Medical Center workers to talk to investigators. There were instances when Slaughter's hospital colleagues clammed up when approached by detectives; they obviously did not want Slaughter to think they were "talking and telling things" to the police.

Meanwhile, the murder task-force investigators were centering their attention on Cecelia Johnson, the nurse who they had learned was one of Slaughter's girlfriends.

The withdrawn Johnson knew considerably more about Slaughter and his activities than she was telling, detectives had decided. Johnson first had been interviewed briefly on July 6, 1991, only four days after the murders. At that time she didn't have much to say, except that Jimmie Slaughter was a fine gentleman who in no way could be responsible for the horrible deaths of Melody Wuertz and precious little Jessica.

But in the days following that initial talk, the investigators had heard statements made to hospital workers by Johnson that convinced them the hefty nurse was far from being unbiased when she talked about Slaughter. There was the remark that she would be "willing to kill" for Slaughter; there was the unsigned postcard suggesting that police talk to her and a coworker, Elmo Meredith, to whom she had expressed her feelings; and to take a look at the record of long-distance phone calls made from the ward on the hospital's watts lines.

The phone log had proved revealing, especially one series of calls made on June 19, 1991. That was the date the results of Slaughter's blood test by the DHS had been forwarded to Melody Wuertz, showing that Slaughter was the father of Jessica Wuertz by a 99.39 percent certainty provided by the DNA testing of his samples given on May 7.

Wuertz had told friends about the results, and word had spread quickly on the ward. On that June 19, the phone

records revealed that calls had been placed by Cecelia
Johnson trying to reach Jimmie Slaughter at the Irwin
Army Hospital, his Carr Hall apartment, his home in
Guthrie, and even the Tulsa, Oklahoma, hospital where
his mother was critically ill in the final stages of cancer.

Had Johnson been calling to give him the blood-test
results, which had just been disclosed by Wuertz, the detectives wondered. If not for that reason, what had been the
obvious urgency of Johnson's phone calls to her boyfriend?

The more they learned about Cecelia Johnson, the more
the task-force sleuths pondered her complicated personality. She had been a friend of Slaughter's wife, Nicki, when
the two worked at the VA Medical Center.

It was a friendship that extended into numerous visits
in the Slaughter home with Nicki and the two girls; also,
according to a report of at least one ex-girlfriend of Slaughter's, Nicki and Cecelia both had taken part in the purported Druid activities in a field near the Slaughter home
at Guthrie.

In spite of this close relationship with the family, Johnson ultimately had become deeply involved, probably in a
sexual relationship, with Slaughter, at least based on other
ward workers' observations of conduct between the two
while on duty.

And, she apparently had been one of the most arduous
admirers of baby Jessica after the baby was born, and
became almost sisterlike toward Melody, witnesses said.
She had paid for new clothes for the baby, for photographs
and frequently expressed that she would like to have Jessica
for her own.

Witnesses had said Cecelia had been devastated at the
news of the murders of Melody and Jessica. But even when
detectives again talked with her in September, Cecelia
Johnson obviously was as infatuated with Slaughter as ever,
speaking in glowing terms about him, and scoffing at the
suspicions that he might have killed the mother and baby.

* * *

As police would learn later, on October 9, 1991, after a long phone conversation with Jim Slaughter, Cecelia Johnson attempted to kill herself by taking an overdose of drugs. She had been prescribed an array of different sedatives and drugs for her emotional and mental problems, it was reported.

Elmo Meredith, the sometime confidant of Slaughter who had made up his mind to tell all he knew about Slaughter and Johnson, later recounted an episode that evening on the ward after Cecelia's suicide attempt became known.

Meredith and Slaughter were working in the ward office when Slaughter asked, "Did you know Cecelia tried to kill herself?"

Meredith nodded affirmatively. That kind of news got around fast.

Slaughter said, "I understand she wrote some checks to her mother and a letter to her lawyer." He paused. "This may seem vicious to you, Elmo, but I wish she had finished the job. I wish that she had killed herself—maybe it would have taken the focus off of me."

Meredith understood that Slaughter meant the police interest in him as a suspect in the killings of Melody and Jessica Wuertz.

The detectives talked to still another nurse, Emelia Grayson, who remembered Slaughter's reaction to Johnson's attempted suicide. When Slaughter came to work at 3:30 P.M. the next day, he had told Grayson that he had gone by St. Anthony's Hospital to check on Johnson. He said she was comatose and "it doesn't look good for her."

He thought she was going to die, Slaughter added. Grayson noticed he didn't appear unhappy about the prospect of her dying. In fact, he said, "I hope that if she killed Melody and the baby that she left a note." He even smiled.

"Well, knowing Cecelia, I feel like she would have," Grayson said.

"Well, you just never know what people will do."

Slaughter said he had no idea, however, what motive Cecelia could have had to kill them. But then he speculated it might have been jealousy.

"I guess it might be because Melody had things that Cecelia couldn't have, like a house she could afford and a baby." Emelia Grayson knew Melody Wuertz had a small house, but she wasn't sure whether she could afford it or not. She doubted Wuertz could afford the baby.

Grayson asked him, "Well, if she did kill them—don't you think that you would have a feeling about that? I mean, you would know it if she did it, knowing her like you do?"

"Yeah, I've had a feeling. But even if I thought she did it, I wouldn't tell the police because I'm not that kind of person. I wouldn't talk to the police about such things."

Grayson recalled that Slaughter said he certainly had no motive for the crime. She was surprised when he volunteered, "I wouldn't kill somebody just over child support. That's not motive enough to kill somebody."

The nurse said Slaughter mentioned that Cecelia was "such a nice person, very responsible, the kind of person who always did the right thing, as compared to Melody who was always wanting something, and was something of a money-hungry bitch."

Calling the deceased Wuertz such a name shocked Grayson.

Slaughter volunteered that he probably was the best friend that Johnson had in the world. He became more candid, saying that, in spite of all the rumors, he and Cecelia had not had a sexual relationship.

"If for no other reason, she is a good friend of my wife, Nicki, and I wouldn't have an affair with one of my wife's friends."

He said his only association with Cecelia Johnson outside the hospital was during "family-type things," when he was with Cecelia and Nicki and his kids.

"I've never been in her home," he said.

Slaughter's attitude when he said Cecelia might be dying struck Grayson as entirely inappropriate. He was excited and smiled when he said she might die.

He told Grayson that the police "were trying to set him up and that, failing to have enough evidence to charge him, were going to force him to go before a grand jury."

"Well, you can't expect the police to just let this thing go—a baby was killed," Grayson responded.

"There were thousands of babies killed in Vietnam and it was no big deal. All of a sudden this one baby is a big deal. We killed thousands of babies in Vietnam and it was no big deal."

Slaughter was wound up now. "I wouldn't be going to the grand jury if people hadn't said so many bad things. I'm going to remember who talked to the police and what they said. I'll probably be indicted, but I won't be convicted, and I'll remember what people said." He was aggressive and agitated.

Grayson recalled later that he looked her straight in the eye, and she felt he was speaking to her personally with the remark. Emelia knew that Cecelia was aware that she had spent a long time talking to the police, and she believed if Cecelia knew that, then Slaughter knew it.

Grayson felt Slaughter's words were a warning. She was scared. As it turned out, Slaughter was wrong on one statement, partially right about the other.

Cecelia Johnson did not die. She spent two days in the hospital and then was released. She began seeing a psychiatrist, as she had in the past.

Slaughter was correct about the grand jury. He would wind up before one within a short time. He could not be "forced" to testify, however. He could claim the Fifth.

But he didn't.

If ever they needed a reminder about Jimmie Slaughter's cocksureness, arrogance and denial-type attitude toward anyone trying to tell him what to do, all the investigators had to do was pick up the copy of the letter he had written to the Oklahoma Department of Human Services on the night he threw a tantrum in Irwin Army Hospital. He had gone into the fit of rage after receiving a notice from the DHS that he was obligated to pay child support to Melody Wuertz.

As Darlene Ellis, the former Irwin Army Hospital nurse, later told Detective Pfeiffer and D.A. investigator Andrews when they interviewed her in Alabama, Slaughter had gone ballistic, was "almost apoplectic," when he ranted to Ellis about the DHS letter, and wrote the agency before cooling off.

The hostile letter, the furiously scribbled words showing it was written while he was angry, read:

To Whom It May Concern:

I recently received notification of child support from your office.

This is a great surprise to me as I have no biological affiliation with the mother of the child. Apparently your office is somewhat one-sided in your listening abilities and collaborates only with those who hone their whining abilities to your doorstep.

I would not say this had your office been up front with your assumed allegations, but to simply be arrogant enough to present a person with notification of payment due is unpardonable.

I suggest an apology is in order from your office. I also expect an explanation as to how you came to believe that I am, in fact, responsible for the support of one Miss Wuertz or her child.

I do have my own children to support and am an excellent father and do my best to deny my children nothing.

But I cannot condone any bureaucratic extortion from the DHS or any other office.

Please remember that my tax money supports your quasi-legal operations as much as any other citizen.

Thank you,

J.R. Slaughter

It was the letter that sealed Melody Wuertz's determination to file a formal paternity lawsuit against Slaughter, and to fight for it all the way.

Chapter 27

More keys that would unlock the answers for finding the killer of the hapless mother and child were beginning to fit, literally. Among them were two keys attached to the key ring recovered from the ashtray of Slaughter's Dodge Shadow on the day after the slayings when Detective Meador and Sergeant Griffin made their search at Fort Riley.

Rockie Yardley took the keys to the Wuertz home and found that one of them unlocked the dead bolt on the front door. The other key belonged to the apartment where Dr. Beatrice Alexander had lived, and where someone, thought by Dr. Alexander to have been Slaughter, had removed several items—including a large hunting knife.

Yardley also made a test to determine if shots fired in the Wuertz house could have been heard in the houses of neighbors, such as the teenage boy who recalled hearing what he was sure was a shot at about 12:30 P.M. on July 2.

Yardley fired .22 Stinger bullets into a sandbag inside the Wuertz residence under the same conditions that existed in the homes where witnesses had thought they heard shots, that included a television turned on in the teenager's home.

Detectives in positions at the locations heard the shots fired by the evidence technician.

"No one has a motive to kill the child but him," said Larry Andrews speaking of Jimmie Slaughter. "We don't know of anyone that had a motive to kill the mother but him. But there absolutely is not anyone who has a motive to kill the child but him."

Andrews and the other investigators had come a long way in the murder probe since that day so many weeks ago when District Attorney Bob Macy assigned him to the case, with the cautionary advice of not to overfocus on any one suspect to the exclusion of other possibilities.

There seemed little doubt now that Slaughter was the killer. This was based on sound investigative techniques, the careful screening of all evidence, the autopsy reports and statements from scores of witnesses questioned by the task force, as well as scientific reconstruction of the heinous crime by top crime analysts in the field, spearheaded by the notable specialists in the FBI's Behavioral Science Investigation Support Unit at Quantico.

Everybody agreed that no one would have had any reason to kill baby Jessica Wuertz—had reason to fire two gunshots into her head to insure she was dead—except the man who had reacted so explosively to the paternity suit for child support. That extreme hatred was behind the gruesome overkill of the mother, Melody Wuertz, was undisputed. Both victims without question had been targeted for death when the killer went to their house.

No way could it have been a random kill, for reasons of burglary or rape or homicidal mania. This could be nothing but carefully premeditated murder, precisely planned in every detail.

The murders had been an organized, cold-blooded lightning-strike by a ruthless killer, who was experienced in the use of guns and knives. One who staged the crime scene to lead investigators on a phony trail away from the person who might surface as a logical suspect from a known relationship with the mother and child.

In the theory advanced by the task-force probers, the paternity suit had to be the core motive, although it by no means was the only reason for the murderous raid. The investigators believed that suspect Slaughter had multiple motives: the feared revelation of his illicit affair, which might bring divorce, loss of his children, and financial ruin; and, not the least of reasons, his loss of ultimate control in a matter he deemed should be left to his voluntary discretion—all this brought about through the folly of a woman, as Slaughter must have seen it.

Factoring in that Slaughter had displayed a belief in the occult, and that killing babies gave him power, it pointed to a murder machine switched on.

Combining these with his possessing a box of the rare ammunition from which the FBI lab experts had said the death bullets in all probability came; his having the key to the victims' front door; the identification by two witnesses as his having been in a car a half block from the crime scene at the estimated time of the murders; the flaws in his alibi; the threats he had voiced against the victims to several people; his propensity for enjoying mutilation and killing during the Vietnam war as attested by witnesses— it all pointed directly at Jimmie Slaughter.

Now, Andrews and the rest of the murder task force planned two other moves to cinch the tightening case.

They planned to seek a judge's writ to put a wiretap on Cecelia Johnson's telephone, and the District Attorney's Office would call a special grand jury to investigate the

Wuertz murder case. Principally, the grand jury would function to question under oath, and to jar loose, potential witnesses who were obviously holding back because of fear of possible retaliation by a killer who was still free. These scared witnesses felt the culprit might well be their fellow hospital worker, Jimmie Slaughter.

The writ for the phone tapping was granted by a judge. Unknown to Cecelia Johnson, or to any of the parties who would talk to her, the wiretap was put in place on November 7, 1991. From then on, Cecelia's phone conversations were live and on the earphones of listening investigators.

The grand jury for digging into the brutal murders was to hold its first session on the following day, November 8, 1991. The task force had launched a double-barrel attack to bring down the killer.

Assigned by District Attorney Bob Macy was an assistant district attorney whom the D.A. felt was well qualified to head up the grand-jury investigation. Richard M. Wintory, had been an employee of the district attorney's office for ten years. He was a member of the Special Prosecutions Unit and had prosecuted Oklahoma's first state wiretap cases.

During his career, and as a special assistant United States attorney, Wintory took part in trying drug cases, among them the successful prosecution of what the United States Department of Justice believed to be the third largest domestic heroin ring in the country.

As a member of the Oklahoma District Attorneys Association legislation committee, he assisted in drafting Oklahoma racketeering-money laundering, drug trafficking, forfeiture and wiretap laws. His wide experience in criminal and forfeiture law led him to serve on task forces on the Uniform Controlled Substances Act and the Model Asset Forfeiture legislation. This work resulted in his receiving the president's award by the National District Attorneys Association, and the exceptional service award from the U.S. Department of Justice.

From 1990 until June 1991, Wintory served as director of the National Drug Prosecution Center in Alexandria, Virginia, which is funded by the Department of Justice. In the summer of 1993, he was recognized by Attorney General Janet Reno for his representation of state prosecutors in negotiations with the Department of Justice and congressional leaders to reform habeas corpus laws and shorten death-penalty appeals.

By taking on the special grand-jury probe of the Wuertz murder case, he was guaranteed to have his hands full.

Chapter 28

Jimmie Slaughter was questioned again by OSBI agents at their office in Oklahoma City on October 30, 1991, a week before the grand-jury investigation was to begin.

Slaughter changed his story from what he had told the Edmond police officers when they quizzed him at Fort Riley on July 3. At that time the nurse had acknowledged barely knowing Melody Wuertz or her baby. But he finally had admitted in July that he had signed the paternity affidavit at the hospital as the father, saying then, "I did something really dumb. I signed the paternity affidavit."

Now, however, he was taking a different tact, claiming to have put his signature on the hospital document because he thought it had been the right thing to do. He had signed the affidavit because he wanted the child to have a legal father.

His feeling was prompted by the fact that he himself had been a bastard child, Slaughter said. "When I did it I had no idea she was going to be such a bitch about it," he said to the OSBI agents in the tape-recorded interview.

Slaughter had little else new to add to his first interrogation. He denied any involvement in the murders, as he had done from the beginning. Once again he claimed to have been shopping with his wife and kids in Topeka, whether some of the clerks remembered him or not.

The investigators manning the wiretap surveillance of Cecelia Johnson's telephone noticed that when Slaughter talked to her, he seemed to be careful about what he was saying. He obviously was surveillance conscious, though he showed no signs that he thought the phone might be tapped.

Slaughter's tone of voice, what he said, the way Johnson responded so meekly, left no question as to who was in control of their relationship. Johnson was mousy and compliant about everything Slaughter had to say, almost worshipful in her attitude toward him.

Slaughter revealed little that interested the monitoring detectives, except to convince them that he and Johnson were intimately involved—if for no other reason than the manner in which he spoke and she assented. But as the grand-jury probe got under way, the conversations would heat up on her phone line—and not from a romantic aspect.

Richard Wintory met with members of the task force at length to plot the course of the grand-jury probe. When the series of conferences ended, the assistant district attorney had a list of over one hundred names to whom subpoenas would be sent.

Other than the detectives, crime-scene techs, Medical Examiner personnel, friends of Melody Wuertz and Slaughter, the witness list was weighted heavily with nurses and other workers from the VA in Oklahoma City and

Irwin Army Hospital in Fort Riley. No small number had appeared reluctant to talk because they were afraid of Slaughter.

The grand jury would hold its sessions behind closed doors at the Oklahoma County Courthouse. From one perspective, it would be like a reunion of Jimmie Slaughter's girlfriends—ex-girlfriends and those on his active list—and his wife, too.

Slaughter's harem, one investigator cracked.

Long after each day's grand-jury testimony ended, Wintory and the task-force officers huddled to discuss developments, and pursue the ongoing murder probe outside the grand-jury room.

Cecelia Johnson's tape-recorded phone conversations with Slaughter, her parents, and others were still monitored daily, around the clock. Before the grand-jury probe began, things had been picking up in the investigation.

The Edmond detectives and the OSBI agents and Wintory believed that Cecelia Johnson, following her suicide attempt, had things on her mind that might be pushing her to the breaking point. They felt that the despondent nurse could break the probe wide open if she decided to tell all she knew about Jim Slaughter and the murders.

The VA Medical Center record of the many phone calls Johnson had made to Slaughter while he was at Fort Riley—particularly the frantic attempts to locate him on the date the paternity blood-test results were revealed, and the lengthy call to him a few minutes past midnight on June 30, 1991—convinced the investigators that she was deeply involved somehow in the homicides.

Aware that Slaughter had talked to her on the phone the night she overdosed from her substantial supply of drug prescriptions, the detectives at their listening post would hear other phone conversations in which Johnson still talked about taking her own life. Once when Johnson had brought up suicide, Slaughter said he did not want her to kill herself. Yet, she asked him, "If I write a suicide note, if I kill myself, what do you want me to put in the note?" Devoted to him to the end, the sleuths thought, shaking their heads in wonderment.

And when Slaughter answered, "I don't want you to kill yourself," he did not sound all that convincing to the listeners. It was their theory, backed by what they were hearing these days from witnesses, that Johnson's self-inflicted death would not displease Slaughter.

After her release from the hospital, the detectives and agents questioned Johnson and her mother, too. The troubled Cecelia talked by phone frequently to her mother. On October 22, an OSBI agent told Cecelia's mother that Jimmie Slaughter was talking to some of the hospital workers about how jealous her daughter was of Melody Wuertz, especially over baby Jessica, whom Cecelia adored and wished had been her child. Slaughter had hinted that if Johnson had been the killer, jealousy probably would have been her motive, the agent revealed.

After Cecelia heard from her mother about Slaughter's remarks aimed at her, investigators sensed the beginning of an attitude adjustment in Slaughter's subservient girlfriend. Whether she discussed with Slaughter what he had said was unclear.

But some time later when Johnson talked to her mother after appearing before the grand jury, she said, as the eavesdroppers listened, "You know, if it wasn't for you and Daddy, I think I would just go ahead and confess to it and get it done with. I don't know that I would, but I think it would just be easier. Just say, oh hey, I did it, you know. You've solved your case. Now you can let other people alone."

At one point in their past, when Johnson was a fervent follower of Slaughter's tutoring in the occult, she had said she would be willing to be a human sacrifice for Slaughter in the rituals he often described. The investigators had learned this during their look into her life. To the detectives, this "confession" statement to her mother sounded like Johnson again was willing to put her life on the line for Slaughter's benefit.

Key words in that remark were "so you can let other people alone," the detectives thought. It was apparent that the devoted nurse who once told a hospital worker she would "kill for Jimmie" also would say anything to cover up for him.

When Cecelia Johnson first came before the grand jury on November 21, she had trumpeted the merits of Jimmie Slaughter. But the news that Slaughter was telling people she might have done the murders devastated her. That he no longer loved her was the reaction that hammered at her unstable emotions.

Both Johnson and her mother testified before the grand jury in December. Cecelia spent three consecutive days in the witness chair before the investigative panel, with Wintory doing the questioning. The assistant D.A. had the advantage of knowing the details of Johnson's and Slaughter's recent phone conversations.

Chapter 29

Slaughter surprisingly had volunteered to answer questions before the grand jury. Later, he said that his lawyer at that time had advised him to testify. But the attorney said he advised Slaughter not to answer questions.

Richard Wintory asked Slaughter about his beliefs in the occult, the meanings of symbols in Slaughter's books on witchcraft and black magic, his tattoos, a report of him once shooting to death his wife's two dogs, and his possible killing of three men in Mexico.

The line of questioning arose from what the task-force investigators had been hearing from coworkers and ex-girlfriends of Slaughter's in the weeks since the murders. Though none of this was information that would or would not link Slaughter to the murders, the incidents and his responses gave the grand jurors some insight into Jimmie Slaughter's bizarre lifestyle, and afforded them the chance to see for themselves his attitudes, and judge his truthfulness.

Answering Wintory's question about one of the witchcraft books police had found in his quarters, Slaughter said there was no special inference to be drawn from a page that dealt with occult symbols whose corner had been turned down. He wasn't sure if he or someone else had marked that place in the book. The book was titled *Necronomicon,* a textbook on black magic, demons, and communicating with the spirits of the dead.

Wintory flashed up on a large screen photographs of Slaughter's tattoos. There was one on his wrist, a Gemini, as it was described, and a blue-colored dragon etched into his chest.

Replying to Wintory's question of whether the qualities attributed to the dragon by Chinese culture, as set forth in the book, influenced his tattoo choice, Slaughter said the only reason for his selection was that he "simply liked the dragon tattoo." He denied his choice was related to the book's statements that the dragon in Chinese culture was a symbol of "might and kingship."

Wintory quoted a portion of the text that said in both Asian and Western Europe cultures the dragon or serpent resided "somewhere below the earth, is a powerful force, a magical force which is indemnified [sic] with mastery over the creative world. It is also a power that can be summoned by the few but not for many."

Said Slaughter: "There's no way in the world I can associate my tattoo with anything stated in this book. . . . If you interviewed everyone that went into a tattoo parlor to have a tattoo put on and tried to figure out why they did, it would drive you mad."

Wintory asked, in relation to the book's "might and kingship" quote: "You've never said to anybody, I'd like to be able to rule the world for a little bit?"

"Oh, I say that every day of my life. I would like to rule the world right now," Slaughter responded.

"Okay, what would you do if you were ruling the world right now?"

"Take a vacation."

Slaughter also was questioned about a purported violent episode in Mexico, which he had mentioned in the past to several associates. Three Mexican men had tried to rob him while he was visiting in Nuevo Laredo several years ago, Slaughter said. He recalled he was twenty-five at the time and training in San Antonio.

He testified that while the three were riding in his car, one of the men pulled a gun and they tried to rob him of his diamond ring and watch.

"Basically, I just beat the guys up. They got out of my car. They got behind my car and they were firing shots into the air, and I tried to back over them. I don't know whether I hit them or not."

"You told others you believed you had run over them and killed them?"

Slaughter said he didn't remember.

"You did the best you could to run over them, is that right?"

"Yes, sir."

"Did you run over them?"

"I really don't know. I didn't have any bent-up places or anything on my car."

But he had decided he better not remain in Mexico and headed back across the border immediately.

Wintory continued to ask about Slaughter's apparent tendency toward violent acts.

"Did you shoot two dogs belonging to your wife Nicki because they were sleeping on the bed?" he asked.

"I only shot one of the dogs, and it was at her behest.

The dog was injured. She asked me to shoot the dog. I wouldn't have shot her dog without her saying it was okay."

"Could you have told people at the hospital [Irwin Army Hospital] that you shot the dogs just for getting on your bed, that you told people, By God, you're a man of action, or anything like that?"

"No, no, I don't believe so, no."

"I mean, you have pretty consistently represented yourself to the grand jury as the kind of guy who doesn't tell stories, fishing stories or that sort of thing, in order to make himself look tougher than he really is, right?"

"That's correct."

"Well, have you any explanation why more than one person would indicate they had conversations with you where you described shooting the dogs because they were on the bed?"

"Not unless one person misconstrued the story and told it around the same way."

"Okay. So if the circumstances were that there was one person that talked to you, and the others said 'I heard from so-and-so this,' then we could have had one kind of those misconceptions, misconstruing of the story?"

"That's true."

"But if we have more than one person here and at Fort Riley who say they spoke with you personally and that's the way you have characterized it, I guess that explanation wouldn't make sense, either, that there was one person who got the story wrong?"

"I can't imagine mentioning anything like that to someone at Fort Riley. This has [sic] been years ago. We're talking years ago. I don't remember mentioning that to anyone."

"I'm sorry. When you say this incident happened years ago, where you shot Nicki's dog after it had been injured, how long ago was it?"

"Jeez, years. That's hard to say how long ago. Maybe six

or seven years ago or longer. I don't know what year it was."

"Well, can you see how if anyone, even under the mistaken impression, had the idea that you're the kind of guy who was tough enough or mean enough to shoot dogs that got on the bed, that might—even if they're under a mistaken impression—cause them to have some fear of you?"

"No, that sounds bizarre to me."

"Granted, it sounds bizarre indeed. I think any reasonable person would agree that sounds bizarre. So if that conduct were attributed to you even indirectly, is that a bizarre thing that might cause some reasonable person to have some fear of you?"

"I don't think a reasonable person would believe anything like that."

"Well, we read in the paper every day about people who do bizarre things, don't we?"

"Yes, we do, sir. But if you were to ask anyone where I work, anyone I've ever worked with, if I have ever raised my voice, lost my temper or acted in any way bizarre . . . I'm just a regular person.

"I don't do crazy things."

One night after testifying before the panel, Slaughter phoned Cecelia Johnson and told her he might have made a mistake with the answer he gave to one question.

Wintory had asked, out of the blue, "Mr. Slaughter, if you wanted to shoot someone and paralyze them but not kill them, what kind of shot would that take?"

Perhaps it appealed to Slaughter's vanity, the chance to show off his knowledge of guns and medical wisdom. Or maybe he answered too quickly. His own attorney would say later that Slaughter often ran his mouth before putting his brain into gear.

Slaughter had replied, "Well, that would be like a spinal-type shot."

When he talked to Johnson that evening, he told her, in effect, "I may have kind of stepped on myself today with this spinal-cord injury thing."

That, of course, was exactly what had happened to Melody Wuertz—one shot was fired into her spinal cord that left her alive but unable to move as her baby was executed before her eyes in the hall of their home.

He also told Johnson that for the grand jury's benefit he had been playing down his anger toward Melody Wuertz, really minimizing it and telling the grand jurors there was no way he could have done such a thing.

Slaughter also disclosed in the phone talks one of his worst fears: that Cecelia Johnson would reveal their sexual relationship. He almost seemed more concerned with that happening than his being a suspect in the murders.

He believed that if his wife Nicki found out about the sexual intimacy between her husband and her good friend, it would blow him out of the domestic waters. He felt sure there would be a crushing divorce, loss of his favorite daughter and financial ruin.

It was weird, but that was what really worried him as indicated in his phone conversations with Johnson, the investigators noted.

Chapter 30

Cecelia Johnson, defeated, despondent, plagued by nightmares of her guilt, dropped the bomb on Jimmie Slaughter at the end of her long and difficult testimony before the grand jury.

She broke, and when she did, the pent-up frustration, grief and stricken conscience poured forth in a stream of information that removed all doubt that might have been in the minds of the weary investigators that Jimmie Slaughter was the man who shot to death Melody and Jessica Wuertz. Unquestionably, the psychiatric male nurse was the murderer who vented with fury his rage against the young mother in acts of butchery that would have done credit to any sacrificial cult ritual from the ancient days of barbarism.

In tears and full of inner turmoil, Cecelia Johnson gave a handwritten statement to the detectives. In it she admitted supplying Slaughter with the black Negroid hair bunched in the comb. She also provided the pair of men's Jockey shorts. This evidence had been planted to lead crime investigators on a far different trail than that of Jimmie Slaughter, who recognized his paternity fight with Wuertz would make him a suspect in her death.

Johnson said that Slaughter had asked her to commit the slayings, but she only had helped him to set the stage with false clues. In part of her statement she wrote that Slaughter "said he wished both [Melody and Jessica] were dead."

Johnson said that Slaughter had made the suggestion to her that hair from a black male could be left at the crime scene to confuse and mislead the homicide investigators. She said she had obtained the hair later found in the comb, and the filthy undershorts, from the room of a transient black patient at the hospital.

In the normal day-to-day routine of the alcohol- and drug-addiction and dependency unit, from 6 to 7 P.M., all patients are out of their rooms, attending the required regular Alcoholics Anonymous meeting on the ward. It was a simple matter for Johnson to go into the patient's room and obtain the hair from his hairbrush and comb, and the pair of shorts. She had mailed the incriminating evidence to Slaughter at Fort Riley.

In that drawn-out telephone call to Slaughter shortly after midnight on June 30, 1991, she had informed her boyfriend that Melody Wuertz was leaving on a two-week vacation to her parents' home in Indiana on the afternoon of July 3. If Slaughter was to accomplish his carefully constructed plan of murder, it had to be before Wuertz's scheduled departure date.

The time period was critical, too, in respect to Slaughter's being off duty, and having his family present to afford an alibi for his whereabouts at the time of the murders, the sleuths realized. From the first day of the investigation, the detectives had been sure that the time that the slayings went down, at midday, pointed to Slaughter. Most killers usually strike under cover of darkness, but Slaughter did not have the luxury of choosing the nighttime.

Johnson later told Detective Pfeiffer and Agent Jordan that after the detectives questioned her at her home on July 6, she had disposed of a .22-caliber pistol she owned. Not because it was involved in the murders—it was not the weapon—but because she feared the consequences if the investigators learned she had such a weapon, the same caliber that had killed Melody and Jessica Wuertz.

She had often carried the weapon to work in her purse, apparently for protection when she finished her shift in the early-morning hours.

After telling everything she knew, after implicating herself in having helped Jimmie Slaughter to get the phony evidence for staging the murders to resemble a sexual attack by a black man, Cecelia Johnson agreed to cooperate fully with the sleuths to gain evidence against Slaughter. She agreed to wear a wire and to record conversations with Slaughter. Johnson convinced the investigators that she personally had not participated in the homicides other than to furnish the false evidence.

On December 26, 1991, the day after Christmas, the District Attorney's Office entered into a signed agreement with Cecelia Johnson that if she cooperated fully and told the truth, and if no evidence was forthcoming that placed her at the murder scene when Melody and Jessica Wuertz were slain and showed she personally participated in the killings, then the state would "evaluate her cooperation."

Time was running out for Jimmie Slaughter.

At 6 P.M. on Friday, January 3, 1992, the special Oklahoma County grand jury returned a multiple-count indictment against Jimmie Ray Slaughter charging him with first-degree murder of Melody and Jessica Wuertz. The jury brought additional charges of perjury against Slaughter, saying in the grand jury's final report on the intensive probe that he had committed "blatant perjury" during his testimony before them. Now, the task force moved quickly to obtain an arrest warrant for Slaughter.

Winter was upon the land in earnest on this eventful night of the long and hard-pressed murder investigation. The temperature was headed down as the officers prepared to grab Jimmie Slaughter.

The task force planned carefully how the arrest of Slaughter would be made. They knew that Slaughter had told people that if the police ever tried to arrest him, he would get his guns together and there would be a shoot-out. He had waxed graphically about it, saying that he would "just back up to a tree and shoot it out with the Keystone Kops."

It sounded like more Jimmie Slaughter braggadocio, but the task force intended to exercise extra caution when taking the accused murder suspect into custody. He certainly had the guns and the proven ability to use them.

They knew that his wife and children were with him in their home four miles southwest of Guthrie on this night. There was the possibility that Slaughter would take his family hostage or even kill them. As family men and women, they did not want Slaughter's two small daughters to witness his arrest, either.

It was decided the posse of heavily armed city, county and state lawmen would surround Slaughter's house and wait him out. They wanted him outside the home, away from his wife and children, before they took him down.

The key investigators who had worked so long for this moment were present: Larry Andrews, now coordinator of the task force after it had moved its headquarters to the District Attorney's Office; Detectives Pfeiffer and Ferling, the tenacious primary detectives of the Edmond PD; Rockie Yardley, the evidence expert who had a major role in building the case against the suspect; and the OSBI agents and others.

Driving separately in unmarked cars to the Guthrie residence to avoid attention, the officers quietly took up concealed positions around the home. With binoculars they studied the house, looking for signs of movement from within. There was none. The lights burned on into the night. It was going to be a long and cold night for the waiting lawmen.

They maintained radio silence for fear their communications might be picked up on police scanners, maybe even inside the Slaughter home. When they saw all lights go off inside the house, they settled into their cold makeshift stations to await daybreak.

It was doubtful that Slaughter would come out during the night, but the contingent of lawmen who encircled the house still kept attentive vigil.

The hours dragged on, and to the east the sky slowly lightened. The tension, however, increased.

Slaughter worked today. The officers knew his schedule at the VA, but he could emerge from the house at any time to run an errand, or the whole family might come out together for some purpose before Slaughter was due to leave for work. If that happened, a further delay would result until Slaughter was alone.

Fortunately, no one came out of the house until Jimmie Slaughter walked out and got into his Dodge Shadow to drive to the hospital in Oklahoma City. His route of travel would be south on Interstate 35.

It was shortly after 3 P.M. when Slaughter left, unaware of the caravan of automobiles that dropped into a staggered line behind him. Those lawmen who were known by sight to Slaughter kept at a distance where they could not be recognized. There were no marked police units in the procession moving toward the Oklahoma County line. Other motorists on the interstate, which was not as busy on Saturday as the usual bumper-to-bumper traffic during the workweek, were unaware of the tense drama unreeling on I-35.

At 3:15 P.M., Slaughter glanced into his rearview mirror and saw two black-and-white patrol cars of the Edmond Police Department that had moved up behind him. They had not been part of the motorized posse.

The sight of the police units may have been the suspect's first indication that he was about to be arrested. The marked police cars had come into his sight barely past Waterloo Road, in the Oklahoma County limits. Slaughter began to slow down.

Larry Andrews, pulled out and drove ahead of the other units so he could get in position and signal the Edmond marked units when they passed. He knew the patrolmen in the black-and-white units did not know that Slaughter was driving the Dodge Shadow.

Inside the city limits of Edmond, after the order went out to move in, the officers in the first marked unit behind the suspect switched on the emergency lights and used the car's loudspeaker system to order Slaughter to pull over and get out of his car slowly and to keep his hands in the air.

Slaughter pulled to the side of the street and slowly stepped out with his hands up. He did not resist as the officers hurried forward and ordered him to stretch out on the pavement. The patrolman snapped on handcuffs with Slaughter's hands behind his back. Slaughter did not say anything.

After being read the Miranda warning informing him of his legal rights, the suspect was taken before a magistrate, who denied bond, and Slaughter was booked into the

Oklahoma County jail. His nurse's greens gave way to the county jail's orange coveralls.

Unknown to Slaughter, or to his wife Nicki or the news media, the grand jury also had issued a sealed indictment at the time the true bill was returned against Slaughter. The sealed indictment charged Nicki Slaughter in the murders.

Not making the sealed indictment public was a strategy move by the investigators, hoping to accrue more evidence before revealing their hand. They thought it possible Slaughter's wife might still tell them something. They knew that once someone is charged or indicted, they usually clam up.

Finally, the sealed indictment was opened, and Nicki Slaughter, the loyal wife who had backed up the alibi of her husband and whom the grand jury had not believed, surrendered to authorities accompanied by her attorney. She was lodged in the county jail.

News of the indictment and arrest of Jimmie Slaughter rocked Oklahoma City like no other murder case had in years. The national news media, print and electronic, also pounced on the shocking story.

Two reporters on the staff of the *Daily Oklahoman* had been working behind the scenes. In the early Sunday edition of the newspaper published on the evening of January 11, 1992, a startling story all about Cecelia Johnson's implication in the Wuertz murders was spread across the front page.

Chapter 31

On Saturday, January 11, 1992, Nelda Emerson, a nurse, was working the evening shift at the VA Medical Center when the nurses'-station phone rang.

The hospital's evening clinical coordinator, who was the hospital supervisor for the evening shift, was calling. She said, "There's an article in the paper that has Cecelia Johnson's name all over it, and it's really going to upset her."

Johnson also was on duty this evening. Later, after some-one had brought a clipping of the newspaper story to the nurses' station, Johnson began reading the story and flipped.

As she read, she suddenly stood up and began waving her arms around and exclaiming loudly, "How could they do this? How could this happen?" She threw down the clipping and dialed a number on the desk phone. She was breathing hard and fast in obvious anger.

Johnson yelled into the receiver, "How did this happen? You were supposed to protect me! You promised to protect me!" As she talked, she alternately sat down and stood up, still waving her arms, shouting into the telephone.

Emerson saw that Johnson was really mad, pacing back and forth as far as the phone cord would extend. Psycho-motor agitation was how it was described in the textbooks, Emerson recalled. Really pissed was how she viewed the actions.

Johnson read from the newspaper clipping in her hand and slammed it down on the desk. After she banged down the receiver, Johnson raved on to Emerson.

"They used my exact words!" she cried. "They promised they would protect me! They didn't have to be so explicit! They could have been more vague!"

She apparently meant the newspaper people when she said "they," Emerson decided. She noticed the angry expression on the ranting nurse's face had changed to one of terror—that's the only way she could describe it, a look of real fear.

"I'm a goner! I'm going to get killed over this! He's going to kill me!" Her fright gave way to a rush of tears.

"Who, you mean Jimmie Slaughter?" Emerson assumed Johnson meant the former male nurse on their ward who had been charged in the murders of Melody Wuertz and her baby.

Emerson had read the clipping, which went into great detail about Johnson's role in furnishing false evidence for Slaughter to leave in Wuertz's house. The story was full of statements quoted from Johnson about what she had done for Slaughter.

"Don't worry, he's in jail, he can't hurt you, Cecelia." Emerson tried to console the overweight nurse before she had a stroke or heart attack. Her face, at first flushed deep red, was now as white as paste.

Emerson's remark brought a scornful glare. "Sure, he's in jail! And would have an alibi! A perfect alibi! You don't understand! He knows people who kill people! He could have me killed!''

"Did you send this stuff they're talking about?"

Johnson replied she got hair from a patient's brush in his room, and she also mailed Slaughter a pair of underwear the patient left behind when he checked out.

"Oh, God, he's going to kill me, or have somebody kill me!" Johnson moaned. "I don't know why they did this to me! They promised I would be protected! But they used my exact words, my exact words! Damn! Damn!"

Emerson saw that Johnson was far too upset to finish her shift. She phoned another nurse and asked her to come in and work in Johnson's place.

Cecelia Johnson left the ward in tears and went home. It was all out in the open now, everybody who could read a newspaper knew about it, the shameful things she had done, the terrible things. Everybody in the hospital knew it now, and Cecelia knew she probably would lose her job.

But she was scared, badly scared. She feared her ex-lover, Jimmie Slaughter, would kill her some how, do it himself or get somebody to do it. He would do it. He could do anything he set out to do. He always told her that, and she believed it. Cecelia Johnson knew she was doomed.

Nelda Emerson was glad Johnson did not know about the unsigned postcard she had mailed to the police mentioning that Cecelia said she carried a loaded .22-caliber pistol to work in her purse all the time. Emerson had reported this to the ward supervisor, too.

And it was Nelda Emerson who suggested the police investigate the watts-line phone calls Johnson made from somewhere on the ward when Emerson needed and couldn't find her.

But now, Emerson realized Johnson couldn't help herself. She felt really sorry for her.

* * *

On Saturday, February 29, 1992, Cecelia Johnson's mother was unable to contact her daughter when she phoned repeatedly from her Texas home. Knowing her daughter's despondent condition and past emotional history, the anxious mother called the sheriff in her Texas county and requested that he have authorities in Oklahoma check on her daughter.

After the sheriff called, Agent Tom Jordan was sent to Johnson's residence to see if something was wrong. He had talked to her several times in the course of the murder investigation. Something *was* wrong.

The agent found Cecelia Johnson dead in her home in northwest Oklahoma City of an apparent drug overdose. She had left a suicide note, the contents of which were not revealed publicly.

Later, one poignant line of a note she scribbled three days before her death told the whole story. "Now, my worst fear of all has come true. I am alone."

In her last days, Cecelia Johnson had been seeing a psychiatrist, as she had for several months. During that time a large quantity of various drugs had been prescribed for her severe depression: drugs such as Prozac, Anafranil, Dalmane, Xanax, and Novane. She had a plentiful supply to do what she decided to do.

Johnson had been despondent about the preliminary hearing to be held soon for Jimmie Slaughter to determine if he would be bound over for trial on the murder indictment. He would be sitting there in the courtroom watching as she testified against him. She would have been a key witness in that hearing, and in the later trial, if and when one was held.

Slaughter may have felt a surge of optimism when he

heard about Johnson's death. Not only was a vital witness against him dead, he undoubtedly hoped her death might raise some suspicions that she, and not him, had slain the mother and child.

District Attorney Robert Macy said that the story in the newspaper figured prominently in the suicide note. "That article put a chain of events in motion that led to her suicide," he said. "The revelations in that article gave rise to many of her pressures, and I feel it may have brought about her death."

The newspaper story didn't help her feelings, of course, but Johnson had been heading in a suicidal direction long before the story ever was written and published (Like her October 9, 1991 attempt). She always seemed to be talking about killing herself.

As for her death's bearing on the Slaughter murder case, the district attorney said, "The loss of any witness affects a case, but this tragic event won't stop our prosecution, and we are still prepared to go to trial."

The prosecutors were getting more prepared by the day. One move the state made immediately was to obtain an expert's psychological analysis of Cecelia Johnson's personality and her relationship with Slaughter, with special reference to the deaths of Melody and Jessica Wuertz.

John A. Call, a forensic clinical psychologist in Oklahoma City, prepared the analysis. He based his conclusions on police and OSBI investigative reports; the letters and writings of Johnson; transcripts of phone conversations between her and Slaughter; and her psychiatric records and interviews with the therapists who had treated Johnson at various times starting in June 1991 up to the time of her death.

Call said Johnson had been diagnosed as suffering from deep depression. He said that she "had no real sense of self-worth, was kind of a victim-type person who would seek people who would victimize her." She had "an avoidant and dependent personality, was obese and hyperthyroid."

Johnson, said the psychologist, "demonstrated a severe personality disorder associated with a long history of recurring depression and self-defeating personality traits, saw herself as defective, undesirable and worthless." In plain language, Johnson had not liked herself.

Her predominant fears were of "being alone, unloved and dispensable," the psychologist said. These insights were especially pertinent to her relationship with Jimmie Slaughter, which she began when she was in an unhappy marriage that was ending. Her life pattern was "submissive and dependent behavior wherein she sought to elicit positive affection by meeting the needs and requests of significant others in her life no matter how inappropriate."

The psychologist reported that Johnson "acquiesced to Slaughter's description of women as being 'garbage receptacles for his sperm,' had offered to be a human sacrifice so that Slaughter could receive more powers from Satan and evil, and had offered to help Slaughter with financial support for Jessica Wuertz. What she craved most was his approval, affection, and attention."

Although she denied having any sado-masochistic sexual activities with Slaughter, that was the nature of their relationship, the report said.

Johnson still had positive feelings for Slaughter in December 1991 and January 1992 after she knew he no longer cared for her and was telling people that she might have been the killer of the mother and child. "Her suicide was the culmination of a maladapted life script," concluded the psychological analysis.

The overall psychological conclusion about Cecelia Johnson was that she was far more likely to do violence to herself than to other persons, especially baby Jessica Wuertz whom she had been so taken with.

Even when he testified before the grand jury, Jimmie

Slaughter had said that Cecelia Johnson would never hurt Jessica.

After a preliminary hearing for Jimmie Slaughter in the spring of 1992, he was bound over for trial on the murder charges with bond still denied.

The preliminary hearing for Nicki Slaughter, conducted at the same time, had a different outcome. The presiding judge ruled that evidence was insufficient to bring her to trial on the murder indictment. The judge ordered that the charges against her be dismissed.

It had been a drawn-out process for Nicki Slaughter, who maintained all along that she was innocent and had no complicity in the slayings, and needed to be out of jail to be with the Slaughter children. After she was freed from jail, she still stuck to her story that her husband had been shopping with her and their two daughters in Topeka stores during the time period that the murders were thought to have happened in Edmond, Oklahoma, about 300 miles south of Fort Riley.

Investigators were still trying to track down the source of the one Negroid hair found on Melody Wuertz's abdomen, which remained unidentified. It was different from the hair of the black patient in the VA hospital that Cecelia Johnson had obtained from his hairbrush.

The lone unidentified hair had characteristics of female hair, a hair examiner noted. With this information, the detectives arranged for the Army CID investigators at Fort Riley to collect hair samples from all black hospital employees who worked on the psychiatric unit where Slaughter was assigned while at Irwin Army Hospital.

When all of the new hair samples were checked under the microscope, it was determined the unidentified hair apparently was that of a black female psychiatric specialist who had worked with Slaughter. When questioned, she recalled that all of the unit workers shared the same bathroom, and that she had combed out her hair, which was badly "crimped" and falling out, in the bathroom on the night of June 29–30, 1991. The finding would be especially incriminating against Slaughter. How could a hair from a female nurse at the Irwin Army Hospital wind up on the body of Melody Wuertz unless Slaughter had taken it from the hospital bathroom and placed it on his slain former girlfriend?

The nurse remembered that Major Slaughter had been on duty that night and received a telephone call at the unit desk shortly after midnight from a woman. She thought he had talked until nearly 5 A.M. The detectives surmised this had been the call from Cecelia Johnson informing Slaughter of the plans of Wuertz to leave on a two-week vacation on July 3.

That night Slaughter apparently had collected some of the hair of the woman who had combed out the falling strands in the commonly shared bathroom on the unit. It was ironic, too, because this was the same coworker whom Slaughter had told once that it would be easy to kill somebody, to get away with a crime. He had said that to the nurse when they were discussing a patient admitted because he was homicidal in feelings toward someone in his unit.

The hair expert said the female unit worker's hair and the one on Melody Wuertz's abdomen had the same characteristics. All foreign hairs on the victim's body had been accounted for.

Chapter 32

Slaughter's trial for murder did not start until three years after his indictment by the grand jury.

The jury to hear the case was completed on July 5, 1994, in the State District Court of Judge Thomas C. Smith after six weeks of examining prospective jurors.

Slaughter, whose mother had left him a sizeable sum of money after her death from cancer, employed two notable defense attorneys, John W. Coyle of Oklahoma City and Patrick Williams of Tulsa.

Assigned by District Attorney Robert Macy to prosecute the high-profile case were assistant district attorneys Richard Wintory, who had headed the grand-jury probe, and Wes Lane.

Detective Pfeiffer, in charge of the custody and organization of the state's exhibits, also would be seated with the prosecuting attorneys to ride herd on the many exhibits to be introduced into evidence. Detective Ferling also would assist in this task.

John Coyle, Slaughter's lead attorney, was a criminal

attorney with a reputation of being a tough battler for his clients. Coyle, who has a deep, well-modulated voice and a sometimes salty vocabulary, is well respected and liked even among Oklahoma's law-enforcement officers who have been witnesses in cases in which Coyle was the defense attorney. They know he can be grueling on a cross-examination.

"He's a sharp attorney and a good old boy, but he can sure be hell on wheels sometimes when he's fighting for a client," one veteran investigator said.

There is a plaque on a wall in Coyle's office that reads, "Gunfighters don't get paid by the bullet."

Coyle and Williams, a gray-bearded lawyer with a professorial look, made a good team in the courtroom. Slaughter, dapper with a trimmed mustache, spectacles, and wearing slacks and a sport coat, looked as if he might be part of the legal team when he entered the courtroom and took his seat with his lawyers.

After Slaughter had entered a plea of not guilty to the murder charges, Richard Wintory stood before the jury of eight women and four men to open the sensational trial, which would extend over five months and become the longest criminal trial in Oklahoma County history.

In his opening statement to the jury, Wintory outlined the state's case against the defendant.

"The evidence, ladies and gentlemen, is going to show this is a case about a man who believed in his right and ability and power to control his own world ... about a man [who], when that control was threatened by the eleven-month-old child that he fathered, decided to test his belief that it is easy to kill and get away with it, and he planned and carried out and acted on his belief."

By just looking at him, it would be difficult for the jury members to reconcile the neatly dressed, quiet-appearing defendant with the description of the brutal atrocities that were committed in the modest home on a quiet residential street in Edmond on that sultry Tuesday, July 2, 1991.

Wintory described how Slaughter parked his car on a street one-half block away, climbed over a back fence, entered the house by the front door with a key he possessed, and in a blitzlike attack, shot both the mother Melody Wuertz, and her baby, Jessica, in the hallway of the home.

The shootings occurred outside the bathroom door. Melody was curling her hair, preparing to drop Jessica at the baby-sitter's house and go to work, the prosecutor said.

The violent attack occurred around high noon, said Wintory, a time that would figure strongly in the case against Slaughter, who then had been assigned to night duty as a psychiatric nurse at Irwin Army Hospital.

The motive for the murders was Slaughter's white-hot anger over a paternity suit filed against him by Melody Wuertz seeking child support for the baby he had fathered. The defendant's anger, hatred if you will, was demonstrated in the terrible things he did to Melody Wuertz's body with a scalpel-sharp hunting knife, all perimortem-type wounds, meaning they were inflicted while the woman was still alive.

The killer, Jimmie Slaughter, had shot his baby daughter in the head while she played on the hallway floor. It was the second shot he fired, said Wintory. The baby was shot immediately after her mother had been shot in the spinal cord, a shot that paralyzed her but left her conscious to see Slaughter execute her baby.

He then dragged Melody Wuertz down the hall to her bedroom, where he did the deplorable things with his knife, and also shot her in the head.

After butchering the mother, Slaughter returned to where Jessica lay dead in a pool of blood, calmly turned over the infant and shot her a second time in the head.

He wanted to be absolutely certain that he would not be paying child support in the future, the prosecutor told the jury.

The heinous knife wounds on the body of Melody Wuertz were unimaginable, Wintory said.

"The evidence from this crime scene shows that the wounds . . . were as cold-blooded as can be envisioned by man. Both of her breasts were slashed to the point where her ribs were cut through and her lungs were exposed.

"Another X is carved above her pubic mound. Her vagina has the knife plunged into it, down through—out of her vagina, through her rectum, out her buttocks, into the T-shirt that has been dragged underneath her, cutting through the T-shirt.

"This is a massive wound which leaves no castoff, only the blood that flowed from her body, which is to say that the evidence and testimony will be that it was slow, careful, and exceptionally cold-blooded and deliberate."

In other words, done with almost surgical skill.

Slaughter sat motionless, his face showing no emotion, as the prosecutor hammered away at the viciousness and horror of the knife assault.

Wintory's remarks to the jury continued in the exceptionally quiet courtroom. "Melody Wuertz has one more knife wound which is skillfully placed to penetrate her heart.

"Next, she has a symbol carved on her abdomen with the tip of the knife. It is not an accident. They [the cuts] are a personal expression of some need that the defendant had, and you'll hear evidence concerning that."

Leaving the slashed and stabbed body in the bedroom, Slaughter went back to the hallway, rolled Jessica over facedown and "takes a pillow probably from the sofa in the living room, folds it over the top of his handgun, a .22-caliber revolver, and presses the barrel into the back of the baby's head and fires," said Wintory. There is an audible gasp from someone in the courtroom.

"The baby is already dead, dead when this shot is fired, but he has to make absolutely certain this baby is dead. Otherwise, all of this means nothing."

He had worn gloves to avoid leaving any fingerprints. Since he would be an obvious suspect because of the paternity-suit dispute, Slaughter had planted false evidence at the scene and arranged Melody's body to suggest a sexual attack, Wintory told the jury.

Everything was so carefully thought out and planned, but when Slaughter left the murder scene and returned to his parked car, he encountered one of life's little fateful intangibles. He was spotted by two boys who happened to be walking by, the prosecutor told the jury, and they will definitely identify Slaughter from the witness stand as the man they saw in a car parked a half block from the murder scene about 12:30 P.M., when the killings were thought to have occurred, said Wintory.

That is about the time that Slaughter would claim he was far away from Edmond, Oklahoma, eating lunch with his wife and kids in a restaurant in Junction City, Kansas, a small town next to Fort Riley, where he was stationed as a nurse.

The prosecutor spoke to the jury for 3½ hours, outlining step-by-step how the state would prove beyond a reasonable doubt that Jimmie Slaughter was the killer. Wintory said, although the paternity suit was the primary motive, there were multiple motives that finally pushed Slaughter over the edge.

"Understanding those motives explains why, out of all the persons in the world, this is the man who killed them," said Wintory. "For Jim Slaughter, understanding his motive requires you to understand him to the point that you know for him control is everything. His ability to control the world around him is paramount."

The prosecutor said the paternity suit filed against him was "the worst nightmare that Jim Slaughter could confront."

Wintory said after Melody Wuertz filed the paternity action, "the defendant angrily denied having any biological affiliation in a letter he wrote in his hand to the Department of Human Services.

"The defendant actively sought any way he could to avoid taking a paternity action. He was absolutely enraged at the prospect that a court, triggered by a woman and an eleven-month-old infant, could wrest from him the control over his life.

"A woman with whom he had an illicit affair, not being willing to accept what he thought would be a fair and equitable arrangement.

"For Jim Slaughter, a fair and equitable arrangement would be for her to tell him how much she needed, for him to decide whether or not that amount, and for the purposes intended, was fair, for him to give only that amount, and before any other monies are given to her, him to decide whether or not the earlier monies had been properly spent. No court intervention. He's not comfortable with that. That's not what he wants.

"Jim Slaughter had the prospect of a court telling him how his money was spent."

In fact, Slaughter had made statements to witnesses, one coworker in particular, that if Melody Wuertz did not back off from the paternity action, "I'll kill her and I'll kill the baby," said Wintory.

Wintory pointed out Slaughter also was worried that his wife would divorce him if she knew of his affair with Melody and of the birth of Jessica.

And a divorce would be "an unacceptable consequence" to him because it would require him to start over.

"Jim Slaughter made it clear in no uncertain terms he was not prepared to start over, not prepared to pay child support to his wife Nicki, and he was not prepared, absolutely not prepared, to lose access to his oldest daughter Betsy.

"His oldest daughter was, as he put it, his 'daddy's girl,' his special girl, the one he was very, very close to. He cared so little for his youngest daughter that she was utterly inconsequential to him," Wintory told the jury.

Wintory said ordinary people find it hard to believe that someone could kill a child, his own child at that.

"But, ladies and gentlemen, you will hear evidence that the defendant participated in a belief system that did not consider the death of his child a tragedy, that the death of a child he is responsible for increased his power."

The nature of this Satanic belief system was not on trial, Wintory stressed, but it was important to the case to show that Slaughter used the belief system to rationalize his own behavior.

"He used this belief system in such a way that not only did Jim Slaughter not have the normal reservation that one might expect of a father, he had the exact opposite. The death of a child was a good thing to Jim Slaughter," the prosecutor said.

Referring again to the estimated time of the murders, 12 to 12:30 P.M., Wintory asked the jury, "Why would anyone plan to kill at midday? If you were going to kill, why not in the dead of night? The only person, ladies and gentlemen, who had a motive because of their circumstances, to kill at midday, the only person who could establish an alibi at midday is Jim Slaughter.

"The only person to whom it made sense to kill at midday, despite the increased risk, is Jim Slaughter, only Jim Slaughter."

Why did he choose July 2 to do the murders? Wintory asked. Because he knew, after a call from his girlfriend

Cecelia Johnson, that Melody Wuertz was leaving on July 3.

"Tuesday, July second, was the only day that Jim Slaughter would have access to Melody and Jessica and an alibi. And the only time he can get there with a four-and-one-half-hour drive is midday, and he made it there just after noon."

He did the murders, drove back to Topeka, and bought a T-shirt from a woman clerk in a mall at 5:14 P.M.

Said the prosecutor: "That clerk is the only nonfamily witness who can absolutely confirm that Jim Slaughter was at that mall. And by five-fourteen P.M., Slaughter would have had time to drive back from Edmond.

"That clerk is the only nonfamily witness who you will hear say, 'I know it was Jimmie Ray Slaughter who I did a business transaction with on this day from five-fourteen P.M. forward. No other nonfamily witness will testify that they recalled that specific date conducting a business transaction with the defendant, within minutes of the exact drive time going the speed limit."

Wintory turned again to the symbol carved on Melody Wuertz's stomach. He said that "despite the increased risk, Slaughter showed a familiarity with, and a desire to carve, a symbol on Melody, a symbol that resembled one that he habitually had placed on his knives, knife sheaths, and holsters. It was composed of half circles and straight lines."

The symbol seemingly resembled one contained in *The Complete Book of Black Magic and Witchcraft*, which describes how witchcraft symbols often are reversed and inverted.

In her final days, Melody Wuertz lived in fear, said Wintory. "Melody felt fear of one person alone—Jim Slaughter—because he had a key to her house.

"She didn't have the money to replace the dead bolts. She locked the door every time she came in, and once she was in, she threw the dead bolt again, but the fear that she expressed to her friends was that some night she would come home—and no one else in the world did she fear but this man—she feared that he would be waiting for her one night.''

He came at midday instead, said Wintory.

As for little Jessica, who was playing contentedly and watching her mother curl her hair, she would have seen nothing more than her mother being struck and then heard a loud noise. Jessica Wuertz would feel nothing more than her father's hand pressing down on her head and then she would feel a pressure on the temple of her head, and then—nothing.

Chapter 33

The opening statement by the defense came the next day. Prosecutor Wintory's opening address had been lengthy, but Defense Attorney John Coyle would exceed the state's time, talking to the jury for five hours.

Coyle was ready with blowup maps showing the Oklahoma-Kansas border area, especially Edmond, Oklahoma, and Fort Riley, Kansas, and the area in between. He used a pointer to show the vitally important locations of towns and the mileage between them.

Coyle, his strong voice reaching out in the quiet of the courtroom, said casually:

"Welcome back to the courthouse, and this is the time when we get to tell you what we believe the evidence in this case will show."

He paused a few seconds. "It will show that Jim Slaughter did not kill Melody Wuertz. That Jim Slaughter was with his wife, Nicki Slaughter, and his daughters, Betsy and Caroline, in Kansas."

Pointing to the map enlargements, Coyle said, "The

murders occurred here in Edmond. The Slaughters were up here in Junction City, Kansas [which is next to Fort Riley].''

He indicated the city of Topeka, Kansas, and its location relative to Fort Riley.

"I'll show you where they went and tell you about the witnesses and the people that saw them, real people, not anybody they knew before.''

Coyle explained that Nicki Slaughter had made plans to visit Jimmie at the Army base over the Fourth of July holidays a month earlier. She arrived with their two daughters on Sunday afternoon, June 30, 1991.

Slaughter went to work on his night shift at the Irwin Army Hospital at 7 P.M. Sunday until 7 A.M. Monday.

On Monday the family went to eat at a Mexican restaurant at Manhattan, Kansas, a small nearby town, then attended a movie, came back to his apartment and retired after watching TV.

Now, the defense attorney began the rundown on his most important evidence in the defense of Jim Slaughter: what he claimed was the timetable of the Slaughters' activities on that fateful Tuesday, July 2, when Melody and Jessica Wuertz were murdered in their home at Edmond, Oklahoma, more than 300 miles away.

In his opinion, John Coyle emphatically told the jury, Jimmie Slaughter had an alibi that cleared him of any possible involvement in the homicides.

Coyle related that the Slaughter family slept until about 11 A.M. on Tuesday, July 2, in Slaughter's apartment in Carr Hall on the Army base.

Coyle said: "When they get up, the family goes to a restaurant in Junction City, getting there about twelve-thirty P.M. They eat breakfast.''

A nineteen-year-old waitress at the restaurant later positively identifies Nicki and the girls as having been there at that time, Coyle said.

"She does not remember Jim Slaughter, cannot identify him, but she recalls there was a man with Nicki and her daughters," said Coyle.

"The family leaves the restaurant about one-thirty P.M. and drives to nearby Milford Lake [twenty-eight miles away]—the kids had never seen the lake, and I don't think Mr. Slaughter had ever been up there. It is about a ten-minute drive from the restaurant, and they just drive around the lake for a while. It doesn't look particularly appealing to them, so they get on the highway, and the first place they go is Hypermart."

Hypermart is a large discount store in Topeka, Kansas. The drive to Topeka took about forty-five minutes to an hour, and they arrived there about 2:45 or 3 P.M., said Coyle.

If the jury was paying close attention to the time elements in the case, Jimmie Slaughter already was accounted for in Kansas before, during, and after the murders happened according to the timetable that Coyle said he would prove with witnesses.

According to Coyle's statement to the jury, Slaughter bought a watch for Betsy from a woman at the Hypermart. When arriving at Hypermart, Slaughter and the children left Nicki to shop in another area of the store. They were separated about twenty or thirty minutes.

When Nicki encountered them again, Betsy ran to her and said, "Look, Daddy got me a watch," and showed her a Timex watch she had on, said Coyle. Slaughter also bought Caroline a "little denim purse."

Then about 4:16 P.M. Nicki and the kids buy a coloring book and other items at Hypermart.

Then the family goes to the Westridge Mall, located about a half mile from Hypermart.

They go into the mall through the outside entrance at Dillard's, Coyle related.

"Now, they go out into the mall, and they don't remember the exact time frames of whether they went out in the mall first and then came back, or they bought the T-shirt at Dillard's first. But at five-fourteen P.M. Mr. Slaughter buys a peach-colored T-shirt . . . there's no question about that," Coyle explained.

"Then they go out in the mall—I'm going to put five o'clock approximately—and I'll tell you why in a minute. And they buy Betsy a ring. Now, they're not sure whether they bought this first or the T-shirt first, and the evidence will show you that this may well have been before five o'clock."

Coyle took a break from the timetable at this point, explaining he would return to the rest of the Slaughters' day in a moment. "First though, let's go through some of these witnesses. I forgot to tell you, a Korean maid cleaned the rooms at Carr Hall, and she remembers the family being there. She's not sure whether it was July 1 or July 2, but she remembers seeing them in the room.

"Now the next witness is very important to you. A young lady by the name of Patsy Restine. She says Nicki did most of the ordering, and that Nicki looked like one of her friends' moms, that's why she remembered Nicki."

Coyle explained to the jury one reason, in his opinion, that Slaughter had not been identified by the waitress.

Investigators had shown a photograph of the Slaughters to Patsy, but she was able to only identify Nicki and the girls. And later, when Slaughter accompanied an investigator to the restaurant, and another time when he went there with a lawyer, the waitress refused to come out and look at him "because police told her this is the guy who had like twenty affairs, that he was under suspicion for murdering a lady and her child. They told her things that made her afraid of Mr. Slaughter."

Sales tickets showed Nicki was at the restaurant about thirty minutes, from 12:28 P.M. to 1:03 P.M.

Coyle switched back to the timetable. He said a woman clerk at Hypermart would testify that she sold Slaughter a Timex watch for his daughter at 3:26 P.M. but she could not be certain of the date. The clerk later had identified Betsy and her father as being the ones who bought the watch.

Coyle said that Slaughter in a videotaped interview with police on July 3 said that he bought his daughter a watch at Hypermart, and it was not until January 6, 1992, that an investigator went there to check on it.

Coyle said that Betsy had been wearing the watch on July 3, when the Edmond officers questioned Slaughter at Fort Riley, but they had not talked to the Slaughter children.

According to Coyle, when Betsy was questioned on November 21, 1991, she told the detective, "Well, I think we got up and went to the restaurant, we went out to the lake, we went to Hypermart, my daddy bought me a watch, and we went to the mall." The defense attorney didn't think she even remembered the name of the mall, but she talked about what they did that day.

"Someone asks her, 'You really remember that day real well, don't you?' She said the reason she remembered that day is 'because it was the day before the police came to see my daddy,'" Coyle said.

"One of their reasons for not interviewing the children [on July 3] is because they didn't find a receipt in the trash in his apartment for the watch, where they found receipts for the other items they bought. You know, 'He must be lying about the watch, so we're not going to check that out.' So now the theory you're going to hear is that he must have bought the watch after July third."

Coyle told the jury that the day the police searched Slaughter's quarters, "They almost had to step over the kids to get in the door. They're playing on the porch. And the whole time Betsy had on the watch, and no one ever asked her if her daddy bought her the watch.

"Because they didn't want to know, didn't want to do anything to upset their plan to make him guilty instead of proving him guilty. . . . There is no question that Jim Slaughter should have been a suspect in the homicides, but rather than investigate it . . . they have tried repeatedly to make him guilty, to ignore the things that point to other persons.

"If Jim Slaughter was there at three-twenty-six P.M., he couldn't have been at Edmond when the state says the murders occurred," said Coyle.

(The state and the defense had stipulated that the driving time from Carr Hall at Fort Riley, Slaughter's Kansas residence, to the home of Melody Wuertz in Edmond, Oklahoma) was four hours and twenty-three minutes. The mileage between the two locations had been stipulated at 282.7 miles. The driving time from the Wuertz home to the Dillard's store at the mall in Topeka where Slaughter was shopping at 5 P.M. was four hours and twenty-four minutes.)

"Slaughter, his wife and the girls returned to Hypermart about a week after July second and tried to retrace their steps and talk to the people who they had been with," Coyle told the jury.

The attorney said a woman clerk at Hypermart recalled selling a watch to Slaughter for his daughter, but she could not say for certain it had been on July 2.

"The clerk is uncertain of the date she sold the watch because it was at least a week later before the Slaughters were able to get back to the Hypermart on the same day, they thought the same salespeople would be there," said Coyle. "Because of that hiatus of time, she's not able to testify to the date."

Continuing the July 2 shopping timetable, Coyle related

the Slaughters bought a coloring book and other items, and were checked out at Hypermart's front register No. 1 at 4:16 P.M. They went from there to the Westridge Mall, arriving about 4:30 P.M., where Slaughter bought the T-shirt at Dillard's at 5:14 P.M., and either right before or after that, Slaughter bought a ring for Betsy at a small shop out in the mall.

Next stop for Slaughter was a speciality shop in the mall where he talked with a clerk about guns and knives, which was confirmed. At 5:45 P.M. Slaughter bought Nicki a pair of earrings.

At 6:45 P.M. Nicki bought a black T-shirt for Slaughter, charging it on her credit card. They went to a movie, *Only the Lonely,* at 7:30 P.M., got out two hours later and went home to the Fort Riley apartment, said Coyle.

There was no argument by anyone that Slaughter had been at the mall at 5:14 P.M., but from the time the murders were believed to have happened until he bought the T-shirt, that would have been ample time to make the drive from Edmond, as the prosecution had stressed.

During his lengthy statement to the jury, the defense attorney attacked, from one angle or another, almost every witness or piece of evidence the state planned to introduce, not a surprising defense move by any means.

He harped on the theme that many people had said many bad things about Jim Slaughter—his womanizing, his macho war stories, his occult interest, his bad temper arising from the paternity suit, but none of those things linked him to the murders of Melody and Jessica Wuertz.

He dwelled at length on the deceased Cecelia Johnson, whom Slaughter thought committed the murders, emphasized her infatuation with Slaughter and her jealousy of Melody Wuertz.

"Cecelia becomes horribly jealous of Melody, jealous of

her for more than one reason. "She's jealous of Melody because she had the affections of Jim Slaughter, but more important, she had Jim Slaughter's baby. She is insanely jealous of the child. But at the same time she wants the child."

When the defense opening statement finally ended, the jury had a mountain of suggested evidence and theories to ponder, including the intricate timetable movements of the Slaughter family on July 2.

Chapter 34

The hot summer day, July 6, 1994, that the state began its parade of witnesses was the day before the birthday of little Jessica Wuertz, who would have been three years old had her life not been so suddenly and violently snuffed out.

Three years ago on this date Melody Wuertz had intended to be in Indiana on vacation with her baby daughter, showing her off to doting grandparents, who now were among the witnesses called for the trial.

In the beginning, both sides thought the trial would go on for five or six weeks, but it stretched into five months. Jury selection had started in the spring, it was summer when the first witnesses took the stand, and it would be autumn before a verdict was reached.

In all, the jury would listen to seventy-nine witnesses and seventy-four taped segments from the grand-jury testimony that spawned the indictment against Jimmie R. Slaughter on two counts of first-degree murder and seven counts of perjury committed during his appearances before the grand jury.

Besides the witness testimony and the grand-jury tapes, the jurors would have 452 evidence exhibits placed before them.

Dr. Beatrice Alexander was the first witness called by the state. The attractive psychiatrist testified of her nearly nine-year romantic affair with Jimmie Slaughter that, among other things, had brought her three pregnancies and three abortions. She blamed the pregnancies on Slaughter's insistence of using the withdrawal method of contraception.

"I remember talking to him about the pregnancies, the pregnancies that ended in abortions, about him taking some responsibility for that, and he was kind of upset," the psychiatrist told the jury.

They had been seated on the love seat in her apartment, she recalled. Suddenly he had stood up, glowering at the turn the conversation had taken. Then he spoke the words that were the beginning of the end of their long romance, the doctor testified.

"He said that he gets power from killing babies," Alexander said. Slaughter then had told her that he would bring her some books that explained what he meant.

"Did you find anything [in the books] that explained or justified the defendant's position?" Assistant District Attorney Wintory asked.

"I found references about the occult, but nothing about killing babies. It all seemed very vague."

Wintory showed the witness *The Complete Book of Magic and Witchcraft,* which she identified as a book belonging to Slaughter. Wintory indicated a symbol, beneath which were printed the words, "All spirits will pay homage to the bearer of this symbol."

Later testimony revealed the symbol had been dupli-
cated on a ring given to Slaughter by Cecelia Johnson.

Another of Slaughter's ex-girlfriends, Annabelle Roberts, a pretty pharmacist's technician at the VA Hospital,
took the stand.

She said she had a relationship with Slaughter for several
months, but broke it off after she felt guilty about going
to bed with him.

But after the murders of Melody and Jessica Wuertz,
when he was back working at the VA Medical Center, he
called and said he needed someone to talk to, Roberts
remembered.

After their shift that night she met him at a restaurant,
and he talked about the murders.

"He was telling me he didn't do it, and he wished they
would get busy and find the person that did. He said there
was some evidence found at the house that indicated a
black man did it."

Once during the discussion, when speaking of Melody
Wuertz, he raised his voice and said, "Well, if Melody
hadn't been so greedy she wouldn't be where she is today."
Roberts said she had been shocked by the angry comment.

As testimony went into the third week, and there
appeared to be no end in sight, the jurors were faced with
a growing concern among their fellow employees and their
employers about when the absent workers were coming
back to work.

When Judge Smith learned of this situation, he spoke
to the jury at the conclusion of testimony on Friday,
July 29, 1994. He said the trial certainly would go through
September.

"If you do have a problem and want the court to do so,

I'll be glad to write a letter to your employer. But I'm absolutely not going to have any of you intimidated in any way.

"And if worse comes to worse, I'll need the names of people who have attempted to intimidate you in any way, and I'll order them to court for consideration to show cause why they should not be held in contempt of court.

"Because you are here under the laws of this State of Oklahoma and under direction of this court, you have absolutely no control over your situation other than to abide by the orders of the court."

The judge later issued such a letter.

Chapter 35

Richard Wintory and Wes Lane, as the weeks rolled along, were presenting the case against Jimmie Slaughter in carefully planned stages, layer upon layer of witness testimony.

A long line of Slaughter's ex-girlfriends and coworkers passed through the witness stand with testimony about Slaughter's conquests and sexual relationships; his oddball remarks about deriving pleasure from killing; getting an erection when he slit throats and cut off ears and noses in Vietnam; his growing rage and threats toward Melody Wuertz after she went to court to prove Slaughter was the father of her baby; his need to always be in control and his domineering influence over weak-willed women who would do anything for him.

Eleanor Reagan, head nurse of the chemical-dependency unit at the VA Medical Center, had heard Slaughter's disparaging remarks about his wife Nicki. "He was angry with her. He would tell me he hated her and didn't have anything in common with her. One time he said angrily he wished she was dead.

"I remember on Sunday he would come in and say he had to wash the children's hair before coming to work. He seemed resentful of that, and it was a weekly chore. He was devoted to his oldest child Betsy, but he said it was a mistake to have had Caroline."

Reagan said that after Slaughter's breakup with Dr. Alexander, who he said he loved very much, he told her it was hard for him not to "get back to witchcraft, that there was a lure to witchcraft and it was trying to lure him back. He was very depressed. I wondered if his life was in danger because he was so depressed."

One time when he was talking about the murders of Melody and Jessica Wuertz, he exclaimed, his face red and lips pursed, "You know, there are people dying in other parts of the world, including women and children, and no one is making a big deal about that."

Cross-examined about whether she ever told police about Slaughter's comments, Reagan said, "My first thought when I heard about the murders was that, he, Slaughter, did it. I don't remember if I told that to the police."

Elmo Meredith, retired now after twenty-three years with the VA hospital, who had worked on the same unit with Slaughter, testified about statements the defendant made once about how he might have "to take out a contract on Nicki" if she decided to divorce him.

Slaughter had made the remark when talking to Meredith about his breakup with the female psychiatrist, Meredith said.

"She asked him to divorce his wife and go with her, and

he said he explained to her that he could divorce his wife, but he could not divorce his kids," Meredith recalled.

"He said he had been in one divorce before and that the wife had taken everything. He said Nicki would take everything, and he couldn't stand to lose everything again."

"What do you think he meant by 'take out a contract on her'?" the prosecutor asked the witness.

"I understood it meant to kill her."

Meredith also told of a far-out comment Slaughter made one evening when they were watching an Arnold Schwarzenegger movie.

"This guy was butchering up people pretty good, and Jim said something like 'There's nothing to that. I could mutilate a sleazeball like that and he wouldn't be recognized.'

"This guy in the movie was using a knife and a machete, a ghastly type movie, you know."

When Slaughter was being reactivated as an Army nurse during the Desert Storm crisis, he told Meredith that he was "actually glad to be getting away from these pushy women, especially Melody. If she keeps pushing me, I'll have to kill her."

Meredith said his coworker Cecelia Johnson appeared to be having an affair with Slaughter. She once told Meredith, "I like Jim. Jim is the best friend I have. Jim and I think a lot alike. I would help Jim kill if he asked me."

Meredith said he wasn't sure whether Johnson said she could kill "somebody" or "Melody."

He testified that Melody Wuertz expressed fear to him after filing the paternity suit against Slaughter. He had replied, "Melody, you need to not push Jim too far. He could be dangerous."

Meredith remembered a conversation in which Slaughter told him he had signed the birth certificate for Wuertz's baby because he "didn't want the baby to be born a bastard." When he looked up, Meredith said he saw that Slaughter was crying.

Meredith quoted Slaughter as saying while tears rolled down his cheeks that "even though she was a little slut who would lay down with four or five men to get a check, he still loved her and cared about her, and that he was not angry with Melody, he was angry with those sleazeballs who sent him the letter [the Department of Human Services]."

Meredith, in his testimony, recounted how badly upset Cecelia Johnson had been that evening of July 2, 1991, when news of the terrible murders reached the hospital unit.

She was very pale and shaking when she grabbed Meredith by the hand, saying, "Come on, I have something I need to talk to you about." She led him to the small office around the corner, turned and said, "I have not talked to you about Melody. I have not talked to you about Jim."

"Why?" he inquired.

"Well, that's just the way it is," she said, and walked off.

Janet Malin was a nurse working in the coronary unit of the VA Medical Center in Oklahoma City.

She testified that she had been in the room of a heart patient when she accidentally overheard a conversation outside in the hall between Jimmie Slaughter and another man who came along.

She recalled that the passerby greeted Slaughter, "Hi, Jim. How's it going?"

"Not too good," Slaughter answered.

"Do you want to talk about it?"

Slaughter mentioned a paternity suit that was coming up. The substance of the conversation was about a mother and a baby, Malin testified. She said that she heard Slaughter tell the other man:

"One of these days I'm going to have to kill both of them. The bitch is causing me trouble at my job and at home."

The nurse related that Slaughter expressed concern to the other man that the paternity suit might cause him trouble with his military rank—he was about to be reactivated into the Army as a nurse.

The other man said, "That won't solve anything. It's not that bad," responding to Slaughter's earlier threatening statement.

Slaughter had answered "he had been through this kind of thing before and knew what happened," said the witness.

The witness recalled Slaughter saying that "he knew how he could do it so he wouldn't get caught. The other man said something to the effect, 'They would know who did it,' and Jim said, 'Yes, they would know who did it, but they would never be able to prove it.'"

The prosecutor asked, "After you heard these statements, what was your reaction?"

"I was quite shocked. I was standing in the patient's room, talking with the other patient, and he just kind of looked at me funny, and I just kind of stood there real quietly in the corner of the room so I didn't have to walk out in the hallway."

The nurse recalled a previous talk she had with Melody Wuertz while on duty, in which Wuertz told her she had not received any money from Jim Slaughter for three months, and she was going to file a paternity suit.

According to the witness, Wuertz told her that Slaughter had threatened to "kill her and the baby both if she were to file the papers and try to obtain child support, and that he had told her he was not going to help her with the baby, and if she attempted to file court proceedings to get him to do so, that he would kill both of them."

"I said to Melody, well, he probably will, and Melody

said, 'No, he won't.' She said he was going to find out he would have to pay child support and that the court would make him.''

Malin said she did not repeat to Wuertz the conversation she overheard in which Slaughter made the threats to kill her and the baby ''because I had already heard her say that Jim had made statements threatening to kill her, so I was aware that she knew this.''

Another registered nurse, Bobbye Rutledge, who worked with Slaughter at the Irwin Army Hospital, told the jury that he tried to get her to move to the Oklahoma City area. She said the women who worked on the same unit referred to Slaughter as ''the silver-tongued devil.''

Rutledge recalled Slaughter tried to persuade her to leave her husband, who she was having trouble with, telling her there was a better life for her than that. He promised to pay her moving expenses and to help her get a job at the Medical Center in Oklahoma City, where he would return after being deactivated.

''He said he had a home I could live in, an older home in an older neighborhood. He said it was a small, gray, frame house that recently had been redone—very nice but an older home in an older neighborhood.''

Rutledge said she turned him down and they never became involved beyond their on-the-job association. He made his offer of the ''older house'' only a short time before the murders. When she saw the newspaper story about the slayings of Melody and Jessica Wuertz, she noticed the story described the residence where it happened as ''an older home in an older neighborhood.''

Reading this, she had talked to Detective Pfeiffer about her suspicions that the house Slaughter had proposed moving her into sounded similar to the one mentioned in the murder story. To the investigators it sounded as if Jimmie

Slaughter was thinking about setting up a new girlfriend in a house he knew would be vacant soon.

Rutledge also told the detective that the last night shift that she and Slaughter worked together, Sunday, June 30, 1991, he had talked about his wife Nicki.

"He was upset because Nicki was going to bring the kids to see him over the Fourth of July weekend and he had wanted to go visit his mother, who was critically ill in a Tulsa hospital. He said Nicki was going to bring the kids and do some shopping."

Rutledge testified that Slaughter frequently complained about his wife, her poor housekeeping and not taking care of the kids as she should. He also said he had a "sexless marriage," that his wife was spoiled because her mother was rich and bought her a new sports car every year.

Chapter 36

The prosecution team was ready for another phase of evidence: testimony from the family and friends who knew the victims best.

By no stretch of the imagination could Melody and Jessica Wuertz have been considered high-risk victims, the legal term used by crime analysts to describe people who set themselves up for murder by engaging in a so-called high-risk kind of lifestyle.

Victimology, as the crime analysts call it—meaning learning everything known about a victim and how they lived—is the core of determining murder motive. It is the starting place for any homicide investigation.

As David C. Gomez, special agent for the FBI assigned to the Investigative Support Unit of the National Center for the Analysis of Violent Crime Center, testified during the trial: "In this particular case the victims were determined to be relatively low risk. They weren't involved in any high-risk criminal activity. There was no promiscuity on the part of the adult female victim.

"They were not living in a high-crime area. They were not involved in any activities that would lead anyone to target them as high-risk victims.

"The infant is the most low risk of all. You have to ask yourself, why would an offender kill an infant even to complete a sexually motivated crime, which, of course, this was not. The infant could not have been a witness, posed no threat to the offender. When victims are not a threat to the offender, that is a definite characteristic you look for to suggest this was a staged homicide."

Gomez continued, "The fact there was no evidence of forced entry suggests one of two things: either the victim and offender knew each other, or the offender entered by some surreptitious means, such as having a key."

Gomez testified that the two shots in the baby's head indicated the killer "wanted the infant dead as much or more than he did the adult female victim. The second shot was to ensure death, in my opinion. It indicates the killer returned to the body and fired the second shot because he wanted the baby dead for some particular reason."

Melody Wuertz's good friend from their St. Louis, Missouri, days, Dianna Angell, had many memories. It had been through the Angells that Wuertz got the job at the VA Medical Center in Oklahoma City.

Angell had watched her friend evolve, from the quiet and friendly young woman who had attended St. Louis Christian College in St. Louis, to a changed, withdrawn, edgy and occasionally sharp-spoken individual.

The transformation came, of course, after Wuertz had fallen under Jim Slaughter's spell, Angell knew.

Angell recalled Wuertz had tearfully revealed her pregnancy by the male nurse who spent all his Thursdays, one of his days off, with Wuertz. He spent his other day off, Friday, with his wife and daughters.

Dianna testified how fearful Melody had become of Slaughter after she filed the paternity suit; how she dreaded to go home at night because Slaughter still had a key to her front door. Angell recalled how she and others tried to persuade Melody to change the door locks, but she had said she did not have the money but planned to change them later.

Wuertz had been excited about her plans to take Jessica home to Indiana on July 3 for a two-week vacation. Angell had volunteered to take them to the airport on July 3.

Wuertz had been so full of hope for marriage and a home for her baby—in the early days before she learned the truth that Slaughter was married already. Angell had seen those hopes die in Melody Wuertz several weeks before she and her baby girl died so violently, she testified.

Jack Daniels, Wuertz's friend from their working days in St. Louis, was another witness who testified about Melody's expressed fear of Jim Slaughter after she filed the paternity suit. He told about his trip to Edmond a short time before the murders. He, too, had urged Wuertz to change the locks on her doors. She replied she was going to do that when she got back from her vacation.

Daniels remembered Wuertz had called him July 1, the day before her death, and was upset by a call she had received from Slaughter the previous early morning, June 30.

Pathos filled the courtroom when the attractive matron walked slowly to the witness chair. Susie Wuertz wore an expression of sadness that never had gone away entirely from that terrible July 2, 1991, night when a deputy sheriff was waiting at her home to bring the almost unbearable news of the murders of her daughter and granddaughter.

Susie Wuertz daily lived her faith founded in Jesus Christ, and it was evident in everything she said and did. She was a Christian lady of obvious class, which the most devastating tragedy that a mother could ever encounter had failed to bring down.

She credited the Lord for this, and the love of her church friends who enveloped her and her husband, Lyle, and their son, Wesley, who so deeply loved his sister. Their pastor and the steadfast church friends had surrounded them with an aura of Christian love that saw them through the darkest of those dark days.

Susie Wuertz quietly testified of the life of her daughter, who had overcome so much in her childhood, and as a young woman, including epileptic seizures starting at the age of thirteen.

She told of their last months and weeks and days, which dwindled into emotional catastrophe at a time when both mother and daughter had been looking forward to the happy vacation weeks together.

Susie Wuertz had come to Edmond and had been in the delivery room when Jessica was born. She had severed the umbilical cord as Melody had requested she do.

After Jessica was born, Lyle Wuertz had taken a week off to come to Oklahoma and visit with Melody and his new angel grandbaby, enjoying doing things such as fixing Melody's car and making repairs around her house.

Enjoying most of all sitting and rocking "that precious little angel," as he called his new grandbaby.

As her testimony showed, Susie Wuertz had suffered in those last days, hearing in regular phone calls from Melody of the burgeoning unhappy events in her daughter's shattered life. Here was a young woman undone by the treachery and evil she had discovered too late in the man she thought she loved and expected to marry, the father of her baby, Jimmie Slaughter.

Melody held much of her troubles back, not wanting to

worry her mom, but enough got through that Susie knew the unhappiness her daughter was feeling, Susie said.

"As I said, we didn't see each other that often, but we talked on a regular basis every Saturday and Thursday. Often times when I would call her, or she would call me on Thursday night, she would say, 'Jim is here and we're getting ready to go do this and that' or 'we're doing this,' or you could hear him in the background, or maybe just a voice or laughter perhaps, or something, but I was very much aware that he was there."

Prosecutor Wintory formed his next question carefully. "I read a letter that Melody sent you and Lyle shortly after the year 1990 when she described to you . . . a lengthy letter . . . told you that she was, in fact, pregnant and made a number of statements. Did you receive that letter?"

"Yes, we did."

"Could you tell us, what did you and Lyle do in response to getting that letter?"

"Best as I remember, the very last portion of the letter said, 'Mom and Dad, don't call me right away. Give yourself a little time to think about this, and if you don't want to call me, that's all right. But think about it for a little while, and I need to know how you feel.'

"And we did not wait a day or two to call her. We called her immediately at work to let her know that no matter what state she found herself in, we loved her very much and we would support her.

"We were distressed about the news. There had never been an unwanted or unwed pregnancy in our family, and it was very distressing to us. But our daughter was not distressing to us, so we supported her very much."

Susie testified of the last conversation she had with Slaughter before she returned to Indiana after being in Oklahoma for Jessica's birth. Melody, Jessica and Slaughter were sitting on the living-room couch in the small neat-as-a-pin house on West Seventh.

"Mr. Slaughter, these are the two most precious things in the world to me. Please take good care of them," she had told him, speaking of Melody and Jessica.

Slaughter's response, viewed in retrospect, was a chilling one.

"Oh, yes. I will."

The defense attorneys had no questions for Susie Wuertz.

Chapter 37

Now came the state's presentation of the hard-rock evidence—not theories, not speculation, but the physical evidence that speaks more profoundly of details of crimes than do eyewitnesses.

The forensic experts, the crime-scene technicians, the firearms examiners, the serologists, the hair analysts, the crime-scene analysts who reconstruct events from blood spatters, spots and "blood throw"—all of these specialists have vital roles in today's homicide investigations.

Rockie Yardley, the evidence technician for the Edmond Police Department, led the string of "technical" witnesses.

Using the large presenter screen to show still photographs, as well as crime-scene sketches, or "maps" of the Wuertz home and specific locations of the bodies and recovered evidence, Yardley took the jury on a "walkthrough" of the murder scene.

The specialist witnesses for the state also included Capt. Tom Bevel, noted blood-pattern expert who is head of the Oklahoma City homicide division. Although a supervisor,

Bevel personally visits many murder scenes because of his expert knowledge of blood patterns and stains, with which the events of a murder can be reconstructed.

Also, Douglas J. Perkins, the OSBI criminalist, who performed Luminol tests in the Wuertz home—the application of a chemical that makes bloodstains glow in the dark—took the stand.

Some of the most telling testimony came from Ronald Jones, firearms examiner for the OSBI, who helped trace the badly damaged .22-caliber long-rifle murder bullets. Jones said that none of the guns taken from Slaughter's Army quarters or his Guthrie residence, could be identified as the murder weapon, mainly because of the deteriorated condition of the death bullets.

But through the comparative analysis of Special Agent E. Roger Peele, an FBI lab expert, who at Jones's request examined the composition of the death bullets and bullets found in Slaughter's gun safe. It had been established that the bullets that killed the victims in all likelihood came from the box of Slaughter's .22-caliber Eley long-rifle subsonic bullets found in his Guthrie home.

Ammunition expert George Kass testified to the rarity of that particular ammunition in the United States, and of its effectiveness as a "hunting" bullet because of the low-noise factor of subsonic bullets.

Hair expert Ann Reed, a former OSBI criminalist who had later taken a similar job with the Tulsa Police Department, told the jury that the single Negroid hair found on Wuertz's stomach had the same characteristics as the hair of a woman nurse with whom Slaughter had worked in Irwin Army Hospital on the night of June 30, 1991, two days before the murders.

The woman had combed out loose hair in a bathroom on the hospital unit that all the workers used. Reed said the other hair in the comb and on the undershorts at the murder scene had the same characteristics as that of a black male patient in the Veterans Affairs Medical Center in Oklahoma City. [The hair and shorts Cecelia Johnson had provided for Slaughter, as other testimony revealed.]

Task-force investigator and coordinator Larry Andrews, Detectives Theresa Pfeiffer and Richard Ferling, and agents of the OSBI, testified about their lengthy probe that pointed to Jimmie Slaughter as the killer.

The two boys who had seen the "bald-headed old doober" in a car near the Wuertz home in the estimated time period of the murders took the stand to positively identify Slaughter as that man.

One youth was positive with his identification, and the other boy said it was Slaughter, although he had not obtained as close a look as his companion had.

In his cross-examination of the boy who was sure that the man he saw was Slaughter, Defense Attorney Coyle asked:

"Now, your answer to me was 'I looked back. Okay, when I was walking by I saw him bent over and when he looked up I looked at him for two—when he looked at me and I looked at him at the same time it was about for two seconds, not the whole time I was passing . . . just when he was looking, two seconds. About two seconds.

"Okay. So it could have been shorter?" the defense attorney challenge.

"No, it could have been longer or shorter."

"Well, I asked you a question, did I not, so it could have been shorter?"

"It's possible, yes," the boy admitted.

But he never wavered in his identification.

The other boy testified that Slaughter was seated in a Nissan.

"Wasn't a Dodge, right?" Coyle asked.

"Right."

"So if the car that is in that exhibit (a photograph) is a Dodge car, it cannot be the Nissan car that you saw on Seventh Street, fair statement?"

"Yeah."

"You told the police officer, Ms. Pfeiffer, on July third, the very first time you had an opportunity, the name brand of the car that you saw, didn't you?"

"Yes."

"And you never wavered, never ever questioned the fact that you saw a Nissan, have you?"

"No."

But he still said the car's driver was Slaughter.

Neighbor Lisa West told of the discovery of the bodies, and unsuccessful efforts to resuscitate the baby.

One of the most controversial state witnesses, Dennis K. Hull, a prison inmate of the Florida penitentiary, who had been returned to Oklahoma to testify under a special writ, testified that Slaughter confessed to the murders to him after they met in the Oklahoma County Jail in January 1992.

Hull said, "It started out with a group of us holding a Bible-study class in my cell."

Slaughter first claimed he didn't commit the murders of Melody and Jessica Wuertz but that "some lady who worked in the VA office [hospital] did it," said Hull.

But in a second round of praying after another Bible-study class in an inmate's cell—his "room," the inmate called it—Slaughter started crying and confessing.

"God forgive me for what I did," Slaughter sobbed, according to Hull. "I'm confessing now, and they can stick the needle in my arm if they will let me see my two daughters once more."

"A demon told me to do it," Slaughter was quoted by Hull as saying.

Hull testified Slaughter also said: "She [Wuertz] was threatening to ruin my marriage." Hull testified that Slaughter said he shot the victim in the spinal cord to paralyze her. He said he shot her with "a .22 or a .25." [Hull said he didn't hear for certain the last digit.]

Slaughter's lawyers, when they cross-examined Hull, harped on his long criminal record. He admittedly had been a heroin addict since age twenty. From that time on, he had been out of prison only nine months. He now was in his forties.

Another convict testified that Slaughter told him the police couldn't convict him because the gun "mooshed up" the bullets too badly.

Still another convict, who said he was present during the prayer meeting, got in the act of Christian conscience and said Slaughter had not confessed anything to Hull at the Bible study, and Hull had "better watch his back," being now a marked snitch.

Among the witnesses called by the defense were Nicki Slaughter, Betsy and Caroline, and the employees from the Topeka businesses, to try to prove an alibi for Slaughter at the probable time of the killings in Edmond.

But the defendant was identified positively as being there on July 2 at a certain time at a certain place only by the clerk at the mall store where Slaughter bought the T-shirt at 5:14 P.M.

Slaughter did not take the stand during the trial.

Chapter 38

The long and tedious trial was coming to an end. Testimony was finished on October 4, 1994, but equally long and arduous state- and defense-summation arguments before the jury followed.

The defense hammered away at the deceased Cecelia Johnson. Said John Coyle in his final argument, starting on the subtle side:

"The important thing is that I don't know if Cecelia Johnson killed them. She may have. Maybe she didn't. I don't know. No one does. There's just as much evidence that she did it for sure as Jim Slaughter."

He accused the investigators of never completely checking her out.

Richard Wintory listed all of the evidence against Jimmie Slaughter and concluded with this last thought to the jury:

"You can do nothing to bring them back. You can do nothing to ease the pain his conduct inflicted on the other members of the family.

"An act of justice . . . that's the one thing you can give them. . . ."

It was late on the night of Thursday, October 6, 1994. The lights burned on in the Oklahoma County Courthouse. The jury had been deliberating almost twelve hours spread over 2½ days.

As the task-force investigators and the prosecutors were passing the time by playing the card game UNO in an office in the district attorney's suite, the bailiff appeared. "They're calling for us."

The jury was ready to report.

When Theresa Pfeiffer stood up to go to the courtroom, she discovered she was shaking all over. Nothing like this had ever happened to her.

Racing through her mind as she walked numbly to the district courtroom was a torrent of thoughts: This man, we've been inside his head, he's an evil man. He has used people, manipulated people, probably murdered before. He's a horrible person.

She could not bear to think about him being turned loose on society, possibly seeing him walk out of here a free man.

Suddenly, after the three years of working day and night, it was down to the line.

As she started to enter the courtroom, someone from behind grabbed her hand. Susie Wuertz, tears in her eyes, told Pfeiffer, "Don't worry, Theresa. It's in the Lord's hands, and I know the Lord is always right."

The prosecutors and Pfeiffer sat down at the counsel table. The lawyers went up to the bench. They were permitted to look at the verdict before the judge gave it to the clerk to read.

The lawyers sat down. Wintory reached over and tightly

squeezed Pfeiffer's arm. She didn't know what that meant. She saw tears in Wintory's eyes, but that did not tell her which way it had gone.

At the first "guilty" read by the court clerk, tears streamed down Pfeiffer's face. She couldn't stop them. No sound, no crying out loud, but a deluge of tears.

Defense Attorney John Coyle asked the judge to poll the jury individually. Each of the jurors answered "guilty," the most beautiful twelve words Theresa Pfeiffer had ever heard.

In addition to finding Slaughter guilty of two counts of first-degree murder, the jury also convicted Slaughter of five counts of perjury related to his grand-jury testimony.

Slaughter, obviously stunned by the verdict, told reporters, "I did not do the crimes."

The punishment phase began the next day. The state was seeking the death penalty on two grounds that the law stated justified it: that the defendant knowingly created a great risk of death to more than one person, and that the murder of Melody Wuertz was especially heinous, atrocious, and cruel.

Wuertz family members testified about the cruel impact of their loss. None of the burly investigators sitting in the back row were dry-eyed when it was over.

Then, finally, came the jury's decision.

The jury gave Jim Slaughter the death penalty, plus a total of fifteen years to be served consecutively on the perjury charges.

The judge formally decreed that the State of Oklahoma "shall legally and fully put to death Jimmie R. Slaughter by continuous intravenous administration of a lethal quality of an ultra short-acting barbiturate in combination with a chemical paralytic agent until death is pronounced by a licensed physician."

* * *

This writer sat thumbing through the thick court file that had been tucked away in the dusty archives of the "old case" record room in the basement of the County Office Building.

Two documents that became part of the court file on the murder case caught the writer's attention. They had a bitterly ironic ring to them.

They referred to the paternity suit filed by Melody Wuertz against Jimmie Slaughter way back in 1991.

One stamped document said, "Notice is hereby given that the annual disposition docket will be held and this case will be dismissed without prejudice unless counsel appears and shows cause why the case should be allowed to remain on the docket."

The second document read: "An order of dismissal is entered that the parties in the cause have failed to diligently prosecute this case. The action should be dismissed by the court and is hereby dismissed without prejudice to either party."

Of course, in the real world of how things are, it did not matter one whit now to either party. One "party" in the cause was dead, along with her baby daughter. Pending appeals, the other "party" was well on the road to being that way.

And Theresa Pfeiffer, who spent so many hours away from the first days and weeks of her new baby's life, continued to be asked by people, "How's your baby?"

"She's six years old now," Detective Pfeiffer said.

About the same age that Jessica Wuertz would be.